Strategic Writing

Multimedia Writing for Public Relations, Advertising, Sales and Marketing, and Business Communication

Charles Marsh
University of Kansas

David W. Guth
University of Kansas

Bonnie Poovey Short
Short Solutions

PEARSON

Boston   New York   San Francisco
Mexico City   Montreal   Toronto   London   Madrid   Munich   Paris
Hong Kong   Singapore   Tokyo   Cape Town   Sydney

*The authors dedicate this book
to their mentors, their colleagues
and their students*

Series Editor: *Molly Taylor*
Series Editorial Assistant: *Michael Kish*
Marketing Manager: *Mandee Eckersley*
Editorial-Production Service: *Omegatype Typography, Inc.*
Manufacturing Buyer: *JoAnne Sweeney*
Composition and Prepress Buyer: *Linda Cox*
Cover Administrator: *Linda Knowles*
Electronic Composition: *Omegatype Typography, Inc.*

For related titles and support materials, visit our online catalog at www.ablongman.com.

Between the time Web site information is gathered and then published, it is not unusual for some sites to have closed. Also, the transcription of URLs can result in typographical errors. The publisher would appreciate notification where these errors occur so that they may be corrected in subsequent editions.

Many of the designations used by manufacturers and sellers to distinguish their products are claimed as trademarks. Where those designations appear in this book, and Allyn and Bacon was aware of a trademark claim, the designations have been printed in initial or all caps.

Library of Congress Cataloging-in-Publication Data

Marsh, Charles
    Strategic writing : multimedia writing for public relations, advertising, sales and marketing, and business communication / Charles Marsh, David W. Guth, Bonnie Poovey Short.
      p. cm.
    Includes index.
    ISBN 0-205-40573-8
    1. Business writing—Problems, exercises, etc. 2. Business report writing—Problems, exercises, etc. 3. English language—Business English—Problems, exercises, etc. I. Guth, David. II. Short, Bonnie Poovey. III. Title

PE1479.B87M35 2005
808'.06665—dc22

2004044491

Printed in the United States of America

Contents

Introduction: How This Book Works

Once upon a time (longer ago than we want to admit), the three authors of this book were young professionals. Our careers took us through jobs with corporations, government bureaus, nonprofit organizations and marketing agencies in addition to freelance work. Then we went crazy (according to some) and decided to become professors. As professors, we quickly learned three things about textbooks that teach writing for such careers. Although there are many good books,

- Most tend to cover only one area of writing, such as public relations or advertising.
- They're long.
- Being long, they don't always give concise instructions about how to write particular documents.

As working professionals, we hadn't been limited to just one area of writing. All of us wrote speeches (public relations), print advertisements (advertising), direct-mail packages (sales and marketing), business reports (business communication) and more. We wrote for print, for video and, more recently, for the Internet. We believe that kind of multidisciplinary, multimedia convergence is increasing for today's writers. We wanted a book that prepared students for that diversity.

As professional writers, we worked on tight deadlines. Therefore, we wanted a book that got right to the point. For example, if your professor assigns a news release that's due in 90 minutes, we wanted you to have a book that offered a clear set of instructions—a recipe, basically—for writing a standard news release. We wanted a book that you could use as a desktop reference while you wrote. And we wanted a book you could take to the job after graduation.

Finally, we wanted a book that emphasized the importance of strategy. As young professionals, we weren't always sure *why* we were writing *what* we were writing. Sometimes we wrote documents just because the boss told us to; we didn't always examine *why* we were writing those documents. We didn't always wonder *how* those documents helped move our organization toward the achievement of its goals. We want you to be better than that. We want you to realize that, ideally, every business document you write—whether it's a business report or a script for a radio commercial—advances the organization toward a specific business goal. We want you to understand that every document should aim at a desired effect. We even want to help you identify what the goal-oriented message of each document should be. Our name for this goal-oriented writing is *strategic writing*. We describe strategic writing in the next section.

We've divided this book into five sections:

- The first section gives you the background on strategic writing. It's packed with information, but we've tried to keep each chapter short.
- The second section gives instructions for public relations documents.

- The third section gives instructions for advertising documents.
- The fourth section gives instructions for sales and marketing documents.
- The fifth section gives instructions for business communication documents.

The book concludes with six appendixes that offer guidelines for punctuation, grammar, style, editing, proofreading and tips for oral presentations.

We hope the purpose of this book is clear: It explains strategic writing. It offers instructions—recipes—for more than 35 different strategic documents. And it offers help with punctuation, grammar and style. It's designed to be a user-friendly tool that helps make you an effective writer.

Acknowledgments

The authors wish to thank the many people who helped make this book possible, including Dean James Gentry and the faculty, staff and students of the William Allen White School of Journalism and Mass Communications at the University of Kansas.

As the book progressed from draft to draft, we greatly appreciated the educators and professionals who generously offered advice: Karen Boros, University of St. Thomas; Tania H. Cantrell, Brigham Young University; Cynthia A. McCune, San José State University; Lowell Scheiner, Polytechnic University; and Lisa Sisk, University of South Carolina. In moving from manuscript to the book you now hold, we relied on the indispensable expertise of the teams at Allyn and Bacon and Omegatype Typography, Inc., particularly Molly Taylor, Michael Kish and Karla Walsh.

And, as always, the authors thank their families for love, patience and knowing where the dictionaries are.

Part of good communication is feedback, and we invite you to write us with questions or comments on this book.

Charles Marsh
University of Kansas
marsh@ku.edu

David W. Guth
University of Kansas
dguth@ku.edu

Bonnie Poovey Short
Short Solutions
Hendersonville, N.C.
bshort@mchsi.com

Section I
Strategic Writing

Objectives

*In Section I: Strategic Writing, you will learn what
strategic writing is. In doing so, you will learn about*

- The importance of good writing
- The writing process
- Writing for electronic media
- Integrated marketing communications
- Ethics and strategic writing

- Diversity and strategic writing
- Persuasion and strategic writing
- The law and strategic writing
- Jobs in strategic writing

Strategic writing is goal-oriented writing. Well-managed organizations have specific, written goals they strive to achieve. Strategic writing helps those organizations achieve those goals.

Another title for this book could be *Writing That Helps Organizations Achieve Their Specific Business Goals*—but that's too long. We prefer *Strategic Writing*. In the paragraphs that follow, we'll further explain what we mean by strategic writing. Right now, however, you'll start well in this exciting profession if you focus on the following key idea: Whenever you write a specific document for public relations, advertising, business communication or sales and marketing, you should know what the purpose of the document is and how that purpose relates to a specific organizational goal. Imagine what a successful strategic writer you'll become if every document you produce moves your organization closer to the fulfillment of its specific goals.

The word *strategy* itself comes to English from Greek. In Greek, *strategos* means *military leader* or *general*. As a strategic writer, you are like a general: With each document, you direct your words and ideas on a specific mission. Most dictionaries define the word *strategy* as meaning something like "planned actions in support of a particular policy." In strategic writing, your "planned actions" involve the process of writing, and the "particular policy" is the business goal you're helping to achieve.

As a strategic writer, you should be familiar with business goals, so let's examine where they come from. Many organizations have a values statement, a brief set of core values that ideally guide their actions. Those general values often lead to a mission statement that more precisely describes the organization's purpose. In order to fulfill that mission, organizations usually create annual business goals.

As a strategic writer, your job is to help your organization achieve its values-driven, mission-related business goals. That sounds like a big job—and it is. If you're writing a newsletter story, you need to know what business goal or goals your story and the newsletter are helping to achieve. The same is true for a print advertisement and a direct-mail package. Ideally, everything you write on behalf of your organization moves it toward the fulfillment of its mission.

Your communication skills will be particularly important to your organization: To achieve their goals, organizations rely partly on resources controlled by other groups. For example, nonprofit organizations rely in part on the resource of contributions made by donors. For-profit companies rely on the resource of purchase decisions made by customers. Both nonprofit and for-profit organizations depend on the resource of fair coverage that the news media hold. In every organization, top management relies on the resource of productivity held by other employees. Your mission as a strategic writer is to secure those resources through effective communication. Much of your work as a strategic writer will involve building productive relationships with resource holders.

In building those relationships, the documents that you produce can be divided into two groups: on-strategy and off-strategy. On-strategy documents remain focused on a clear message that helps an organization achieve a particular goal or goals. Off-strategy documents fail to connect with business goals. Either they began with no consideration of business goals, or they attempted but failed to create a goal-oriented message. Off-strategy documents can be worse than a waste of time. Their nonstrategic messages can confuse target audiences, who become unsure about what message you're trying to send and what kind of relationship you seek.

We'll close this chapter with some cold, hard truth. Although strategic writing is the ideal for successful organizations, it's not always the practice. Some organizations lack leaders who understand the importance of strategic communications; other organizations become distracted and overwhelmed by the many demands of successful management; still others may lack writers with your knowledge and skills. The authors of this book are professors as well as professionals, and we occasionally receive slick media kits or brochures from our graduates. Sometimes a former student will include a note that says something like this: "I know this is off-strategy, but the client insisted" or "This seems off-strategy to me, but my boss made me do it this way because it's how we've always done it."

As young professionals, the authors of this book encountered the same problems. We've been there, and we sympathize. Our best advice is to try some strategic communication with your boss and your clients. Surely they want to succeed. If you can politely illuminate the advantages of strategic writing (without sounding like a pushy know-it-all), you may succeed in transforming your organization's communications.

On-strategy: That's our message.

The Importance of Good Writing

As professionals, the authors of this book hired our own writing staffs. As professors, we get to have gossipy lunches with employers who want to hire—you. And we, as professionals, and those employers say the same thing: "Please give me someone who can *write!*" Yes, employers want diplomatic team players. And they want hard-working students with experience. But they almost always begin by asking for good writers.

A few years ago, we secretly studied the guest speakers we brought into our classes to see what job skills they stressed to students. We gave up the study when, after several dozen speakers, it became clear that each put good writing at the top of the list.

We've noticed a similar trend in management textbooks. When successful CEOs and other leaders discuss the talents that took them to the top, communication skills—both written and oral—almost always receive prominent mention.

This book is all about helping you become a first-rate strategic writer. As you already know, strategic writing involves delivering goal-oriented messages—messages that are on-strategy. Strategic writing also involves carefully crafted sentences. You don't want to distract your audiences with bad grammar, sloppiness or wordiness. The appendixes of this book contain guidelines on punctuation, grammar, style, editing and proofreading. We hope you'll review those. What follows here are tips for strengthening sentences.

TEN TIPS FOR WRITING BETTER SENTENCES

1. **Challenge *to be* verbs.** Challenge every appearance of *am, is, was, were, be, being, been* and every other form of the *to be* infinitive. Sometimes a *to be* verb best suits the needs of a sentence, but often you can find a stronger, more evocative verb.

Original	Revision
He *will be* a good communicator.	He *will communicate* well.
We *are inviting* you . . .	We *invite* you . . .

2. **Use active voice.** By active voice, we mean active subject. In active voice, the sentence's subject does the action described by the verb. In passive voice, the subject doesn't do the action.

Passive Voice	Active Voice
Our profits were affected by a sales slump.	A sales slump affected our profits.

Passive voice is grammatically correct, and it's the right choice when the action is more important than the action's doer (for example, "She was fired"). But passive voice can seem timid, and it requires a weak *to be* verb. In contrast, active voice is confident and concise.

3. **Challenge modifiers.** Modifiers (adjectives and adverbs) can strengthen a sentence by sharpening your meaning. But sometimes they prop up poorly chosen words, especially imprecise nouns, verbs and adjectives. A precise, well-chosen word needs no modification.

Original	Revision
We are *very happy*.	We are *ecstatic*.
Quickly take your report to the client.	*Rush* your report to the client.
He is *rather tired*.	He is *tired*.
Please deliver the package to our headquarters building.	Please deliver the package to our *headquarters*.

4. **Challenge long words.** If a long word or phrase is the best choice, use it. Otherwise, use a shorter option.

Original	Revision
utilize	use
revenue-enhancement measure	tax

5. **Challenge prepositional phrases.** To tighten sentences, turn prepositional phrases into shorter adjectives when possible. Avoid a string of prepositional phrases.

Original	Revision
I will present the report in the meeting *on Thursday*.	I will present the report in *Thursday's* meeting.
We will meet *on* Thursday *in* Weslaco *at* the Lancaster Hotel *on* McDaniel Street *near* the park.	We will meet Thursday at Weslaco's Lancaster Hotel, 1423 McDaniel St.

6. **Challenge long sentences.** How long should a sentence be? Long enough to make its point clearly and gracefully—and no longer. Challenge sentences that are more than 25 words; realize, however, that some good sentences will exceed that length. As discussed above, you can tighten sentences by eliminating *to be* verbs, modifiers and prepositional phrases.

7. **Avoid overused expressions.** Clichés such as "It has come to my attention" and "I regret to inform you" lack original thought. They sound insincere. Overused figures of speech such as "He's a fish out of water" don't create the engaging image they once did. Overused expressions suggest to readers that you didn't take the time to devote clear, serious thought to the message you're sending.

8. **Avoid placing important words or phrases in the middle of a sentence.** The beginning of a sentence breaks a silence and calls attention to itself. The last words

of a sentence echo into a brief silence and gain emphasis. The middle of a sentence generally draws the least attention. A writer friend of ours says, "Words go to the middle to die."

9. **Keep the focus on the reader.** Tell readers what they want and need to know— not just what you want them to know. Keep the focus on how they benefit from reading your document. Talk to them about themselves and what your message means to them.

10. **Read your sentences aloud.** Or at least whisper them to yourself. That's the surest way to check for effective sentence rhythms. Reading aloud also can be an effective editing technique.

Good writing is also concise, so we'll end this segment.

The Writing Process

Good writing is more than just good luck and natural talent. Good writing is the result of a logical process. Because the writing process can seem intimidating (or just plain hard), some writers prefer to just rush in and start writing. But that's like planning a Spring Break trip with no destination, no map, no budget—and no hope. Other writers may feel so overwhelmed that they avoid the job until it's too late for their best work.

Good writing isn't easy. There's nothing wrong with you if you find writing to be hard work. You can, however, make that hard work a little easier by following a nine-step writing process.

Step One: Research

This book shows you how to write more than 35 documents for public relations, advertising, business communications and sales and marketing. And for each document, we begin with an analysis of purpose, audience and media. We recommend that you do the same.

Begin your research by defining the document's purpose: What is its goal? What should it accomplish? What business goal does it support? With your answers to these questions, you should begin to answer another purpose-related question: What should be the one, key strategic message of this document?

Now extend your research to the target audience of the document. To whom are you writing? Audience research generally falls into two categories: demographic and psychographic data. Demographic data consist of nonattitudinal information such as age, income, gender, educational level, race and so on. Psychographic information contains attitudinal details about values, beliefs, opinions and, of course, attitudes. Psychographic information can include political and religious beliefs, personal ethics codes, goals in life and so on. Use your research to deeply understand your readers. Perhaps the most important question you can answer is why members of your target audience should care about your document. What's in it for them?

With your understanding of your target audience, you might want to refine the one, key strategic message you've begun to identify.

Finally, you should gather information about the medium or media you'll be using. Will you use speeches? News media? Special events? Web sites? Knowing the characteristics of your chosen medium can help you further refine your one, key strategic message. One of the best ways to select the best medium for your message is to study your target audience. Which media does it prefer in this situation?

Step Two: Creativity/Brainstorming

Some documents, such as advertisements, newsletter features and direct-mail packages, call for a high degree of creativity. Other documents, such as news releases and business reports, are more straightforward. When your one, key strategic message requires a creative approach, consider using a basic five-step approach to developing ideas. In the mid-20th century, advertising expert James Webb Young wrote that the creative process consists of these steps:

- Gathering research
- Thinking about your research
- Concentrating on other matters and letting your subconscious go to work
- Recognizing when your subconscious reports back a great idea
- Refining the great idea

A process known as brainstorming can assist the creative process. Brainstorming usually is a group activity in a comfortable setting. Group members toss ideas back and forth, building on one another's ideas, reviewing key research findings and encouraging everyone to be innovative. Brainstorming works best when two rules apply: No one's idea gets ridiculed, and no one worries about who gets the credit.

Step Three: Organizing/Outlining

You've gathered all the necessary information. You've identified a key message and, perhaps, developed a creative approach. Now it's time to determine what to include and how to organize that information.

Many things affect organization, including the target audience's interests, the type of document you're writing and the importance of each piece of information. The best general guidelines for good organization are to consider your audience (what order of information will keep it interested?) and to be logical: You should have a reason for the order of presentation: One part of the document should lead logically to the next.

Writing an outline, whether it's formal with roman numerals or just notes scribbled on an envelope, will help you refine and remember your document's organization. Don't be surprised if you change or reorganize items as you write. New options may appear as you progress. (Experienced writers sometimes can create outlines in their heads—or, as they begin to type, they type a few organizational ideas and then begin composing.)

Step Four: Writing

Finally. Now for perhaps the hardest part of the writing process. Again, writing is tough work for most of us. If you just can't get the beginning, start somewhere else. Your outline allows you to do that. And don't worry about getting the words just right in your first draft. It's more important to get the ideas and meanings right.

Step Five: Revision

One cliché about writing says, "Good writing isn't written; it's rewritten." Even if you love your first draft, set it aside for as long as possible. Return to it fresh, and be critical. Approach the document now not as a writer but as a reader. Poet and novelist Robert Graves recommends imagining that your intended reader is looking over your shoulder and saying, "But what does that mean? Can't it be clearer? What's in this for me? How do I benefit by reading this?"

You might also try reading your document aloud. This can be a good way to catch mistakes or language that doesn't flow well.

Writers who get serious about revision sometimes find that they have accidentally memorized all or parts of a document. With the document temporarily lodged in their memories, the writers are able to revise it as they eat lunch, ride in an elevator or drive home. This may sound excessive (even weird)—but it illustrates the point that good, successful strategic writers don't settle for first drafts.

Step Six: Editing

Sure, colleagues may edit your document. But you should be the document's first editor. Think of editing as the last fine-tuning before you hand the document to your boss. Editing breaks down into two parts—macroediting and microediting—and you should do both. Macroediting involves looking at the "big picture" of the document. Is the document's key message clear and goal-related? Does the document appeal to readers' self-interests? Does it cover the important parts of who, what, when, where, why and how? Is it well-organized—does one section lead logically to the next? Is the format—the way it looks on the page (or computer screen)—correct?

Macroediting also can involve a final revision. Can you find a precise noun to replace a current adjective-noun combination? Can you find a precise verb to replace a current adverb–verb combination? Are you using boring *to be* verbs too often? Can you find more interesting verbs?

Microediting is proofreading. It involves going through the document one sentence at time and double-checking grammar (including spelling and punctuation) and accuracy. *Double-check all names, dates, prices and other facts.* Use your computer's spell-check program, but don't rely on it exclusively. Use a dictionary to look up every word or phrase that could be wrong. Double-check the accuracy of quotations. Microediting is best done backward, starting with the document's last sentence. Moving backward breaks up the flow of the too-familiar document. Moving backward makes the document sound new and different; it helps you focus on each sentence. You'll see what you actually wrote instead of what you meant to write.

Included in Appendix D of this book is the ACT Agenda, a nine-step system for editing and proofreading strategic documents.

Step Seven: Seeking Approval

What could be hard about this stage? All you do is give the document to your boss and anyone else who needs to approve it before distribution. But serious writers know that this can be one of the toughest steps in the writing process. You've done your best with the document, and you're committed to your approach. What if someone with authority wants to change part of it—or all of it?

Keep an open mind. Would the proposed changes make the document more strategic? That is, would they help it reach its goal more effectively? If so, swallow your pride and realize that a successful document often requires a team effort. But if the proposed changes seem to hurt the document's strategic value, do your best to politely debate the revision. Keep everyone's attention focused on the goal.

Never send a document to the target audience without undergoing this approval stage. By this point in the writing process, you're probably too close to your document. It's hard for you to be objective. The document now needs other reviewers and editors. And that can be hard. Avoid being a prima donna—that's the term given to temperamental opera singers who won't accept advice because they think they're perfect.

Step Eight: Distribution

You must now send your document out into the world—or at least to the target audience. You may not be responsible for distribution, but you have a major investment in the document's success. Be sure you know where it's going and how it's getting there. And then be sure that it got there. As we said earlier, the best way to deliver a document is whatever way the target audience prefers. Be sure your research includes *how* the target audience wants to receive the information.

Step Nine: Evaluation

In one sense, you began to evaluate your document much earlier in the writing process. When you considered different creative approaches and when you revised and edited, you were evaluating. In the approval stage when others edited your document, they were evaluating.

But now it's time for the big evaluation: Did your document succeed? Did it accomplish its strategic mission and fulfill its purpose? Learning the answers to these questions can help you do an even better job next time. If your document succeeded, why? If it failed, why? Did it have the desired effect on the target audience? Was its distribution effective and efficient?

Because strategic writers are so busy, evaluation can get overlooked in the rush to the next assignment. However, evaluation of past documents leads to future successes.

The top three problems your authors see in student writing are a lack of research, a lack of strategic (goal-related) focus and a lack of polish (too many first drafts with small errors and awkward passages). We know that the writing process recommended here can seem like busywork. It can seem like something that authors write just to fill pages or professors say just to fill class time. If you're doubtful about the writing process, we ask you to try it before rejecting it. We think that experience will make you a believer—and a better writer.

Writing for Electronic Media

President Abraham Lincoln's speech at the dedication of a battlefield cemetery in Gettysburg, Pennsylvania, in 1863 numbers among the greatest in history. In a mere 268 words, Lincoln captured the essence and the tragedy of the U.S. Civil War.

However, by today's standards, the Gettysburg Address would be the opposite of good oral communication. Consider the last sentence of Lincoln's speech, which was 82 words long:

> It is rather for us to be here dedicated to the great task remaining before us—that from these honored dead we take increased devotion to that cause for which they here gave the last full measure of devotion—that we here highly resolve that these dead shall not have died in vain, that this nation, under God, shall have a new birth of freedom, and that government of the people, by the people, and for the people shall not perish from the earth.

Think of how a modern-day newscaster might have covered the speech:

> And now, Gettysburg. President Lincoln says we honor the nation's dead by preserving the nation. His comments came at the dedication of a military cemetery in Pennsylvania.

Was Lincoln wrong? Of course not. He spoke his eloquent words in a style common to his day. Without rhetorical flourishes that sound antiquated to today's listeners, Lincoln easily could have lost the attention of his audience. Is our newscaster wrong? No, because the newscaster crafted those remarks in a style best suited for today's short attention spans and for the electronic media that helped to create them: broadcast style.

Broadcast style can be adapted for use on the Web, in speech writing and in any situation that requires clear, simple and direct communication.

There are three major similarities between print-style writing (which is created for the eyes) and broadcast-style writing (which is created for the ears—and eyes, in the case of television). We write each in a manner that best suits the audience. We write each in a manner best suited to the purpose behind the message. And we write each in a manner best suited to the medium used to convey the message.

The major difference is that broadcast-style writing uses language and formats that make it easier for the announcer to read the copy and for the listener to understand it. Aural communication, what we hear, is linear. That means there are no second chances. Newspaper readers can pause, reflect and reread a sentence. However, that doesn't happen in radio and television. Once the message is delivered, it's gone. For this reason, broadcast-style writing features short, active voice, subject-verb-object sentences with key information at the start of a sentence. This style remains the same regardless of the message.

Other major differences separate print- and broadcast-style writing. Print media are better suited for details. A radio listener or television viewer easily can get lost in an avalanche of facts and figures. That's why broadcast-style writing favors the use of broad concepts, tangible examples and big ideas. It's also why broadcast writers repeat key phrases and names—especially in advertising, in which the purpose is to have the message remembered.

And, of course, major differences separate writing for radio, which has no pictures, and writing for television, which is dominated by pictures. In television, words and pictures must work in unison. For example, strategic writing for television commercials and video news releases involves designing images as well as crafting the words that enhance them.

TEN BASIC RULES OF BROADCAST-STYLE WRITING

1. **The announcer has to breathe!** Stick to short sentences of 20 words or less. The shorter, the better.

2. **One at a time.** Only one major idea per sentence. Stay away from compound sentences. (The word *and* should raise a red flag.)

3. **Write the way people talk.** The best broadcast copy is conversational. Sentence fragments—just as long as they make sense—are acceptable.

4. **First things first.** In contrast to writing for print media, attribution of paraphrased quotations should be at the beginning of the sentence, before the paraphrase. Because broadcast media are linear, the writer must first let the listener know who is speaking. Otherwise, the listener may not be able to distinguish between the opinions of the announcer and the source. All titles go before a person's name. That goes for official titles, such as "Mayor Mary Smith," and unofficial titles, such as "community activist Mary Smith."

5. **Write S-V-O.** Use simple subject-verb-object sentence structures. Eliminate *to be* verbs whenever possible.

6. **Use active voice.** Make the subject the doer of the action. "Lincoln wrote the Gettysburg Address" is better than "The Gettysburg Address was written by Lincoln."

7. **There's nothing like the present.** Use present tense—except when past tense is necessary. Broadcast media are instantaneous.

Present tense expresses this sense of immediacy. It is especially important that attribution be in present tense, preferably using the neutral *say* and *says*.

8. **Write it as you would say it.** Avoid bureaucratic jargon. Speak the language of your audience. When using initials instead of an organization's name, use hyphens between the letters if the announcer is expected to pronounce each letter. (For example, "F-B-I" for the Federal Bureau of Investigation. However, the common second-reference pronunciation for Mothers against Drunk Driving is "MADD.")

9. **Know your numbers.** In a broadcast script, write words for single-digit numbers (for example, "six" and "nine"). Use figures for two- and three-digit numbers (for example, "23" and "147"). For numbers with four or more digits, use a combination of figures and words (for example, "156-thousand"). Because broadcast media are better suited for big ideas than details, round off large numbers and fractions unless precision is required (for example, "more than 25-thousand" is better than "25,389"). And spell out *dollars* instead of using the dollar sign.

10. **Hit and run.** When writing for television, you have the added dimension of pictures. The challenge is to convey the words and the pictures in a complementary way. This involves what is known as "hit and run writing." Words and pictures are connected

during the first shot of a sequence of camera shots. During the remainder of the sequence, the relationship between words and pictures does not have to be as strong. But when the scene changes, the words and pictures should reconnect during the first shot of the new sequence (hence the name "hit and run").

The format used for broadcast-style writing focuses on the needs of the announcer. Each script serves as a road map for how to present the message. In addition to the words that the announcer will read, the script contains instructions for the use of music, sound effects or prerecorded voices. Television scripts also contain visual instructions. To make it easier for the announcer to follow, you should use large typefaces and double-space the lines. This book will go into greater detail about script formats in later discussions of specific documents.

One important detail of broadcast scripts is the special language strategic writers use to communicate with broadcast producers, directors and editors. We'll close this discussion with a brief glossary of terms you should know to write broadcast scripts and talk the talk with broadcast pros.

Actuality: A recorded quotation that can accompany a radio news release. Also known as a *soundbite.*

Chyron: Words shown on a video screen. Also known as a *super.* A slash (/) indicates a line break in a Chyron message in a script.

CU: A close-up shot in a TV script, often of a face, hands or feet.

Dolly: To physically move a TV camera forward or backward rather than zooming, panning or tilting the camera from a fixed location.

Establishing shot: In a TV or film script, a wide shot (WS) that clarifies the scene for an upcoming sequence of shots.

Establish, then under: A description of playing music at full volume for a short time to attract attention or allow recognition then lowering the volume to allow use under narration.

Fade: In radio, a gradual decrease of volume. In TV, a gradual darkening of a visible scene.

MS: A medium shot in a TV or film script, often of a person shot from the waist up.

Pan: To move a camera's lens from left to right (or right to left) without moving the camera itself from a particular location.

RT: Running time. Specified at the end of radio and TV production scripts.

Sequence: A group of related shots in a TV or film script.

SFX: Sound effect or sound effects.

Shot: A camera placement. When the camera physically moves to a different location, a new shot begins.

SOT: Sound on tape. Often designates natural background sound beneath an announcer's voiceover.

Soundbite: A recorded quotation that can accompany a radio news release.

Tilt: To move a camera's lens up or down without moving the camera itself from a particular location.

Under: A description of quiet background sound or music that runs unobtrusively beneath voices in a radio or TV spot.

VO: Voiceover. Words spoken by an unseen announcer.

WS: A wide shot in a TV or film script, often of a building, a room or a group of people.

Integrated Marketing Communications

Integrated marketing communications—more commonly known as IMC—is a valuable concept for strategic writers. The philosophy of IMC suggests that your target audiences receive several different messages from your organization: ads, news stories triggered by news releases, speeches and even unintended gossip. IMC suggests that all those messages should be coordinated and "on-strategy." Otherwise, your target audiences will receive mixed messages from your organization and will become confused. To better understand IMC, let's look at each of its three words, beginning with *marketing*.

At its core, *marketing* means making consumers want to buy your product and helping them to do so. The "marketing mix" consists of everything from product research and design to packing, pricing and product demonstrations. The marketing mix even includes the product's name. Years ago, marketing professors Philip Kotler and Jerome McCarthy defined the marketing mix with what they called the "Four P's" of marketing:

- Product (including name, design and packaging)
- Price
- Place (including moving the product to where the consumer can buy it)
- Promotion (including tactics from advertising, public relations and sales and marketing)

Strategic writers sometimes believe marketing means only the fourth P, promotion. But marketing means much more.

Now for the word *communications*. The IMC philosophy says that each of the four P's communicates something to consumers. The name, design and package of a product send a message about quality to members of a target audience. So does price ("Wow, that's expensive; it must be luxurious") and place ("Hey, that's an upscale store; this must be a good product"). It's easy to see the communications aspect of the fourth P: Promotion directly involves the strategic writer, who will create ads, direct-mail packages and other sales-related documents.

Finally, the word *integrated*. As you know, the IMC philosophy says that each of the four P's sends messages to consumers. The word *integrated* means that all those messages should work together. In other words, those messages should pursue a single strategy. The messages should not be haphazard and contradictory. For example, a luxurious product with a shockingly cheap price would send mixed messages to a target audience ("I thought that product was prestigious—but not at that price, I guess"). Or that luxurious product, now with a high price, would be out of place in a discount store ("I like that product, but it just loses its prestige by being sold here").

Strategic writers should create promotions with consistent messages. That luxurious product shouldn't have an ad campaign that stresses one benefit, while a related public relations campaign stresses a different benefit and an in-store sales campaign stresses yet a third benefit. Who could blame the target audience for being confused about the product's image? Strategic writers should not just ensure that all written messages are integrated; they should also help ensure that all the messages from the marketing mix—from the Four P's—are integrated.

There's more to IMC than just integration. IMC practitioners

- Try to focus on individual consumers. As much as possible, they develop products for individual consumers, and they create sales messages to target specific consumers' self-interests.
- Use databases to target individual consumers rather than huge target audiences. These databases contain a wealth of information on individual consumers' wants, needs, preferences and buying habits.
- Send a well-focused message to each targeted consumer through a variety of communications, including ads, news releases, direct-mail packages and all other forms of marketing communication, including packaging and pricing.
- Use consumer-preferred media to send their marketing messages.
- Favor interactive media, constantly seeking contact with and information from consumers. New information goes into the databases mentioned earlier. Media such as interactive Web sites can be ideal for IMC.

IMC is a logical extension of strategic writing. Strategic writing begins with the philosophy that a document's message should be on-strategy. IMC extends that philosophy to all related messages, ensuring that a variety of coordinated communications will send the same message to a target audience.

Ethics and Strategic Writing

An ethics code establishes guidelines for behavior. Ethics codes go beyond legal codes into the sometimes confusing world of right and wrong. Something legal, for example, isn't always ethical.

Knowing the right, honorable course of action is often easy. But sometimes difficulty arises in *performing* that action. Sometimes, an unethical alternative can appear easier and less troublesome. For example, announcing and taking responsibility for a serious error—when that error is your own—can be difficult. In other cases, knowing the right, honorable action seems impossible. In an ethics dilemma, every possible course of action seems to cause unfair damage.

The origins of the word *ethics* suggest the challenges of behaving ethically. The Greek origin is *ethos* or *character*. But the earlier, Indo-European root of the word, according to the American Heritage Dictionary, is *s(w)e*—which means that related words include *secret, solitary, sullen, desolate, idiot* and even *suicide*. Even the history of the word *ethics* suggests the difficulty of ethical behavior.

Rewards of Ethical Behavior

Ethical behavior is good for business. Although scholarly studies disagree about whether ethical behavior leads to financial success, they do agree on the opposite: Unethical behavior hurts profits and organizational success. Who would want to do business with crooks and liars? Ethical behavior is a goal-oriented strategy. It can help lead to the fulfillment of an organization's goals—especially long-term goals.

But there are other reasons for practicing good ethics. Ethical behavior is part of most of the world's religions. Greek dramatists (and others, certainly) believed that we all eventually face a moment of *anagnorisis*—a moment of ultimate self-understanding. Most of us, in facing such a moment, would like to see a life well-spent, a life built on honorable, productive relationships with others.

Ethics Codes

Ethics codes—written and unwritten—exist at several levels:

- Social or cultural codes (for example, the Ten Commandments)
- International codes (such as the Caux Business Principles, www.cauxroundtable.org)
- Professional codes, including the following:
  Public Relations Society of America (www.prsa.org)
  American Advertising Federation (www.aaf.org)
  Marketing Research Association (www.mra-net.org)
  International Association of Business Communicators (www.iabc.com)

- Organizational codes (such as the Credo of Johnson & Johnson, www.jnj.com)
- Personal codes (an individual's ethics code, written or otherwise)

Probably the ethics code that matters most to you is your personal code. As a writer, you know that writing down your thoughts stimulates precise thinking. Therefore, consider writing a personal ethics code. Draw upon social, international, professional and organization codes to help create your own.

In writing your ethics code, you may wish to consider some of the great ethics principles of the past millennia. In addition to focusing on principles established by important religious figures, university courses in ethics often emphasize these key philosophers and ideas:

- Both Aristotle and Confucius believed that virtue was a point between the extremes of excess and deficiency. For example, courage is the virtuous mean between cowardice and foolhardy bravery.

- Immanuel Kant believed that before committing ourselves to an action, we should ask ourselves if we would want to live in a world in which everyone did the same thing. For example, could we live in a world in which *all people* broke their promises? Kant also believed that the end did not justify the means. In other words, he believed you couldn't justify a bad action that produced a good conclusion.

- Unlike Kant, John Stuart Mill believed that the end could justify the means. Mill believed that in an ethics dilemma, we should take the action that creates the greatest good for the greatest number of people.

- John Rawls believed that justice involved fairness in the distribution of advantages and disadvantages. He recommended that we empathize with every stakeholder in an ethics dilemma to ensure a fair and tolerable distribution of pleasure and pain.

Your personal ethics code may involve considering each of these philosophies before you make a tough ethics decision. The best times to create and revise your code are when you are *not* facing an ethics crisis. In the depths of such a crisis, you'll need the clear, well-reasoned standards you established when you were free from doubts and fears. A crisis, of course, can prompt you to revise your ethics code.

Ethics Challenges

As a strategic writer, you may face many ethics challenges:

- *Dilemmas,* in which every course of action causes damage. Dilemmas occur when important values clash and it seems impossible to find a solution that honors each value.
- *Overwork,* which can lead you to inadvertently overlook important ethical considerations
- *Legal/ethical confusion,* stemming from the dangerous belief that something legal is always ethical—and that something ethical is always legal

- *Cross-cultural ethics,* in which important values from different cultures clash
- *Short-term thinking,* which promotes a solution that postpones and increases pain and damage
- *Virtual organizations,* which consist of independent employees who temporarily unite to tackle a particular job. Can such organizations agree on ethical behavior?

As you encounter these ethics challenges, remember that your mission is to build honorable, productive relationships that move your organization toward its goals. Ethical behavior isn't easy—but its rewards are deep and lasting.

Ethical Strategic Writing

As an ethical strategic writer, you probably will seek to build honorable, productive relationships between your organization and the groups with which it communicates. In building those ethical relationships, you may want to consider these values: honesty, completeness, timeliness and fair distribution.

Honest Documents
- Context can affect honesty. For example, if you note that a production quota was met for the first time, you might also need to note that the quota had been reduced so that it could be met.
- Hard truths sometimes can hurt. Be diplomatic. Put yourself in the place of those affected by those truths.
- For legal and competitive reasons, documents cannot always contain every detail about every matter. But your documents should include accurate details in an honest context.

Complete Documents
- As noted above, you can sometimes ethically withhold information. Justifications for withholding information include legal restrictions, individual rights to privacy and loss of competitive advantage. However, you should not withhold controversial information that a group has a right or a need to know. To paraphrase a famous politician, "If bad news will come out eventually— and it will—it should come out immediately."
- *Complete* is a relative term. In your documents, you should give groups the information they need and deserve. Most groups don't want to be buried in an avalanche of details. If there's any doubt about information a group needs, ask its members. Or use your best judgment and offer to provide more information upon request.

Timely Documents
- Important information should be distributed quickly. This is especially true during crises for your organization or the groups with which it communicates.

Fair Distribution of Documents

- The goal of distribution should be to reach every person who needs to see that message. Meeting this goal means using the communication channels preferred by recipients—which may not be the channels that you would prefer.

We hope you'll agree that ethical communication is not just the right thing to do; it's also a smart business decision. Strategic writing builds productive relationships. Good ethics are a strong foundation for productive relationships that will stand the test of time.

Diversity and Strategic Writing

Diversity is a familiar concept in the 21st century. Many organizations aggressively seek employees from groups that sometimes are underrepresented in the work force, including

- Women
- Members of racial and ethnic minorities
- The physically and mentally challenged
- Gay and lesbian individuals
- Older workers
- Members of non-Christian religions

Organizations seek diversity for several reasons: Diversity is often a moral goal; it can be a regulatory requirement; it improves the organization's public image; it attracts the best employees.

The authors of this book want to offer an additional benefit of diversity: good writing. Appreciation of diversity will make you a better strategic writer. Specifically, we recommend that strategic writers seek and study diversity in three areas:

- Strategic communication staffs
- Sources of information
- Target audiences

Diversity in strategic communication staffs is more than a moral policy or compliance with regulations; it's a good business decision. Even within the same country, people from different cultural backgrounds have different values, concerns, hopes and communication traditions. For example, a word or image can be innocent to one person yet highly offensive to someone from a different culture. As international strategic communication becomes a daily reality, the dangers of cross-cultural blunders increase. Having a diverse communication staff—and seeking knowledgeable partners in other nations—increases the likelihood of recognizing and preventing cross-cultural blunders.

Diversity of sources also helps ensure successful strategic communication. In gathering research for the documents you write, draw upon diverse individuals—especially those you will quote or cite by name. Sources whose backgrounds offer different views of an issue may provide valuable new insights that help you achieve your strategic goal. In many organizations, it's easy to rely on a steady stream of white Anglo-Saxon males in their 40s and 50s. Although these men aren't necessarily bad sources, a diverse group of sources can offer more perspectives.

The diversity of target audiences can vary widely. Although strategic writers should carefully study the values and concerns that unite members of a target audience, they also should be aware of differences within the target audience. To address a large group, strategic writers often must focus on the values of the majority. Whenever possible, however, strategic writers must know and avoid things that might alienate different minority groups or individuals within the target audience. Strategic writers should avoid stereotyping members of the target audience.

Strategic writers can show appreciation for diversity by following these guidelines:

1. Balance personal pronouns (*he* and *she*). For unnamed generic individuals, such as *supervisor* or *client,* balance the use of *he* and *she.* Don't, however, include illogical shifts: A hypothetical supervisor shouldn't change gender within a paragraph. Another solution is to use plural nouns—*supervisors* and *clients*—that can be replaced by *they.*

2. Avoid words that describe particular relationships: *your wife, your husband, your boyfriend, your girlfriend, your parents, your children.* The term *your wife* generally excludes female readers, just as *your husband* can exclude male readers. Let your target audience be your guide as to what is appropriate.

3. Know the dates of major religious holidays and events. When is Rosh Hashanah? When is Ramadan? When is Easter?

4. Don't describe individuals by race, ethnicity, religion, age, sexual orientation, or physical or mental characteristics unless the information is relevant to your document's purpose. If an individual must be so described, consider applying the same exactness of description to every other individual mentioned in the document.

5. If you are responsible for a document's design, apply your quest for inclusiveness to photographs and other visual representations of individuals. Even if you're *not* in charge of the design, don't hesitate to point out lapses of diversity.

The array of terms for ethnic and racial groups can present challenges for strategic writers. A landmark 1995 U.S. Bureau of Labor Statistics survey of almost 60,000 households revealed these preferences:

- Blacks prefer *black* (44 percent) to *African American* (28 percent) and *Afro-American* (12 percent).
- Hispanics prefer *Hispanic* (58 percent) to *of Spanish origin* (12 percent) and *Latino/Latina* (12 percent).
- American Indians prefer *American Indian* (50 percent) to *Native American* (37 percent).
- Multiracial individuals prefer *multiracial* (28 percent) to *mixed-race* (16 percent).

In many ways, diversity can be an asset for your organization. Be aware of its value in your quest to be a successful strategic writer.

Persuasion and Strategic Writing

Persuasion is a controversial concept. People often see persuasion as a win–lose game: One side wins, and the other side loses. However, persuasion in strategic writing works best when it promotes a win–win scenario. Effective strategic writing seeks benefits for all sides in a relationship.

How can strategic writers create win–win scenarios? One way is to understand the target audience. Dean Rusk, a former U.S. secretary of state, once said, "The best way to persuade anyone of anything is to listen." When strategic writers listen to the hopes, fears, concerns and desires of their target audiences, they are better prepared to create strategic messages that satisfy both the organization and the target audience. Strategic writers who listen can help shape persuasive messages that unify rather than divide.

As you listen to members of a target audience, seek an answer to the all-important question of WIIFM: What's in it for me? In other words, how will members of the target audience benefit from the information in your document? What's in it for them? If you're writing an advertisement, how will consumers gain from purchasing your product? If you're writing a news release, why is the news important to journalists and their audiences? If you're writing a proposal, why should readers want to use your ideas? Imagine that every target audience is ready to greet your message with two shouted responses: "So what? What's in it for me?" If your message can answer these questions and present benefits to the target audience, you can probably reverse the process and get *them* to listen to *you*.

In some situations, listening becomes dialogue—and dialogue becomes negotiation and persuasion. You do this frequently when you listen to a friend, consider his concerns and attempt to move him toward an action that will benefit you both. Communication scholars George Cheney and Phillip Tompkins have developed four principles that they believe should guide persuasive negotiations:

1. **Empathy.** You should truly listen, motivated by a desire to find a solution that's best for everyone.
2. **Guardedness.** Just because you're willing to listen doesn't mean you have to agree and change your own opinions.
3. **Accessibility.** On the other hand, be willing to consider changing your own opinion. Consider that you might be wrong.
4. **Nonviolence.** Threats have no place in ethical persuasion.

By following these four principles, you can support your organization and still keep an open mind as you search for a win–win solution.

Just as listening is key to successful persuasion, so is your character as a persuader. Personal credibility is one of the most powerful tools of persuasion. Almost 2,500 years ago, Aristotle wrote that there are three approaches to persuasion: *logos* (an appeal to the target audience's intellect); *pathos* (an appeal to the target audience's emotions); and *ethos* (an appeal based on the speaker's character). Communication scholars today still agree with Aristotle's analysis. Of those three approaches, Aristotle wrote that *ethos* was often the most powerful. (We've all heard that "virtue is its own reward"—but in negotiations, virtue provides an additional reward: persuasive power.) As you learn more about a target audience, you should consider what combination of *logos, pathos* and *ethos* would be most persuasive.

Almost a century ago, communication scholar Alan Monroe developed a blueprint for persuasive messages. Today, many strategic writers use "Monroe's Motivated Sequence," which consists of five parts:

1. **Attention.** Grab the target audience's attention. Chances are, the target is overwhelmed by messages. Cut through the clutter. Get noticed.
2. **Need.** Describe an important problem that the target audience faces—a problem that needs a solution. (You'll discover this need/problem by listening.)
3. **Satisfaction.** Offer a solution that benefits both you and the target audience.
4. **Visualization.** Explain the consequences of inaction.
5. **Action.** Tell the target audience what it can do to solve the problem.

Monroe's Motivated Sequence can work in several documents described in this book: speeches, memos, ads, sales letters, proposals and many more.

Persuasion is unavoidable in strategic writing. Ethical persuasion, based on listening and seeking win–win relationships, can create enduring, successful relationships.

The Law and Strategic Writing

In the United States, courts have ruled that strategic writing is similar to speech—and freedom of speech is protected by the First Amendment to the U.S. Constitution:

> Congress shall make no law respecting an establishment of religion, or prohibiting the free exercise thereof; or abridging the freedom of speech, or of the press; or the right of the people peaceably to assemble, and to petition the government for a redress of grievances.

So strategic writing has constitutional protection. That means strategic writers can legally write whatever they please—right?

Wrong.

Freedom of speech in the United States has limits. For example, you can't legally shout "Fire!" in a crowded movie theater. You can't legally create, publish and distribute obscene material. You can't legally threaten national security. Freedom of speech is a relative term. Strategic writing operates within some legal restrictions.

Legal restrictions on strategic writing depend on the purpose of the writing. U.S. courts have ruled that free expression falls into two general categories: political speech and commercial speech. When your organization expresses its opinion on a social issue—such as support for literacy programs—that communication is political speech. Political speech faces few legal restrictions because, the courts have ruled, the free exchange of ideas is essential to democracy. However, when your organization communicates in pursuit of a financial goal—such as an advertisement designed to sell your product—that advertisement is commercial speech. Commercial speech faces more legal restrictions than political speech.

Communication laws constantly evolve, and strategic writers should strive to keep up with those changes. Traditionally, strategic writers should keep up-to-date in five areas: libel, invasion of privacy, deceptive advertising, copyright and financial disclosure. These five areas don't divide neatly between political speech and commercial speech. Advertising, for example, usually would be commercial speech. However, an ad that supports local literacy programs might be considered political speech. Strategic writers should never assume that their documents automatically are political speech and, as such, enjoy greater freedom of expression.

Libel, according to the Associated Press, is "injury to reputation." If a strategic document includes an untrue claim that exposes an individual to public scorn, hatred or ridicule, that message may be libelous—and, therefore, subject to legal action. For a message to be libelous, it must have these qualities:

- *Defamation.* The message must expose an individual to public scorn, hatred or ridicule.
- *Publication.* The message must be published. However, courts have defined publication very broadly. Sending an e-mail message to another person can constitute publication.

■ *Identification.* The message must identify the defamed individual. However, identification need not be by name. If a description of the individual is so complete that a name is unnecessary, identification has occurred.
■ *Negligence.* The message must be inaccurate, and there must be little excuse for that inaccuracy. However, public figures such as politicians have a higher burden of proof for negligence. The U.S. Supreme Court has ruled that public figures must prove that the writer acted with *actual malice,* which is defined as "knowing falsehood or reckless disregard for the truth."
■ *Damage.* The message must have damaged the identified individual. Damage can be as specific as financial losses or as vague as loss of reputation.

The U.S. Constitution doesn't guarantee a citizen's right to privacy. However, communication law does protect some areas of privacy. Illegal invasion of an individual's right to privacy usually comes in one of four forms:

1. *Intrusion* involves a physical violation of an individual's privacy. Trespassing to sort through a competitor's garbage could constitute intrusion.
2. *False light* involves portraying an individual in an improper and unfair context. Publishing a photograph of a competitor walking through a door seems inoffensive. But an inaccurate suggestion that the photograph shows the competitor entering your business to purchase your product would be portraying the photograph and the competitor in a false light.
3. *Publication of private facts* involves the disclosure of information that isn't newsworthy or part of any public record. For example, writing a news release about the minor personal problems of a competitor could constitute publication of private facts, particularly if that individual is not a public figure.
4. *Appropriation* involves using someone's name, voice, likeness or other defining characteristic without that person's permission. For example, using a photograph of a popular musician in an ad without that person's permission would be appropriation. An act of appropriation is said to violate an individual's *right of publicity* or *right to publicity.* These rights do not end with a person's death.

As databases provide more and more access to information about target audiences (see Integrated Marketing Communications in Section I), strategic writers must understand the legal limits of acquiring and communicating personal information.

In the United States, deceptive advertising doesn't necessarily mean untrue advertising. In this country, advertisers can legally stretch the truth—within limits. For example, a new toothpaste may seem to promise teeth so white that passersby will gasp in admiration and write you love poems. Do consumers really believe that? Probably not: The exaggerations are just a humorous way to make a point. Acceptable exaggeration in advertising is called *puffery.*

But what happens if that same toothpaste ad falsely claims that the product prevents sore throats? If the ad presents that falsehood in a way that could fool a reasonable consumer, it becomes deceptive advertising. The U.S. Federal Trade

Commission determines when puffery deviates into deceptive advertising, and it has a range of punishments it can apply, including forcing the company to run corrective advertising that retracts false claims. To separate puffery from deceptive advertising, the FTC uses the "reasonable consumer standard." That standard says that if an ad could deceive a reasonable consumer who expects exaggeration in advertising, the ad becomes deceptive and, therefore, illegal.

Laws regarding puffery and deceptive advertising differ from country to country—as do laws regarding libel, invasion of privacy and other key legal areas outlined in this chapter. Writers who help create international strategic communications campaigns should be aware of those differences.

Companies that sell stock—publicly owned companies—are subject to disclosure law. Disclosure law governs how and when companies communicate about matters that affect or could affect their stock prices. Disclosure regulations began as a response to abuses that helped create the Great Depression almost a century ago. Their purpose is to ensure that every investor has a fair and equal chance in the stock market. Publicly owned companies must provide quarterly financial reports (Form 10Q) and annual financial reports (Form 10K) to the federal Securities and Exchange Commission. They also must provide annual reports and annual meetings for their stockholders. Publicly owned companies must notify the SEC of unusual events that could affect stock prices (Form 8K). Those companies also must notify stockholders about such news, usually through news releases sent to relevant news media. All disclosure-related communication must comply with SEC Rule 10b-5, which prohibits deceptive or misleading statements in all such communications.

Copyright law protects intellectual property. Federal law defines *intellectual property* as "original works of authorship that are fixed in a tangible form of expression." For strategic writers, copyright law regulates our use of someone else's creative work in our documents. To use such work, we must gain the creator's written permission. Often, we also must pay a fee established by the work's creator. Exceptions do exist: The "fair use" doctrine allows students, teachers, reporters, reviewers and others to use copyrighted works to inform others. However, fair use generally does not protect those who borrow intellectual property for commercial purposes. Even if fair use does protect such borrowing, strategic writers should always credit, in writing, the creator of the work. Although copyrighted material often is marked by the symbol ©, a work has legal copyright protection from the moment its creator establishes it in a fixed, tangible form. For example, a brochure that you create has legal copyright protection even though you have not applied to the U.S. Copyright Office or included the © symbol. You also should know that work completed for an employer generally is "work for hire" and legally belongs to the employer.

If you own this book, you probably are more interested in being a writer than a lawyer. Relax: You needn't know the letter of the law to succeed as a strategic writer. However, you should know the basic regulations of political and commercial speech. And when you know one of your documents contains legally questionable material, it's a good time to start asking questions—of bosses, clients and, yes, even of lawyers.

Jobs in Strategic Writing

Don't let the brevity of this segment alarm you: Jobs in strategic writing *do* exist. As long as businesses communicate, strategic writers will have jobs. Good strategic writers will have choices among good jobs. And really good strategic writers may discover an irony in their careers: Their successes in writing may pull them away from writing. A great ad copywriter may become an agency's creative director—more memos, proposals and business letters, certainly, but fewer ads. A talented writer of newsletter stories may soon become the editor of the newsletter—more money, but less writing. These talented individuals will groom the next generation of strategic writers, searching for writers as good as themselves. Good writers recognize and value good writing.

So where do you start? Start by proving that you're a good strategic writer. Seek internships and volunteer opportunities that will allow you to write. Do real writing for real clients. Enjoy your successes and learn from your failures. Pay attention to your professors. Collect your best work in a portfolio that will impress potential employers.

Every business needs strategic writing. Some businesses do it in-house, others hire agencies and many combine both approaches. One good way to find a satisfying job in strategic writing is to pick a geographic area that interests you—say, Tierra del Fuego (we hope you speak Spanish). Now examine what organizations have offices in Tierra del Fuego. Begin your job search by studying and applying to those organizations.

Another job-search strategy involves combining your talent in strategic writing with a passion in your life. One of our favorite recent graduates was a double major in public relations and art history. She is now marketing director for an art museum.

Jobs in strategic writing tend to cluster in five categories: corporations; agencies; nonprofit organizations and trade associations; government agencies; and independent consultancies. Let's quickly look at each.

Corporations

Corporations are for-profit businesses that can be as large as General Motors or as small as a local dry cleaner. This book, as you know, focuses on four areas of strategic writing: public relations, advertising, business communications, and sales and marketing. Corporations, especially large ones, hire strategic writers in all four areas. Because corporations are for-profit businesses, they have relationships with a wide variety of groups: customers, employees, government regulators, the news media, stockholders and many more. Developing and maintaining these relationships requires strategic writing. Of these five employment categories, corporations tend to pay the highest starting salaries for entry-level strategic writers.

Agencies

Agencies supply advice and strategic communications for other organizations. Some agencies are international, with offices throughout the world. Others operate from spare bedrooms in suburban houses. Three broad categories exist: advertising agencies, public relations agencies and full-service marketing agencies that combine advertising, public relations and other sales and marketing functions. Because agencies are businesses, they rely on business communications: reports, memos, business correspondence and more. Of the five employment categories, agencies tend to have the second-highest starting salaries for strategic writers.

Nonprofit Organizations and Trade Associations

Nonprofit organizations provide services without the expectation of earning a profit. They can be as large as the World Wildlife Fund or as small as the local community college. Trade associations resemble nonprofit organizations in that they offer services without the primary motive of profit. Trade associations include such groups as the National Association of Home Builders. Like corporations, nonprofit organizations and trade associations traditionally have strategic writing positions in public relations, advertising, business communication, and sales and marketing. And because these organizations generally have smaller communications staffs than do corporations, they offer great opportunities for writers who don't want to specialize. A strategic writer for a small nonprofit organization may work on a news release, a print ad, a proposal, a fund-raising letter and a memo all on the same day. Of the five employment categories, nonprofits tend to have the third-highest starting salaries for strategic writers.

Government Agencies

Government agencies exist at the international, national, state and local levels. They can be as big and well-known as the U.S. Securities and Exchange Commission or as small as your local school district. Strategic writing can be a diplomatically sensitive subject for government agencies. If they openly engage in public relations, advertising and marketing to promote themselves or elected politicians, members of the voting public may cry, "Propaganda! Waste of taxpayers' money!" Yet some government programs and projects must be promoted, such as the U.S. Department of Agriculture's food pyramid. Strategic writers for government agencies must constantly be aware of the gray area between legitimate strategic communication and unacceptable promotion. Of the five employment categories, government agencies tend to have the fourth-highest starting salaries for strategic writers.

Independent Consultancies

An independent consultant is a freelancer. A freelancer may often be part of a "virtual organization," a business group that forms for one project and then disbands.

Independent consultants generally specialize in one of the professions discussed in this book—public relations, for example. However, versatility can mean more clients and more profits. In addition to strategic writing, independent consultants carry the burden of finding clients, answering the phone, filing, making coffee and finding time for a life. Of the five employment categories, we rank independent consultancies last in starting salaries—and, in a sense, that's unfair. Successful consultants often earn more than the average corporate strategic writer. However, very few strategic writers begin as independent consultants. Instead, they work for other organizations, learn the ropes, earn a reputation—and then take a deep breath and go out on their own. Consultants usually are experienced professionals. The concept of starting salary takes on a different meaning for consultants.

The authors of this book believe in the value of strategic writing. We believe in the value of *jobs* in strategic writing. So work hard. Do research. Stay on message. Get experience. Build a great portfolio. Somewhere out there, a job in strategic writing waits for you.

Section II
Strategic Writing in Public Relations

Objectives

In Section II: Strategic Writing in Public Relations,
you will learn to write these documents:

- Print news releases
- Media advisories
- Pitch letters
- Radio news release scripts
- Video news release scripts
- Media kit backgrounders

- Media kit fact sheets
- Media kit photo opportunity sheets
- Newsletter and magazine stories
- Annual reports
- Speeches
- Web documents

Public relations often gets confused with publicity. Public relations certainly includes publicity—but it includes much more. A standard definition of *public relations* shows how broad the profession can be: Public relations is the values-driven management of relationships with publics that are essential to an organization's success.

As we noted in Section I, well-run organizations often have values statements that define their beliefs, the principles they hope to follow and how they see their role in society. One challenge for public relations practitioners is to build relationships that honor not only those values but also the values of the other group in a relationship—the values of journalists, for example, or the values of stockholders.

Well-run organizations also have goals consistent with their values. To reach those goals, they often need resources that the organization's managers don't control. For example, to reach its goals a major corporation needs resources held by employees (the willingness to work hard); stockholders (the willingness to buy stock and to vote for the managers in annual meetings); the news media (the willingness to cover the organization fairly); and many other resources held by other groups. Public relations practitioners strive to develop positive, productive relationships with publics that control essential resources. Those relationships are productive when the organization receives the needed resources.

The term *public* has a specific meaning in public relations. A public is any group whose members have a common interest or common values in a particular situation.

Those people don't need to be official members with official T-shirts and secret hand-shakes. A public can be as official as the members of a state legislature or as unofficial as the residents of a neighborhood where your organization wants to build homes for Habitat for Humanity.

Many of us think of public relations as a process of getting different groups to like our organization—of getting our organization's message to people and making them agree with it. Just like publicity, that can be part of public relations. But, again, public relations is bigger than that. We want different publics to like our organization because those groups have resources that we need. Basically, public relations strives to acquire resources by building positive relationships.

The actual practice of public relations follows a process that we also find in advertising, business communication, and sales and marketing. That process consists of four stages: research, planning, communication and evaluation. As straightforward as that seems, sometimes the process moves backward. For example, as we create a plan based on our research, we may discover that we need more research before we can finish planning. Or as we communicate in accordance with our plan, the situation may change, forcing us to go back to the planning stage. Evaluation is a form of research that can lead to more planning. But in general, we conduct research, and we plan before we communicate. Again, this applies not only to public relations but also to advertising, business communication, and sales and marketing.

Professors James Grunig and Todd Hunt have identified four different models of public relations:

1. *The press agentry model* focuses on gaining favorable publicity from the news media.
2. *The public information model* focuses on distributing accurate information to those who request it, such as members of the news media.
3. *The two-way asymmetrical model* focuses on researching and communicating with target publics to get them to agree with an organization.
4. *The two-way symmetrical model* focuses on researching and communicating with target publics to build productive relationships that benefit both sides. In this model, the organization recognizes that sometimes it needs to change in order to build a productive relationship.

Few organizations follow just one model exclusively. For example, an organization may use the symmetrical model or the asymmetrical model depending on the particular relationship or who is in charge of planning. However, new research shows that well-run, successful organizations tend to favor the two-way symmetrical model.

Strategic writing is a foundation for successful public relations. To build productive relationships with different publics, we communicate with them. Much of that communication is written as speeches, news releases, newsletter stories and more.

News Release Guidelines

Purpose, Audience and Media

A news release is a document that conveys newsworthy information about your organization to the news media. Journalists generally agree that a newsworthy story has at least one (and probably more) of the following elements.

- **Timeliness.** The story contains new information.
- **Impact.** The story affects a journalist's readers, viewers or listeners.
- **Uniqueness.** The story is different from similar stories.
- **Conflict.** The story involves a clash of people and/or forces, such as nature.
- **Proximity.** The story describes events geographically close to the targeted readers, viewers or listeners.
- **Celebrity.** The story involves a famous person such as a politician, business leader or entertainer.

Most often, a news release is written as a ready-to-publish news story. You write a news release in the hope that journalists will take its information and publish or broadcast it in their news media, thus sending your news to hundreds or thousands—perhaps even millions—of people.

Don't be hurt if your news release isn't published or broadcast verbatim. Most are not. Journalists often use news releases as story tips, and they rewrite your work, sometimes with additional information. If the journalist's story includes your main points and doesn't introduce any negatives, your news release succeeded.

The news release is often called the press release, a term that is outdated and inappropriate. Most of us get our news not only from print news media (which use a printing press) but also from television, radio and the World Wide Web. The term *news release* seems more appropriate.

Still, news releases generally are written as if they were for newspapers. Other news media, such as television stations, then edit news releases for their particular needs.

In general, three styles of news releases exist, each of which is described in following sections:

1. Announcement (the straight news story)
2. Feature story (a combination of information and entertainment)
3. Hybrid story (a combination of the feature and the announcement)

Three other documents are similar to news releases. Unlike news releases, they are not in ready-to-publish form. Each of these is described in upcoming segments.

1. Short teasers (brief tantalizing descriptions of newsworthy items)
2. Media advisory (quick information on a breaking news story)
3. Pitch letter (an exclusive offer of a story to a particular journalist)

The audience of a news release is a journalist. To be a successful news release writer, you must focus intensely on what journalists like and dislike in news stories. They like conciseness; they dislike wordiness. They like specifics; they dislike generalities. They like reputable sources; they dislike unattributed opinions. They like objective facts; they dislike promotional writing. They like honesty and candor; they dislike dishonesty and evasion. Too often, news releases get written to the wrong audience: They become promotional documents designed to please bosses and clients. Journalists have a time-honored place for such news releases: the wastebasket.

News releases exist in a variety of media: Many are still written on paper and sent through the mail. Others are placed on Web sites. Others are sent as e-mail messages, and still others are burned onto CDs and mailed. You can deliver radio and video news releases via tape, disks and satellite signals. News releases have even been written on the labels of champagne bottles and sent to journalists (attached to a full bottle, of course).

■ **Key to Success:** A news release should contain only newsworthy information. It should not be a thinly disguised advertisement for your organization. A good news release has a local angle; that is, journalists read it and quickly see that the information it contains is relevant to their readers, listeners or viewers.

Format/Design

When possible, a news release should be on your organization's stationery. Use letterhead stationery (with your organization's logo, for example) only for the first page. If the news release extends to a second page, however, don't switch to a different color or quality of paper. Use a blank sheet that matches the paper stock of the first page. In mass mailings, it's all right to use photocopies of letterhead stationery, but if the budget permits, use originals. Some organizations use special news release stationery that clearly labels the document as a news release.

Headings (Format)

If the stationery doesn't label the document as a news release, type "News Release" in big, bold letters—usually 24-point type. Below that, begin the actual news release with headings that specify "FOR IMMEDIATE RELEASE," the composition date and "FOR MORE INFORMATION" data: a contact person, the person's title, a phone number and an e-mail address.

The headings should be single-spaced.

Leave about two inches between the headings and the headline. All together, the headings of a news release should look something like Figure 1.

Organization Letterhead

News Release

FOR IMMEDIATE RELEASE
Nov. 20, 2005

FOR MORE INFORMATION:
Catherine Jones
Public Relations Director
(555) 123-4567
cjones@xyz.org

Circle City Red Cross schedules downtown blood drive

FIGURE 1

The Headline (Format)
Your headline should be a newspaper-style headline (see page 34).

Boldface the headline. Capitalize the first word and any names (of people, buildings, organizations and so on). Lowercase all other words, just as most newspapers do.

The Text (Format)
Double-space the text of news releases written and distributed on paper. Double-spacing provides room for journalists to edit the release. You may single-space digital news releases distributed through e-mail, CDs and Web sites.

The text of a news release should be long enough to tell the story concisely—and no longer. The entire release rarely should be more than two pages—one front and one back, or two separate pages. Make it shorter, if possible. Many news releases are one page.

Page Numbers, Slugs and Similar Items
If the news release is more than one page, type "-more-" or "-over-" at the bottom of each appropriate page. Beginning with page two, place a condensed version of the release's headline (called a "slug") and the page number in the upper-right corner. After the last line of the news release, space down one more line and type "-30-" or "###."

Staple the pages of the news release together. Never trust a paper clip.

Content and Organization

Focus on your audience: a journalist who seeks newsworthy information for her audience. What kind of information is newsworthy?

- Timely information that affects members of a news medium's audience. Such information is said to have "local interest"—an important quality to journalists.
- Timely information that is unusual or exceptional
- Timely information about a well-known individual or organization

For additional qualities of newsworthiness, see page 31.

The Headline

News release headlines are written in newspaper style. Most newspaper headlines are, roughly, complete sentences.

Most newspaper headlines are written in present tense, which, in headline grammar, means recent past tense. For example, "Palmquist University celebrates anniversary" means that the university recently celebrated—probably yesterday. Some headlines, however, require future tense. If the university is planning an anniversary celebration and you are writing a news release to gain support and publicity, the headline would be "Palmquist University to celebrate anniversary."

A good headline includes local interest and summarizes the story's main point. Whenever gracefully and logically possible, mention your organization's name or product in the headline.

The Dateline

Begin the text with a dateline in capital letters and a dash (for example, "DALLAS–"). Datelines give the location of the story. They help establish local interest and answer the reporter's question *where?* Datelines also can include dates (for example, "DALLAS, Jan. 24–").

The Text

With or without a dateline, the first sentence of a news release usually should establish local interest and should move right to the news. A good newsworthy first sentence often concisely covers *who, what, when* and *where.* In a traditional news story, the first paragraph, also called the lead, includes the most important information about the story. It never relies on the headline to supply information. Instead, the headline summarizes information included in the lead.

A traditional news release is structured as an inverted pyramid, which means that the most important information is at the top of the story (the widest part of the upside-down pyramid). As the story continues and the pyramid becomes narrower, the information becomes less and less important.

Include a pertinent, attention-grabbing quotation from a representative of your organization in the second or third paragraph. Such quotations can enliven news releases, making them more attractive to journalists and news audiences alike. Good quotations provide color, emotion or opinion—or all three. Avoid quotations that recite facts or statistics.

Optional Notes to the Editor

If some information, such as the spelling of a name, is unusual, include a single-spaced "Note to the Editor" after the "-30-" or "###" to inform editors that your information is correct. This is not necessary for routine information.

Distribution and Follow-Up

Send all news releases to specific journalists by name and title. Find out who appropriate editors are at each medium. Books such as *Bacon's Media Directories* and *Working Press of the Nation* can be helpful, as can software such as MediaMap. Some local chambers of commerce also can supply local media lists to organizations.

If the news release announces an event, be sure that newspapers, radio and television stations and news Web sites receive it about 10 days before the event. Magazines generally need more advance notice than that; six months isn't too early for some monthly or quarterly magazines.

Consider paying a distribution service, such as PR Newswire or Business Wire, to distribute your news release. Such services can electronically transmit your news release directly to journalists throughout the world. Studies show that editors prefer to receive news releases electronically, via newswire services, e-mail, searches of Web sites and even, in some cases, faxes. However, many news releases, especially those that are part of media kits (pages 65–75) still are printed on paper and sent through the mail. Whenever possible, ask specific reporters how they prefer to receive news releases from your organization.

Send only one copy of your news release to each appropriate news medium. Don't send your news release to several reporters at the same news medium, hoping it will interest one of them. Send it to the most appropriate reporter or editor at each news outlet.

A continuing debate in public relations concerns follow-up calls—that is, telephoning journalists to ensure that they received the news release and to offer assistance. Most journalists resent such calls unless you've offered an exclusive story (see page 36). If your news release presents a story of interest to a journalist's audience, the journalist will call you if he needs more information. Journalists are too busy and receive far too many news releases each day to answer questions from eager news release writers. However, some situations do justify a follow-up call. For example, if you send a media advisory (see pages 47–49) on a fast-breaking news story that you know journalists will want to cover, they probably will appreciate a quick follow-up call to ensure they received the information.

If you must call regarding a news release of crucial importance, be polite. Remember: Journalists are under no obligation to use your story. If you are unable to reach the journalist, don't leave more than two messages. Don't earn a label as a nuisance.

Never ask journalists if their organizations used your news releases. That tells them that you're not reading, listening to or watching their work.

Telephone Pitches

Presenting a story *idea* (instead of a written story) to a journalist is known as "pitching to the media." A pitch can be oral, as in a telephone call, or written, as in a pitch letter (pages 50–53).

Some journalists will consider newsworthy story ideas over the phone. Often, telephone pitches work best when the journalist and the public relations practitioner know and trust each other. Some public relations practitioners, however, are willing to fight the odds and phone journalists they don't know. Such calls as known as cold calls.

Pitches very often are exclusive offers, meaning that when a journalist agrees to a story, the public relations practitioner does not offer the idea to other journalists. Sometimes, exclusives apply only to regions. For example, an exclusive story might simultaneously be pitched to journalists in Cincinnati, Pittsburgh, Denver and similar large cities that don't have a national medium, such as the *New York Times*.

Successful telephone pitches share a basic strategy:

1. Thoroughly understand the needs of the particular medium (a radio show, for example) and the journalist. Be familiar with the medium's recent content.
2. Know the daily deadline times of the journalists you plan to phone—and don't phone at those times.
3. Come right to the point. Show why the idea will interest the journalist's audience.
4. Be well-informed, ready to answer the journalist's questions.
5. Be prepared to act if the journalist wants to start work immediately.
6. Never lie. Never promise more than you can deliver.

Finally, if a telephone pitch fails, accept rejection gracefully. Don't damage a relationship with a journalist over one unsuccessful pitch.

TIPS

1. Ensure that the phone number in the For More Information heading provides 24-hour/seven-day-a-week access to the contact person. Many organizations ensure that contact people have cell phones or satellite phones to guarantee that journalists have immediate access.
2. Avoid using the words *today, yesterday* and *tomorrow* in your news release. Journalists almost always will have to change those words. For example, your *today* probably will be incorrect by the time your news release is published or broadcast. Using an actual date—for example, Jan. 23—can solve this problem. Daily news media, such as newspapers and radio or TV stations, often use days of the week, as in "XYZ Partners will build two factories in Puerto Rico in 2006, the corporation announced Wednesday." The present-perfect verb tense can be used to denote the immediate past, as in "XYZ Partners has announced third-quarter profits of $50 million."
3. Use past-tense verbs to attribute quotes. Use *said* instead of *says* in print-oriented news releases.

4. Be precise and concise. Every word that journalists print or broadcast costs money.

5. Remember the importance of local interest. Ask yourself why your news will appeal to the audience of each news medium that will receive your news release. Use the news release's headline and first sentence to spotlight local interest. (The word *local* doesn't have to mean hometown. For example, a news release about an important new product that will be used by consumers throughout the world has "local" interest to readers on all continents. Finding individual hometown angles, however, can strengthen a news release.)

6. Avoid promotional writing, except in short teasers (pages 44–46). You, as the writer, should be completely objective. Don't include unattributed opinions (your opinions) about your organization's excellence. If the news release is a thinly disguised advertisement for your organization, its chances of being published or broadcast are remote. Strive for the objective voice that appeals to journalists.

7. Be sure that your manager and/or your client reviews the news release before it is sent to the news media. After you review their comments or suggested revisions, you may need to remind them that a news release should be an objective, unbiased news story.

8. Avoid so-called embargoed news releases—that is, news releases that aren't for immediate publication. With an embargoed news release, you ask the editor to hold the information until a specified release date. Don't make a practice of asking journalists to delay the publication or broadcast of newsworthy stories. Embargoes generally work only when journalists and strategic writers agree in advance that a situation merits special treatment.

Going Online

News releases appear online primarily as Web site documents and e-mail messages. Many organizations use their Web sites to feature current news releases as headline links on the site's home page or on an easily accessible screen. Some organizations also use their Web sites to archive old news releases. Those archived news releases help create an official history of the organization.

News releases also move online as e-mail messages. Check with journalists before e-mailing them news releases. Some prefer other methods of delivery, and others will have e-mail addresses reserved exclusively for news releases.

As Web documents and as e-mail messages, news releases should still have the local interest and objectivity that characterize all good news releases.

Announcement News Releases

Purpose

The announcement is by far the most common type of news release. Use announcement news releases for standard "hard-news" stories—for example, the announcement of a new chief executive officer. (Please review the general guidelines for news releases, pages 31–37.)

Format/Design

Follow the general guidelines for news releases, pages 32–33.

Content and Organization

The announcement news release imitates a straightforward news story. The lead (the opening paragraph) covers the most important aspects of *who, what, where, when, why* and *how*. The story follows the inverted pyramid structure (page 34); in other words, the information in the story becomes progressively less important. The least important (but still newsworthy) information comes last in an announcement news release.

Announcement news releases usually are written in past tense. If, in your lead, you need to establish that your news happened in the very recent past, you can use present-perfect tense (using a form of *to have*)—for example, "XYZ Partners has announced third-quarter profits of $50 million."

An announcement news release often includes relevant quotations from appropriate sources, such as members of your organization's management team. Trade magazines, business journals and small newspapers sometimes reprint announcement new releases verbatim. Other media may turn them into brief announcements or use them to generate longer stories. Remember: The news media may ignore a news release altogether, especially if it's poorly written, too promotional or lacks local interest.

PALMQUIST UNIVERSITY
234 COLLEGE AVE.
HOSEA, WIS. 59830
555-876-0864

News Release

FOR IMMEDIATE RELEASE
Sept. 7, 2005

FOR MORE INFORMATION, CONTACT:
Jane Doe
Director of Media Relations
555-654-2986
jdoe@palmquist.edu

Palmquist University names new president

HOSEA, Wis.—The Wisconsin Board of Regents has named Edward Faxon the new president of Palmquist University. Faxon, formerly vice-provost of Weslaco College in Milwaukee, will begin his new duties Sept. 18, said Regents Director Roberta Kramer.

"Edward Faxon was our first choice," Kramer said. "The Board of Regents is certain that he will lead Palmquist University to a great future."

Faxon, 54, served as vice-provost at Weslaco College for seven years. Before that, he was the Burnett Distinguished Professor of Biochemistry at Kasold University in Portland, Tenn. He earned his Ph.D. in biochemistry from Madrid University in 1979.

Faxon will take the oath of office at 10 a.m., Sept. 18, in McDaniel Auditorium at the Student Union.

"I'm both honored and challenged to assume the presidency of Palmquist University," Faxon said. "I pledge to do my best for Palmquist."

Faxon succeeds Richard Warner, who retired Sept. 1. Faxon will be the 19th president of Palmquist University.

###

Feature News Releases

Purpose

The feature news release relates "softer," less important and less immediate news than does the announcement news release. Feature news releases often are human-interest stories that highlight some aspect of your organization. Feature news releases are not as common as announcement news releases. Traditionally, features attract less media attention than do announcements. (Please review the general guidelines for news releases, pages 31–37.)

Format/Design

Follow the general guidelines for news releases, pages 32–33.

Content and Organization

Feature news releases often present entertaining human-interest stories, such as the efforts of an officer of your organization to hire the homeless. Other feature news releases attempt a less direct view of your news by focusing on topics bigger than your organization and using representatives of your organization as experts.

For example, Hallmark Cards writes feature news releases on the history and traditions of important holidays, such as Mother's Day. In addressing these interesting topics, the news release uses Hallmark experts and information for evidence, thus bringing credibility to the company and linking it to holiday traditions. Some feature news releases include information from nonemployee, noncompetitive sources to round out the story.

Avoid the temptation to include unattributed opinions in feature news releases. Like all news releases, features must be objective and unbiased.

Although feature news releases differ from traditional announcement news releases, they generally begin with a traditional news headline (see page 34). However, many feature news releases attempt to include clever wordplay, such as a pun, in the headline.

Feature news releases don't have traditional news leads. Instead, the lead attempts to spark the reader's interest with a question, an anecdote, an image or a similar device.

Feature news releases use storytelling skills, so they're not inverted pyramids, as are announcement news releases. The most dramatic paragraph in a feature news release might be the final paragraph.

Feature news releases often use present tense to attribute quotations—for example, *says* instead of *said*. Present-tense attributions can help create the sense that a story, not just a report, is being told.

Because feature new releases aren't as newsworthy as announcement news releases, they're rarely as successful. Always consider if your feature news release could work as an announcement news release. However, if your organization has an interesting story, but it's not a good hard-news story, you should consider a feature news release or a pitch letter (see pages 50–53).

A more extensive discussion of feature stories can be found in Newsletter and Magazine Stories, pages 77–83.

PALMQUIST UNIVERSITY
234 COLLEGE AVE.
HOSEA, WIS. 59830
555-876-0864

News Release

FOR IMMEDIATE RELEASE
Sept. 7, 2005

FOR MORE INFORMATION, CONTACT:
Jane Doe
Director of Media Relations
555-654-2986
jdoe@palmquist.edu

Palmquist University to sponsor duck race for United Way

Palmquist University sophomore Andrea Smith has hatched a ducky idea for raising money.

"It started in my bathtub," she says. "But that's probably more than people want to know. Let's just say that I was playing with two rubber ducks and got a weird idea."

Smith's weird idea may help feather the nest of the Havelock County United Way. On Friday, Oct. 7, Palmquist University will sponsor its first rubber duck race on Patterson Creek. Five bucks buys two ducks, and the first duck to float to Old Bridge wins its owner $100. The race begins at noon behind Sprague Hall. Anyone age 18 or older may enter.

"We were a little surprised when Andrea came to us with the idea," says Jane Evers, director of Havelock County United Way. "But she's put together a great program."

Ducks go on sale Monday, Oct. 3, in the Student Union.

"Palmquist University is delighted to help the United Way in this manner," says Edward Faxon, university president. "Especially if one of my ducks wins."

###

Hybrid News Releases

Purpose

Hybrid news releases usually are short news releases. They have an attention-grabbing lead, after which they adopt the inverted pyramid style. They are called hybrids because they begin like a feature news release but quickly become an announcement news release. (Please review the general guidelines for news releases, pages 31–37.)

Format/Design

Follow the general guidelines for news releases, pages 32–33.

Content and Organization

The hybrid news release combines the announcement style and the feature style of news releases. It begins with a traditional news headline (page 34). The hybrid has a featurelike lead, designed to attract the reader's attention. Then the hybrid moves to an announcement style, delivering the facts in inverted pyramid form (page 34). Unlike the feature news release, information in a hybrid news release becomes progressively less important.

The hybrid news release can be ideal for a hard-news story that has a whimsical or human-interest angle—for example, a student group's sponsorship of a "weird pet tricks" competition for charity.

PALMQUIST UNIVERSITY
234 COLLEGE AVE.
HOSEA, WIS. 59830
555-876-0864

News Release

FOR IMMEDIATE RELEASE
Sept. 7, 2005

FOR MORE INFORMATION, CONTACT:
Jane Doe
Director of Media Relations
555-654-2986
jdoe@palmquist.edu

Palmquist University to sponsor duck race for United Way

Andrea Smith has hatched a ducky idea for raising money.

Palmquist University will host a rubber duck race Friday, Oct. 7. The event is a fund-

raiser for the Havelock County United Way.

"I got the idea for the race in August and have worked with the university and the

United Way to make it happen," Smith, a Palmquist sophomore, said.

The race will begin at noon behind Sprague Hall. Ducks will be numbered, and the

first duck to reach Old Bridge will win its owner $100.

Ducks cost $5 for two entries and can be purchased at the Student Union from

Monday, Oct. 3, to Friday, Oct. 7. Anyone age 18 or older may enter.

"Palmquist University is delighted to help the United Way in this manner," said

Edward Faxon, university president. "Our goal is to be an excellent citizen in our

community."

###

Short Teaser News Releases

Purpose

Unlike other news releases, short teasers are not meant for direct publication. Instead, they tease, or entice, journalists into contacting your organization for more facts so that they can produce related news stories.

Format/Design

Follow the general guidelines for news releases on pages 31–37.

Each teaser generally consists of its own descriptive subheadline, a paragraph that describes the most interesting aspects of the story and the name, phone number and e-mail address of a contact person for that particular story.

Teasers can be in the format of a pitch letter (pages 50–53), but more often they are a series of bulleted (•), related story ideas under the headings of a traditional news release.

Because short teasers are not meant for direct publication, they are single-spaced. (On paper news releases, double-spacing allows editors room to edit. Journalists don't edit short teasers. They use them as story ideas.)

If your short teasers news release is more than one page, type "-more-" or "-over-" at the bottom of each appropriate page. Beginning with page two, place a condensed version of the release's headline (called a "slug") and the page number in the upper-right corner. After the last line of the news release, space down one more line and type "-30-" or "###."

Staple the pages of the news release together.

Content and Organization

Again, short teasers generally offer several story suggestions in one concise document. Teasers aren't meant to be published verbatim; instead, they're designed to catch a journalist's fancy, to induce her to contact you for more information about a particular story idea. Teasers work well when you want to publicize a large event with several possible stories—and when there's enough time for a journalist to develop a story.

Generally, the headline describes the purpose of the document: "Story tips for Central City's Black History Month events." Because short teasers usually offer several story ideas—several teasers—in one document, the headline often is generic rather than specific. An introductory paragraph below the headline can help explain this document to journalists. Below that, each story idea receives roughly one paragraph.

Although local interest is vital to successful short teasers, objectivity is not as important. Because teasers are not meant for publication—and because you're trying to entice journalists to pursue the story leads—short teasers often use promotional writing that would be inappropriate in other news releases. Short teasers sound more like feature news releases than announcement news releases. You can have fun with them, but remember: Journalists are trained skeptics who, more than anything else, want good stories. In a short teaser, don't oversell or overpromise.

If your document has only one short teaser—that is, only one story idea, consider writing a pitch letter (pages 50–53) instead of a teaser.

PALMQUIST UNIVERSITY
234 COLLEGE AVE.
HOSEA, WIS. 59830
555-876-0864

News Release

FOR IMMEDIATE RELEASE
Sept. 7, 2005

FOR MORE INFORMATION, CONTACT:
Jane Doe
Director of Media Relations
555-654-2986
jdoe@palmquist.edu

Palmquist University announces weekly faculty research highlights

- **The Alphabet and Ethics**

    Marcia Williams, associate professor of classics, believes that the Greek alphabet encouraged analytical thinking and led to modern ethics. Professor Williams will present a paper on the topic to the International Classical Association in October. Contact Marcia Williams, 555-654-3920, mwilliams@palmquist.edu.

- **Not Lost in Translation**

    Aaron Walling, professor of French, recently published his English translation of Nobel Prize–winner Henri Collor's French novel *Goodbye, Paris* (Lancaster Press, 2005). Contact Aaron Walling, 555-654-3871, awall@palmquist.edu.

- **Secrets of Nature's Mouse House**

    Michael Sung, professor emeritus of biological sciences, and Ramon Fernandez, postdoctoral fellow in biological sciences, recently secured a $600,000 grant from the National Science Foundation for their work studying insulation and rodents' winter habitats. Contact Ramon Fernandez, 555-654-8503, rfernandez@palmquist.edu.

- **High Stakes in the Name Game**

    Kris Ann Paderno, assistant professor of political science, will present her findings on local instances of identity theft to the Barry County Planning Commission on Oct. 4, 2005. Her research includes survey results from local merchants and residents. Contact Kris Ann Paderno, 555-654-7205, paderno@palmquist.edu.

###

Media Advisories

Purpose, Audience and Media

A media advisory is a *what, who, when, where, why, how* outline of a news story. It is appropriate in two situations:

- The media advisory outlines news that is extremely timely—so-called breaking news—and you must get the information to the news media as quickly as possible. You don't have time to write a news release.
- You are sending the media advisory as a reminder to journalists of an important, previously sent news release.

Journalists are the audience for media advisories. Like news releases, media advisories are sent to journalists in the hope that they will pass along the information to their readers, listeners and viewers.

Media advisories are e-mailed, faxed, hand-delivered and posted on Web sites. Because media advisories generally deal with breaking news, they are not sent through the mail. A postal delivery would take too long.

- **Key to Success:** Media advisories should outline only very timely news. A journalist should be able to write a short, complete news story from the media advisory alone—or the media advisory should persuade the journalist to attend a newsworthy event.

Format/Design

The headings of a media advisory are the same as those of a news release (pages 32–33), except that the document is labeled "Media Advisory" instead of "News Release." That distinction is important because a media advisory conveys a sense of urgency.

Media advisories are short and to the point—one page, if possible. They are not meant for publication in their present format. Thus, they are single-spaced, with double-spacing between paragraphs.

After the headings, most media advisories arrange their information something like this:

What:	Gov. Jane Smith will tour the Midtown Recycling Center. The tour will be private, but reporters may join. After the tour, the governor will accept questions regarding her visit and her recycling policies.
Who:	Mike Jones, Midtown Recycling Center founder and president, will conduct the tour for the governor. Midtown Mayor Lynn Johnson will join them. Gov. Jane Smith, an independent, was elected in 2004.

When:	Saturday, Sept. 14, 3–4 p.m.
Where:	Midtown Recycling Center, 3309 Riverview, Midtown
Why:	"I'm visiting Midtown Recycling Center because it's a model facility for the rest of the state. It's the perfect example of my administration's recycling policies."—Gov. Jane Smith

Note how similar the media advisory's format is to the fact sheet's format (pages 70–72). Despite the similarity, fact sheets and media advisories are used for different purposes. A fact sheet usually accompanies a news release in a media kit. A media advisory is usually used for breaking stories that don't allow time for the writing of a full news release.

Content and Organization

The traditional media advisory begins with a traditional news headline (page 34). Following the headline, the advisory becomes a *what, who, when, where, why, how* outline of a story's or event's essential facts. That outline begins with the most important set of facts (often the *what*), then moves to the second most important set of facts (often the *who*) and so on. There's no attempt at a story form. However, either the media advisory should persuade a journalist to attend an event, or the media advisory should be so complete that a journalist could write a short news story from the media advisory alone.

TIPS

1. Never attempt to give importance to a routine news story by making it a media advisory. Journalists will feel deceived, and your next media advisory may be ignored.
2. Because media advisories are comparatively rare and highly newsworthy, you may telephone recipients to ensure that they received the advisory and to offer additional help. Avoid this procedure with standard news releases.

Going Online

Unlike many other documents in this book, media advisories rarely exist on paper. Instead, writers compose them on computer screens and either e-mail or fax them to journalists. After such distribution, writers often post media advisories on Web sites, generally in a prominent location to indicate the importance of the breaking news.

PALMQUIST UNIVERSITY
234 COLLEGE AVE.
HOSEA, WIS. 59830
555-876-0864

Media Advisory

FOR IMMEDIATE RELEASE
Oct. 3, 2005

FOR MORE INFORMATION, CONTACT:
Jane Doe
Director of Media Relations
555-654-2986
jdoe@palmquist.edu

**Palmquist University schedules news conference
to introduce new men's basketball coach**

What: Edward Faxon, president of Palmquist University, will introduce Palmquist University's new men's basketball coach at 9 a.m., Tuesday, Oct. 4, in the media room at Collison Fieldhouse.

President Faxon said that no official of the university will comment on the identity of the new basketball coach until that time.

Who: Printed information on the new coach, including a full biography and résumé, will be distributed to members of the news media at the 9 a.m. news conference.

Where: Collison Fieldhouse is at 1200 Palmquist Blvd. The media room is Room 307 in the fieldhouse.

The media room at Collison Fieldhouse includes lighting suitable for television cameras.

When: The news conference will begin at 9 a.m., Tuesday, Oct. 4, and will last 90 minutes. Both President Faxon and the new coach will make statements, and both will take questions. Copies of the statements will be available for members of the news media.

###

Pitch Letters

Purpose, Audience and Media

The pitch letter is a business letter that attempts to persuade an individual journalist to write the story described in the letter. A pitch letter "pitches," or promotes, a story idea.

Strategic writers often send a pitch letter instead of a feature news release (pages 40–41) or a short teaser news release (pages 44–46). It pitches a "soft-news" story idea rather than a hard-news story, such as the announcement of an important charity event. Don't use a pitch letter to replace an announcement news release (pages 38–39) that delivers hard news.

Should you use a pitch letter instead of a feature or short teaser news release? Ask journalists what they prefer. Before deciding to send a pitch a letter, consider these facts:

- Pitch letters generally take less time to read than feature news releases. Busy journalists will appreciate that.
- Pitch letters contain more details than short teaser news releases. Journalists demand details.
- In a pitch letter, as opposed to a feature news release, the story isn't yet written—so a journalist can feel a stronger sense of ownership of the potential story.

Unlike news releases, a pitch letter is mailed to only one journalist. A pitch letter is an exclusive offer to a particular journalist. If the story has relevance for several different geographic areas, you can offer it as an exclusive in each area; that is, you can offer the story to one journalist in each region. However, if the story has national significance, you should approach only one journalist. If the story has international significance, you could pitch it to one journalist in each nation.

The audience of a pitch letter is one journalist. Ideally, you choose this journalist because you are familiar with his work and know that he will do a good job on the story. Don't assume, however, that the journalist will write the story. The goal of your pitch letter is to persuade him to do so.

Pitch letters can be sent as e-mail messages, particularly when you are personally acquainted with the individual journalist. If you know the journalist well, a phone call could even replace a pitch letter. However, the usual medium of a pitch letter remains the traditional paper letter that you put in an envelope and place in the mail.

- **Key to Success:** The first paragraph must hook the journalist. The opening section should spark the journalist's desire to tell a good story.

Format/Design

Follow the general guidelines for the business-letter format on pages 193–195.

Content and Organization

Pitch letters, like bad-news letters and sales letters, are unusual in that they don't use the first paragraph to tell the recipient the main point of the letter.

Part 1 of 4: Start a Fascinating Story

Hook the journalist with the first paragraph. Write the first part of your letter as if it were the lead of the story that you hope the journalist will write. Journalists are storytellers, so spark your reader's attention by beginning an irresistible story.

Often, this first part will not mention your company or organization. That's because you want to direct the journalist's attention toward the story, not toward promoting your organization. Be concise but specific; journalists love details. However, don't hesitate to tantalize the journalist by creating a sense of mystery. Make your reader want to know the rest of the story. Avoid the overused "Did you know . . . " opening.

This first section generally is one paragraph. Don't make the journalist wait too long to discover the reason for the letter. Don't wait too long to make the pitch.

Part 2 of 4: State the Purpose of the Letter

Tell the journalist exactly why you're writing—for example, "I think the *Dallas Morning News* should do a story on David Smith." (Smith, of course, was introduced in the first section.) If possible, praise a previous story that the journalist wrote; explain that's why you think he's the perfect writer for a story on David Smith. (Or, if the letter is addressed to an editor, mention a recent story in that editor's newspaper section, magazine, newscast or Web site that was well done.) Give more information on David Smith. Continue to tell the story in this section.

This section usually is one paragraph.

Part 3 of 4: State the Terms of Your Offer

Note that you're offering this idea exclusively to the recipient; that should help gain his interest. Then explain that, because of the exclusive offer, you'll need a reply by a specific date. In the same paragraph, offer help. List the best contacts from your organization and their phone numbers and e-mail addresses (be sure those contacts know you have included them). Offer to help set up interviews.

Be diplomatic. Now that the journalist knows the idea, he can try to do the story without you. Don't provoke anger by suggesting that the story can be done only on your terms. Present yourself as an interested assistant.

This section usually is one paragraph.

Part 4 of 4: Describe What You Hope Will Happen Next

Mention that you'll call in a few days (name a day, if possible) to see if he is interested and to determine what help you can offer. If your letter pitches a truly good story, the journalist often will phone you before your deadline. End with a thank-you for the journalist's time and consideration. Include a standard "sincerely" sign-off.

TIPS

1. Sell the story, not your client or organization. The journalist has no interest in promoting your cause or your products, but he does want a good story. Keep the focus on information that will appeal to the journalist and his audience.
2. Play fair. Journalists will never forget it if you hide bad news or if the story is old news already covered elsewhere.
3. Never waste a busy journalist's time. The story you pitch must truly be a good story for the journalist's audience.
4. Be sure to include your direct phone number in the letter. Don't just include a business card that might get lost.
5. Make that follow-up call, unless the journalist calls you first. Do your best not to call a journalist on deadline. Find out what times the medium's daily deadlines are. A good way to start a phone call with a journalist is to introduce yourself and immediately ask, "Are you on deadline? Do you have just a moment?" If you can't get through to the journalist, leave a message explaining why you called. Leave no more than two messages.
6. Be ready to respond quickly if the journalist calls. Don't make him wait for interviews, photographs or any other needs.

Going Online

Again, you can send a pitch letter as an e-mail message—if you know that the journalist prefers receiving story ideas online. If you send a pitch letter via e-mail, be sure to use the subject line to attract the journalist's attention. "Nightmares and Profits: Story Idea" probably is more compelling than just "Story Idea."

Interactive Games
2010 Ridglea Drive
San Francisco, CA 55111

September 14, 2005

Mr. John Hardesty
Editor
California Business Today
P.O. Box 11856
Sacramento, CA 30655

Dear Mr. Hardesty:

David Smith hates moonlit nights. In the shadows of his bedroom, the ideas come too quickly—and some are so terrifying that they pin him to the bed. He tries to reach for the notepad, but his hand trembles. "Will I remember this in the morning?" he wonders, torn between hope and fear.

I think the story of David Smith would be ideal for *California Business Today* magazine. David is an award-winning game designer for MGS Interactive Games. Your recent series on California's creative geniuses has been consistently excellent, particularly your recent story on playwright Cheryl Turcot. As the creative force behind such best-selling games as *Night Terror, Are You Sleeping?* and *StarkLight,* David Smith would be a natural for your creative geniuses series. His best ideas come in dreams so frightening that I sometimes don't want to hear about them. You should see the ideas we reject (unless you're prone to nightmares, we could discuss those).

We're offering David's story exclusively to *California Business Today,* so I would need to know fairly soon if you're interested. I can assure you that David would cooperate fully with any writers or photographers you would assign. We also could help you arrange interviews with members of David's staff or with anyone else who works for MGS Interactive Games. We even have copies of some of his bedside notes. Please just let me know how we might help. My direct phone line is 555-498-8871.

I will call Wednesday, Sept. 21, to see if I might be of any help on a possible story on David Smith. Thank you for your time and consideration.

Sincerely,

Angie Perez

Angie Perez
Public Relations Director

Radio News Releases

Purpose, Audience and Media

Radio news releases serve the same purpose as traditional print news releases: to generate publicity for organizations by providing journalists newsworthy information in a ready-to-use format. Although the content is what interests journalists, a radio news release presents that information in a manner that reflects each organization's values, goals and perspectives.

Just like its print counterpart, a radio news release is often a starting point for journalists who may use it as is, change it or ignore it. The obvious difference from print is that radio news releases are specifically designed for use on radio. For that reason, they feature a writing style that is both easy for an announcer to read and a listener to understand. Because broadcast messages are fleeting—here in an instant and then gone—a listener gets only one opportunity to hear and understand the message. The fleeting nature of radio news releases also means that writers are limited in the amount of detail they can include. At best, they can cover only major points of emphasis. These factors place a significant burden on the writer.

Two kinds of radio news releases exist: the radio reader and the soundbite story. Radio readers are exactly what the name implies: a script for an announcer to read. Soundbite stories are radio news releases that contain taped comments from an organization representative, used much as a quote in a print story. Those taped comments—usually 6–20 seconds long—are known as either soundbites or actualities. When you send prerecorded material to news organizations, that material often includes a series of soundbites with suggested announcer lead-ins. Including such information gives news anchors increased flexibility, thus increasing the chances of the material being broadcast.

Radio's specialization makes it easier to target messages to specific audiences. In large communities, stations survive in a competitive marketplace by carving a niche with specialized programming. Most are characterized by the kind of music they play. Others distinguish themselves by presenting news, sports and talk programs. In smaller communities that tend to be overlooked by regional media, such as metropolitan newspapers and television, the radio station is often a valued source of local information. For strategic writers, this segmentation requires an understanding of each radio station's audience. Something that may be considered newsworthy to listeners of one station may not be to those of another.

Radio news releases may take the form of an announcer's script, a prerecorded package or a combination of both. They are distributed through a variety of channels, although dial-up toll-free telephone numbers are the most popular for soundbites and actualities.

> ■ **Key to Success:** Like its print counterpart, a radio news release must contain news, not fluff. It must be ready to use. The more work required by the journalist, the less the likelihood of the release's being broadcast.

Format/Design

Radio news release scripts use broadcast style (see pages 10–12). The scripts use large, easy-to-see fonts, have wide margins and are double-spaced for the benefit of the announcer. Within the script, soundbite transcriptions can be single-spaced. Use 60-character lines. Should a second page be necessary, never print it on the reverse side of the page; use a separate sheet of paper. Radio news releases contain the same header information found on a print news release (date of release, contact information and headline).

Content and Organization

Radio readers generally run 20–30 seconds. That translates into approximately five to seven lines of copy. As with any news release, you must ensure that the story covers the essential elements of news: *who, what, where, when, why* and *how*. As mentioned before, you can cover only major points of emphasis within this brief message form. Therefore, you must clearly understand both the story's purpose and the essential information it must include.

Soundbite stories generally run 40–50 seconds, including the soundbite. Depending on the length of the bite, that translates into six to nine lines of copy. The presence of the soundbite necessitates a prescribed story structure:

■ The lead, the opening sentence of the news release, which contains the most important fact. However, the lead must also grab the audience's attention and orient it before getting into the details of the story. Radio news leads often are general statements that provide a framework for the specific information to come.

■ The body of the story, in which you detail essential information not covered in the lead

■ The lead-in to the soundbite, in which you identify by name the speaker in the soundbite. This should be a complete, substantive sentence that does not echo what is said in the soundbite.

■ The soundbite, which runs from six to 20 seconds. Within the script, identify the soundbite by a short title, its length and its outcue (the final few words contained in the soundbite). For a short soundbite of only a sentence or two, transcribe the entire soundbite. Include an extra space before and after the soundbite to separate it from the rest of the script. (Include transcription of the soundbite when you distribute scripts and tapes.)

■ The close, which is additional information that provides a strong conclusion to the story. The close helps prevent listener confusion regarding when one story ends and another begins.

TIPS

1. Stick to the news. Because of a radio new release's short length, focus on the essential information.
2. Avoid hype. A promotional tone will almost guarantee that the news release will not be broadcast.
3. Remember that the announcer must breathe. Write short, subject-verb-object sentences in active voice. Sentences should not exceed 20 words.
4. Listen to the rhythm. Avoid predictable patterns by varying the length of sentences.

5. Give the announcer a break. If the script contains any unusual names, provide a pronunciation guide. Don't split words or phrases between lines or pages of the script.
6. Give the big picture. Too many details will confuse the listener. Write in broad but tangible terms.
7. Sound it out. The best way to tell if a script flows naturally is to read it aloud during the writing process.

Going Online

The use of audio news releases and soundbites on organization Web sites is increasing. With improvements in Internet technology, the Web also may become the preferred distribution system.

RADIO READER NEWS RELEASE

RIVERVIEW
COMMUNITY MEDICAL CENTER

Radio News Release

Date: January 12, 2005

Contact: Public Information Director Jeremy Marcus, (999) 555-5555

FOR IMMEDIATE RELEASE

Riverview Med Center appoints chief executive officer with local ties

Riverview Community Medical Center has appointed a new leader. Riverview native

Mary Beth Johnson will become the hospital's new chief executive officer. Board Chairman

Leroy Bissette (Bih-SET) announced Johnson's selection following Monday's board of

directors meeting. Johnson served the last three years in a similar capacity at the City of

Angels Medical Center in Los Angeles. She is a 1970 graduate of Riverview High School.

Johnson graduated from Riverview College in 1974. She also earned an M-B-A from

Harvard in 1977. Johnson succeeds retiring C-E-O Margaret Carlton on March First.

###

Radio News Release

Date: January 12, 2005

Contact: Public Information Director Jeremy Marcus, (999) 555-5555

FOR IMMEDIATE RELEASE

Riverview Med Center appoints chief executive officer with local ties

Riverview Community Medical Center has appointed a new leader. Riverview native Mary Beth Johnson will become the hospital's new chief executive officer. Board Chairman Leroy Bissette (Bih-SET) announced Johnson's selection following Monday's board of directors meeting. Johnson served the last three years in a similar capacity at the City of Angels Medical Center in Los Angeles.

SOUNDBITE: Johnson (12 seconds) "I have always loved Riverview and have dreamed of returning to my hometown. I still have family and friends in the community. That only strengthens my resolve to see to it that the people of Riverview get the very best health care."

Johnson is a 1970 graduate of Riverview High School. Johnson graduated from Riverview College in 1974. She also earned an M-B-A from Harvard in 1977. Johnson succeeds retiring C-E-O Margaret Carlton on March First.

###

Video News Releases

Purpose, Audience and Media

A popular tool for generating television publicity is the video news release. As the name suggests, the VNR is a news release in video format. Organizations use VNRs for major announcements, such as the introduction of a new product. VNRs also have been effective in reaching out to key stakeholders during crises; PepsiCo used a VNR in 1993 to restore public confidence in the wake of a product-tampering hoax. And at a time when media economics have forced many news organizations to downsize, VNRs present strategic communicators with an opportunity to help television news producers fill in the gaps on slow news days and on weekends, when staffing is reduced.

Some critics denounce VNRs as "fake news." This charge is unfair: Journalists, not public relations professionals, serve as the gatekeepers for their media. Journalists have the authority to use VNRs in their entirety, use only selected parts of them or ignore them altogether. Therefore, like its print and radio cousins, a VNR must contain information useful to journalists and their audiences.

The primary target audience of a VNR is a television or cable station. Satisfying such an audience requires demographic and psychographic knowledge of each station's or program's viewers. But before you can reach those viewers, you must gain the approval of those stations' reporters and editors. In short, you have to give the journalists what they want. And journalists want stories of interest to their target audiences. For example, many stations covet female viewers, 25–50 years old, who control most household spending. These stations will be receptive to VNRs that address issues important to that audience, such as women's health care and child rearing. Journalists also seek compelling video that they may not be able to obtain from another source, such as laboratory tests of a new drug or the demonstration of a new product. They also seek the unusual and amusing, often as a transition from the day's hard news.

The two most popular media for distributing VNRs are videotape and satellite. Videotapes are more common when used with traditional media kits distributed to reporters at a news conference or newsworthy event. More popular is the use of satellites, which allows broader distribution and a shorter lead time. However, even satellite distribution has limitations. Organizations still must distribute a traditional news release or media advisory to inform the media of when the VNR will be transmitted and where (which satellite and transponder) it can be found. With the increased digitizing of video, DVD and Internet download distribution of VNRs will become more commonplace.

■ **Key to Success:** Successful VNRs address the needs of journalists and the audiences those journalists serve. They include highly visual content.

Format/Design

VNRs are packaged in a manner that encourages journalists to use them. Different stations may have different requirements. Whereas some stations may want a complete news package, others may need only short pieces of video or a brief soundbite. Properly designed VNRs accommodate these different needs. They follow the "beggars can't be choosers" principle: The easier you make it for the journalist, the more likely it is that some or all of the material will be used.

The role of a strategic writer in the production of a VNR is to produce a two-column script (described in more detail in Television Advertisements, pages 133 and 136–137). The Table and Borders function in most word-processing programs allows you to create visible borders around the two columns.

Content and Organization

VNRs are self-contained. By that, we mean that all the information a reporter or editor needs for writing a story is within the video. Because so many VNRs are distributed via satellite, there is often no opportunity to provide an accompanying script and/or background information. Instead, strategic writers convey critical information through "billboards." A billboard is written information scrolled on the screen to alert the journalist about what comes next—much like a highway billboard telling you the distance to the next gas station. Even when you mail VNRs with printed information, the common practice is to produce a video that will stand on its own with no further explanation required.

The organization of a VNR has five parts:

1. Opening billboard. This provides the essential background information about the news story that follows. It clearly identifies the organization on whose behalf the VNR was produced and contact information for follow-ups. It identifies sources interviewed on-camera by name and title. It also includes a suggested announcer lead-in to the story, the running time of the story and its outcue (or closing words).

2. Video news release. This is a 60–90 second television news story, with an announcer voiceover, natural sounds (SOT, meaning "sounds on tape") and soundbites. Two major differences separate the VNR from the news story you see on the nightly news. First, there is not a reporter stand-up, in which viewers see the reporter on camera. Second, the VNR is also a "rough cut," lacking titles and graphics. The reason for these two differences is the same: Stations want flexibility to use their own people and graphics packages to customize the information to fit an established station image. This works to the strategic communicator's advantage: The more the VNR looks like someone else's reporting, the more newsworthy it appears to be. However, remember that ethical journalists should always identify their sources, and strategic communicators should always be willing to be identified as those sources. No one is trying to fool anyone.

3. Video news release without announcer voiceover. The only sounds in this version of the VNR are the natural sounds from the taped footage (SOT) and the soundbites. You do not include the announcer's voiceover. This gives editors additional flexibility, allowing them to use their own personnel. A brief billboard announcing the deletion of the voiceover precedes this section.

4. Soundbites. These include a variety of soundbites, particularly some that were not in the VNR. A billboard of who is speaking, the length of the soundbite and, often, a suggested lead-in precede each soundbite. The more variety, the greater the likelihood that journalists may use the story in multiple newscasts.

5. B-roll. This is additional footage journalists can use to illustrate the story. A brief billboard that specifies content and running time precedes this section.

Before writing a VNR script, be sure to review Writing for Electronic Media, pages 10–12.

TIPS

1. Think again. Before investing the time and expense of producing and distributing a VNR, make certain that this tactic fits within your organization's overall strategy. Always ask if a VNR is the best way to achieve a desired goal. Are there legitimate reasons why news organizations would not be able to generate the same footage and interviews on their own? When stations commit their time and resources to covering a story, they are more likely to air it. The worst reason for doing a VNR is because you can. There must be more to it than that.

2. Check your ego at the door. Only rarely do television news organizations take a VNR and air it without any changes. Just as with a print or radio news release, a VNR often is a starting point. Good journalists often supplement your VNR with their own reporting.

3. Focus on features. Whereas print news releases tend to reflect newspaper journalism's focus on hard, straightforward news, VNRs can address television's thirst for lighter fare. Most local newscasts try to balance the day's bad news with something that will entertain, enlighten or inspire their viewers. Knowing this creates an opportunity for strategic communicators.

4. Remember that news is still news. Even though television stations want softer news stories, they do not welcome anything overtly promotional. If the message in a VNR is a selling message, news producers and reporters won't buy it.

5. Don't do it on the cheap. Many organizations have excellent in-house video production facilities. However, most do not. In those cases, consider hiring a competent agency or independent producer. If a VNR has poor production values that are not up to the standards of commercial broadcasters, journalists will not broadcast it. And it doesn't matter how important your message is. For every lousy VNR tossed in the trash, there's an excellent one ready to take its place.

6. Make pictures and words work together. If the words and pictures have no connection, the viewer will become confused. However, if the words do no more than describe what

is obvious in the pictures, the viewer will become annoyed. Remember the concept of hit and run writing, discussed in Writing for Electronic Media (pages 11–12). Pictures and words should connect at the beginning of each series of images. When that is accomplished, the words can expand the image, adding to what is shown.

Going Online

Because of the sight and sound dynamics of the Internet, VNRs are easily adaptable for use on an organization's Web site. However, in those cases show only the VNR segment itself. Present a complete story, not B-roll or solitary soundbites.

VIDEO NEWS RELEASE PRODUCTION SCRIPT

Project: SW Foundation VNR
Page 1

CHYRON–PAGE ONE: Cardiovascular disease (CVD) claims the lives of nearly 1 million Americans every year. CVD is the leading cause of death in the United States. According to the American Heart Association, at least 58 million Americans—one out of every four—suffer from some form of heart disease.

CHYRON–PAGE TWO: In an effort to reverse this trend, CEO Roberta Robertson of SlimWhims Inc., the maker of a popular pre-packaged diet program, announces the creation of the SW Foundation for the purpose of supporting CVD research. To launch this research, SlimWhims Inc. is contributing $1 million in seed money. The company also hopes to raise an additional $4 million through a Have a Healthy Heart Campaign.

CHYRON–PAGE THREE: This is a video news release on the Have a Healthy Heart campaign. It will feature interviews with Dr. Marco Podestra (poh-DESS-trah), chief cardiologist at Riverview Community Medical Center and Paula Pressman, executive director of the SW Foundation. The announcer is Robert Franks.

-MORE-

VIDEO NEWS RELEASE PRODUCTION SCRIPT

SW Foundation VNR
Page 2

For more information, telephone SW Foundation
Executive Director Paula Pressman at 999-555-1040
or log on to www.swhealthyheart.com.

CHYRON–PAGE FOUR: Suggested lead-in:
"When it comes to fighting heart disease, the creators of
a popular diet plan want to put their money where your
mouth is . . ."

RT: 1:00

FIVE SECONDS OF BLACK

OPENING SEQUENCE OF SHOTS—Dr. Marco Podestra giving a check-up to a heart patient	ANNOUNCER: Approximately one-million people in the United States will die from cardiovascular disease this year. And the American Heart Association says one out of every four Americans has some form of heart disease. That's more than 58-million people. Cardiologist Marco Podestra of the Riverview Community Medical Center says this is an alarming epidemic.
CU: Dr. Podestra in lab.	DR. MARCO PODESTRA: It is unbelievable. In a country where the world's best health care is at our fingertips, I don't understand how one out of every four Americans faces some form of heart disease. We have to do something about that.
SEQUENCE: Exterior shot of SlimWhims Inc., followed by shots of products. Includes close-up of special markings on packaging.	ANNOUNCER: In an effort to stop the nation's number-one killer, SlimWhims is launching the Have a Healthy Heart Campaign. A portion of the proceeds from specially marked SlimWhims diet products will be placed in a fund created to support heart research. S-W Foundation Executive Director Paula Pressman says it is in everyone's best interests to get involved.
CU: Paula Pressman in SW Foundation offices with Have a Healthy Heart logo clearly visible in the background.	PAULA PRESSMAN: It is not enough for our company to make products that reduce the risk of heart disease. We want to join with the

-MORE-

SW Foundation VNR
Page 3

dedicated doctors and researchers who are searching for ways to prevent cardiovascular disease. You might say our heart is into this cause.

CLOSING SEQUENCE—Heart researchers working with patients in a medical laboratory setting. Closing shot is a close-up of a working heart monitor.

ANNOUNCER:

To get the Have a Healthy Heart Campaign off to a good start, SlimWhims has donated one-million dollars to the effort. Pressman says the company hopes to raise another four-million dollars in the fight against heart disease. The money will come from product sales, employee donations and other special promotions. I'm Robert Franks reporting.

FIVE SECONDS OF BLACK
CHYRON: Soundbite #1—Chief Cardiologist Marco Podestra of Riverview Community Medical Center. RT :13.

PODESTRA:

Of the 50-million Americans who have high blood pressure, one-third of them don't know they have it. Every 29 seconds, someone in the U-S suffers a coronary event. About every 60 seconds, someone dies from one.

FIVE SECONDS OF BLACK
CHYRON: Soundbite #2—Paula Pressman, executive director, SW Foundation. RT :14

PRESSMAN:

We are hoping to raise four-million dollars to support heart research. And that is on top of the one-million dollars SlimWhims has already dedicated to this effort. Heart disease touches one in four Americans. We want to help reduce the threat.

FIVE SECONDS OF BLACK
CHYRON–B-Roll with natural SOT; RT 1:30
B-ROLL: A series of shots of Dr. Podestra examining patients. Heart research in medical laboratory. Pressman and foundation workers planning the campaign. Products with special markings.

###

Media Kit Guidelines

Purpose, Audience and Media

Media kits are, in a sense, expanded news releases. Media kits contain at least one news release. They also contain other documents, such as backgrounders and fact sheets. Media kits also can contain photo opportunity sheets, captioned photographs, business cards, product samples, videos and other items that help tell a story. The purpose of a media kit is to deliver to a journalist more information than a news release alone could supply. For example, television networks often send journalists media kits on upcoming television seasons.

Media kits often are called press kits, a term that no longer seems appropriate. In the 21st century, we get news not only from print news media (which use a printing press) but also from television, radio and the World Wide Web. The term *media kit* is more accurate than *press kit*. However, the term *media kit* also describes a packet of information that a medium such as a magazine prepares for advertisers. That type of media kit includes advertising rate cards and reader profiles, among other items.

The audience of a public relations media kit is a journalist. Just as we said for the news release, a good media kit focuses intensely on what journalists like and what they dislike in news stories. They like conciseness; they dislike wordiness. They like specifics; they dislike generalities. They like reputable sources; they dislike unattributed opinions. They like objective facts; they dislike promotional writing. They like honesty and candor; they dislike dishonesty and evasion. Like news releases, media kits sometimes get written to the wrong audience: They become promotional documents designed to please bosses and clients. Such media kits get about three seconds of consideration from a journalist before they begin the downward arc to the trash can.

And like news releases, media kits exist in a variety of media: Many are still written on paper and sent through the mail. Others are placed on Web sites. Still others are burned onto CDs or DVDs and mailed. Web sites and CDs or DVDs allow media kits to include sound and video, elements that are valuable to multimedia news media.

■ **Key to Success:** A successful media kit generally focuses on one core news story, which is reported in the news release. All other elements of the media kit—backgrounders, fact sheets and anything else—support that core news story.

Format/Design

Media kits exist in a variety of formats. Any format that gathers and organizes a small number of documents can be suitable for a media kit. Media kits often are folders with internal pockets, just like those students use for classes (though the folders often feature an organization's logo). Some media kits appear as small boxes with folders inside. Those folders include news releases, backgrounders, fact sheets and other documents. Media kits also can exist as CDs or DVDs that contain written documents as well as audio and visual elements. Media kits also can be stored on Web sites, though Web-based media cannot themselves be mailed to journalists; they require other communication to notify journalists of their existence.

Content and Organization

A media kit must contain at least one news release (pages 31–37). Other traditional documents in a media kit include backgrounders, fact sheets and photo opportunity sheets. Those documents are described in the following sections.

TIPS

1. Journalists are human; they like toys, gifts, novelties and free samples. When appropriate, include a product sample or a novelty with your organization's name in the media kit. Avoid expensive gifts that might appear to be bribes.

2. In old-fashioned paper-folder media kits, place the news release on the right-hand side of the folder. If you have a fact sheet, place it on the left-hand side. Place any backgrounders behind those two documents. However, if you have an important photo opportunity sheet, place it on the left instead of the fact sheet.

3. If your media kit includes photographs with captions, study newspapers and magazines for guidance on writing good captions. The first sentence of a caption generally is in present tense. That first sentence acknowledges the scene in the photograph, but it also tells the reader something more. For example, "Acme Widget employees applaud as the millionth widget rolls off the assembly line." The photo shows people applauding and the rolling widget, but the caption reveals why *this* widget is important.

Because the first sentence is in present tense, it shouldn't include a *when*, which would tear the sentence between present and past tense. Put the *when* in a second, past-tense sentence—for example, "Acme Widget employees applaud as the millionth widget rolls off the assembly line. Workers in the Park City factory paused Tuesday, Oct. 1, to celebrate the event." Captions rarely exceed two sentences.

Some captions begin with a boldface teaser sentence fragment followed by a colon—for example, "**A World of Widgets:** Acme Widget employees applaud as the millionth widget rolls off the assembly line."

Instead of the term *caption*, journalists often use the term *cutline*.

Going Online

Media kits can appear online as multimedia Web site entries that include text, video and audio. Some organizations feature a "News" section on their Web sites. News sections can store news releases and related media kits. Currently, media kits rarely are sent online unless a journalist requests such delivery.

Backgrounders

Purpose

A backgrounder supplements a news release. For example, a backgrounder can be a biography of a key individual mentioned in the news release. Another backgrounder for the same news release could be a history of the relevant organization. Not all news releases need backgrounders. Most do not. Backgrounders generally appear in media kits (pages 65–66).

> ■ **Key to Success:** Backgrounders are not news releases. They do not have news leads or news headlines. They supply interesting, relevant background information. A news release must be able to stand alone without a supporting backgrounder.

Format/Design

The headings for a backgrounder are like those of a news release (pages 32–33) except that instead of "News Release" in large type, a backgrounder, of course, has "Backgrounder."

Give your backgrounder a headline, which usually is simply the title of the subject matter of the backgrounder—often just the name of a person or of an organization.

As with news releases, if the backgrounder is more than one page, type "-more-" or "-over-" at the bottom of each appropriate page. Beginning with page two, place a condensed version of the backgrounder's headline (called a "slug") and the page number in the upper-right corner. After the last line of the backgrounder, space down two lines and type "-30-" or "###."

Staple the pages of the backgrounder together. Don't use a paper clip.

Like news releases, backgrounders appear in a ready-to-publish format. Paper backgrounders are double-spaced to allow room for editing, if necessary. And, like news releases, backgrounders should rarely exceed two pages.

Content and Organization

Unlike news releases, backgrounders are not important news stories. They do not begin with a news headline. Instead, a backgrounder headline is a sentence fragment. The headline often is simply the name of a person or organization. A backgrounder headline is a concise label for the contents that follow.

Backgrounders should not have a *who, what, where, why, why, how* lead—that's the job of news releases. Backgrounders aren't newsworthy. They don't have datelines in the lead. Backgrounders supply background information to news stories. Backgrounders are much more like encyclopedia entries than news stories.

For example, if you looked up Abraham Lincoln in the encyclopedia, you wouldn't find a news flash about his assassination. Instead, you would find a simple headline (his name) and a beginning sentence that defined him. After that first sentence, the entry would begin at the beginning and move in chronological order. Probably, the entry would begin like this: "Abraham Lincoln was the 16th president of the United States and the first president to be assassinated. Born in a log cabin in Kentucky in 1809, he . . . "

Another way to think of a backgrounder is to compare it to hypertext. If you were reading an online news story and you saw a particular name highlighted in blue, you would know that by clicking on that name, you could jump to that individual's biography. Imagine that the main news story is the news release and the biography is the backgrounder.

Your backgrounder should not contain information that should be in the news release; the news release must be able to stand by itself. Some overlap of information in a news release and a backgrounder is inevitable. For example, a news release on a corporate award might note that Jane Smith is the CEO. An accompanying backgrounder on Smith also would name her position, but it would include additional personal and professional information not in the news release.

Like a news release, a backgrounder should not include unattributed opinions. The tone should be objective. Any opinions should be attributed to clear and credible sources.

Backgrounders rarely are published. Journalists may use them to ensure that they understand the news release, or they may pull a paragraph or two from a backgrounder and insert them into the news release.

PALMQUIST UNIVERSITY
234 COLLEGE AVE.
HOSEA, WIS. 59830
555-876-0864

Backgrounder

FOR IMMEDIATE RELEASE
Sept. 7, 2005

FOR MORE INFORMATION, CONTACT:
Jane Doe
Director of Media Relations
555-654-2986
jdoe@palmquist.edu

Edward Faxon

Edward Faxon is the 19th president of Palmquist University in Hosea, Wis.

Faxon was born in 1949 in Butte, Calif. He earned a bachelor of sciences in biology from Coronado University in 1970. He earned a master's degree in biochemistry from Gabriel College in 1972 and a doctorate in biochemistry from Madrid University in 1979.

Faxon began his teaching career as an assistant professor at Kasold University in Portland, Tenn., in 1979. In 1990, he was named the Burnett Distinguished Professor of Biochemistry at Kasold. In 1994, the senior class at Kasold named Faxon the university's top professor.

Tennessee Gov. Harley Anderson named Faxon to the state Science Council in 1985. Faxon served as council chair from 1989 to 1993. Tennessee's Science Council advises the state legislature on scientific matters, including public school programs and the environmental impact of proposed state legislation. Faxon served as vice-provost of Weslaco College in Milwaukee from 1998 to 2005.

Faxon married Janine Henry of Knoxville, Tenn., in 1982. They have two children, Andrew, 17, and Jessica, 14.

###

Fact Sheets

Purpose

- The traditional fact sheet is a *what, who, when, where, why, how* outline of the accompanying news release. Some editors prefer this stripped-down presentation to the news release. Broadcast editors may prefer fact sheets because, listing just facts, they're not written in newspaper style. Other editors may prefer fact sheets because, by listing only facts, they avoid the subjectivity that many editors fear lurks in news releases. Fact sheets generally appear only in media kits.

> ■ **Key to Success:** A fact sheet must be so complete that a journalist could write a short news story using only the fact sheet.

Format/Design

The headings for a fact sheet are like those of a news release (pages 32–33) except that instead of "News Release" in large type, a fact sheet, of course, has "Fact Sheet."

Give your fact sheet the same newspaper-style headline you used for the related news release.

Fact sheets are not meant for publication in their present format. Thus, they are single-spaced, with double-spacing between paragraphs.

Do your best to keep a fact sheet to one page. After the last line of the fact sheet, space down two lines and type "-30-" or "###."

Content and Organization

A fact sheet begins with the most important information (almost always the *what*) and then moves to the second most important information (almost always the *who*). From there, the general order is *when* and *where*—and, if necessary, *why* and then *how*. This order can change, depending on the importance of the information in each section. The more important the information, the higher it should be on the page.

As the name suggests, a fact sheet covers just the facts. There's no attempt at a story form. However, the fact sheet should be so complete that a journalist could write a short news story based on the fact sheet alone.

Everything in the fact sheet should be in the news release. However, the reverse is not true. Not everything in the news release need be in the fact sheet—just the essential details. For example, a news release may contain quotations that do not appear in the fact sheet.

Most fact sheets arrange their text something like this:

What: The XYZ Corp.'s annual barbecue for the United Way. Beef, pork and vegetables will be grilled.

Who: • The XYZ Corp. is the largest employer in Central City. It makes shoelaces for . . .

• All residents of Central City are invited.

When: Sept. 14, 5 p.m.–9 p.m.

Where: Central City Park, 193 Main St.

Why: The barbecue annually raises more than $10,000 for the United Way.

How: Donations of $5 per attendee will be accepted at the park gates. Registration is not required. XYZ Corp. will supply all food and eating utensils. Attendees should bring blankets or lawn chairs.

A different category of fact sheet functions as a backgrounder. This kind of fact sheet does not summarize the accompanying news release. Instead, it provides interesting background facts that support the story in the news release. Unlike a backgrounder, however, this kind of fact sheet is not written as a story. It simply is a list of facts; often, each fact is highlighted by a bullet (•). For example, a media kit for a basketball tournament might have fact sheets that list each team's record for the season: wins, losses and related scores for each team. This kind of fact sheet has a backgrounder-style headline rather than news release–style headline.

PALMQUIST UNIVERSITY
234 COLLEGE AVE.
HOSEA, WIS. 59830
555-876-0864

Fact Sheet

FOR IMMEDIATE RELEASE
Sept. 7, 2005

FOR MORE INFORMATION, CONTACT:
Jane Doe
Director of Media Relations
555-654-2986
jdoe@palmquist.edu

Palmquist University names new president

What: The Wisconsin Board of Regents has named Edward Faxon the new president of Palmquist University.

Faxon will take the oath of office at 10 a.m., Sept. 18, in McDaniel Auditorium at the Student Union.

Who: Faxon comes to Palmquist from Weslaco College in Milwaukee, where he served as vice-provost for seven years. Before that, he was the Burnett Distinguished Professor of Biochemistry at Kasold University in Portland, Tenn. He earned his Ph.D. in biochemistry from Madrid University in 1979.

Where: Palmquist University is in Hosea, Wis.

When: Faxon will begin his tenure as president Sept. 18, 2005, said Roberta Kramer, director of the Board of Regents.

Why: "Edward Faxon was our first choice. The Board of Regents is certain that he will lead Palmquist University to a great future."
—Roberta Kramer, Director,
Wisconsin Board of Regents

###

Photo Opportunity Sheets

Purpose

As its name suggests, the photo opportunity sheet is designed to attract photographers to an event you're publicizing. When you have a newsworthy, photogenic event that you want to publicize, send photo opportunity sheets to print, TV and online journalists.

Not all events merit a photo opportunity sheet. For example, a news release announcing a corporation's quarterly profits probably lacks a related visual event. But if your organization is sponsoring a skateboard race between your CEO and the mayor—all for charity—you have a great photo opportunity.

Photo opportunity sheets often are part of a media kit. However, they can be sent individually to journalists.

> ■ **Key to Success:** A photo opportunity sheet must move quickly to a detailed, engaging description of a forthcoming visual event.

Format/Design

The headings for a photo opportunity sheet are like those of a news release (pages 32–33) except that instead of "News Release" in large type, a photo opportunity sheet, of course, has "Photo Opportunity Sheet."

Like fact sheets and media advisories, photo opportunity sheets are single-spaced, with double-spacing between paragraphs.

Photo opportunity sheets often open with a descriptive, promotional paragraph. After that paragraph, they adopt the two-column format of a fact sheet, focusing on *what, who, where, when, why* and *how.*

Try to keep your photo opportunity sheet to one page—or at least one page, front and back. You may use the reverse side for a map, if necessary. As with news releases, if the photo opportunity sheet is more than one page, type "-more-" or "-over-" at the bottom of each appropriate page. Beginning with page two, place a condensed version of the headline (called a "slug") and the page number in the upper-right corner. After the last line or item on the last page, space down two lines and type "-30-" or "###."

Content and Organization

Unlike most other media kit documents, photo opportunity sheets can have promotional writing. Even the headline of a photo opportunity sheet can be promotional and subjective. Focus the headline on the photogenic event, but write it with wit or drama to attract photographers' attention.

After the headline, write a detailed, promotional paragraph showing why the event is photogenic and newsworthy. Don't go overboard—don't promise more than you can deliver—but journalists will accept promotional writing in this passage.

Again, after the opening paragraph, adopt the style of the fact sheet, focusing on *what, who, where, when, why* and *how.* Be specific about times and places. As we note in the Format/Design section, some photo opportunity sheets include maps to show photographers where the event will be.

In the *how* section, consider specifying what equipment and facilities, including electrical outlets, will be available for photographers.

PHOTO OPPORTUNITY SHEET

PALMQUIST UNIVERSITY
234 COLLEGE AVE.
HOSEA, WIS. 59830
555-876-0864

Photo Opportunity Sheet

FOR IMMEDIATE RELEASE
Sept. 7, 2005

FOR MORE INFORMATION, CONTACT:
Jane Doe
Director of Media Relations
555-654-2986
jdoe@palmquist.edu

New Palmquist University president to take oath of office

Flanked by the colorful flags of the United States, the state of Wisconsin and Palmquist University, Edward Faxon will take the oath of office Sept. 18 to become Palmquist's 19th president. Wisconsin Board of Regents Director Roberta Kramer will administer the oath. Faxon has chosen to place his hand upon a Faxon family Bible that dates back to 1748.

What: Edward Faxon will take the oath of office at 10 a.m., Sept. 18, in McDaniel Auditorium at the Student Union. The Wisconsin Board of Regents has named Edward Faxon the new president of Palmquist University, of Hosea, Wis.

Who: Faxon comes to Palmquist from Weslaco College in Milwaukee, where he served as vice-provost for seven years. Before that, he was the Andrea Burnett Distinguished Professor of Biochemistry at Kasold University in Portland, Tenn. He earned his Ph.D. in biochemistry from Madrid University in 1979.

When: Faxon will begin his tenure as president Sept. 18, 2005, said Roberta Kramer, director of the Board of Regents.

Where: The Student Union is at 1400 Palmquist Blvd.

Why: "Edward Faxon was our first choice. The Board of Regents is certain that he will lead Palmquist University to a great future."
—Roberta Kramer, Director,
Wisconsin Board of Regents

###

Newsletter and Magazine Stories

Purpose, Audience and Media

A newsletter/magazine story is a narrative that delivers facts on an important subject to a large, well-defined audience. A newsletter/magazine story usually can be read in one sitting and is designed either to inform or to entertain and inform. Some newsletters are published daily. However, most newsletters and magazines are weekly or monthly. Therefore, newsletter and magazine stories rarely announce breaking news that readers must know right away.

Most newsletters and magazines are considered niche publications. Niche publications target well-defined audiences whose members share a common interest. Newsletters and magazines can target an organization's employees; members of a profession, such as accountants; members of an association, such as the American Library Association; people with a common interest, such as antique cars; and so on.

The primary medium for newsletters and magazines remains paper. However, newsletters in particular are distributed by e-mail and even fax machines. Newsletters and magazines also exist as Web site entries.

> ■ **Key to Success:** Newsletter and magazine stories must quickly show readers why they'll benefit from reading the story. Readers must quickly realize that they'll learn useful information and that they might even be entertained as they learn.

Format/Design

Newsletter/magazine stories ultimately will be formatted by a publication designer. In all likelihood, you will submit your stories to an editor as a file attached to an e-mail message. Always consult your editor for format preferences.

At the top of page one, include a proposed headline, a subheadline if necessary and a byline (your name).

You may wish to double-space the text of your story. Double-spacing makes it easier for the publication's editor to read your text. If you are submitting the story on paper, definitely double-space to give the editor space to edit. Newsletters and magazines rarely double-space the text of articles. However, if your story exists as a computer file, the editor can easily change your line-spacing.

Indent paragraphs. Don't extra-space between them.

Hit your space bar only once, not twice, after periods and other punctuation marks that end sentences. Have only one space, not two, between sentences.

At the end of your story, type "-30-" or "###" or some other closing symbol.

If you are submitting a paper version of your story to an editor, put "-more-" at the bottom of each appropriate page. Beginning with page two, in the upper-right corner, place a slug (a few words that identify the story), a page number and your last name. For example, a heading for page two could be "Bubblegum-2-Smith." (Your computer version of your story probably would not include these format items; check with your editor for formatting preferences.) At the end of your story, type "-30-" or "###" or some other closing symbol. Staple the pages of the manuscript together.

Content and Organization

Newsletter stories generally are short and tightly constructed. In most newsletters, space is at a premium. Magazine stories, however, can be longer and can more thoroughly develop a topic.

Most newsletter and magazine stories fall into one of three categories:

- Straight news stories or announcements
- Feature stories
- Hybrid stories

Straight News Stories

Straight news stories begin with a headline that summarizes the story's main point. The lead (a first paragraph) of a news story includes the most important details of *who, what, when, where, why* and *how.* The first sentence of the story often includes *what, who, where* and *when.* Leads don't have to include every detail of *who, what, when, where, why* and *how;* that's what the rest of the story is for. Leads should include only the basic, essential details that a reader must know.

In a straight news story, information appears in descending order of importance—the inverted pyramid organization (page 34). The last paragraph is the least important paragraph and could even be deleted from the story without serious damage.

The straight news story is, except for the format, basically identical to the announcement form of the news release (pages 38–39). Straight news stories focus on informing readers, not on entertaining them.

Feature Stories

Like straight news stories, feature stories inform—but they also entertain. Storytelling skills are important in features. For example, the headline of a feature usually doesn't summarize the story's main point. Instead, it teases and beguiles readers, making them want to read the story to satisfy their curiosity. If necessary, a subheadline can summarize the content of the story.

A feature lead—unlike the lead of a straight news story—need not present all the most important facts. Instead, the first paragraph should "hook" readers, making them want to read the story.

You can present details creatively in a feature. For example, a writer once was assigned a story on the sale of a national retailer's one-millionth pair of pantyhose. Instead of writing a straight news story, he calculated that a kicking chorus line of one million pantyhose wearers would stretch from New York City to Little Rock, Ark.

He then determined how far into space the unraveled thread from one million pairs of pantyhose would reach. Readers praised and remembered the story; they were informed and entertained.

In a straight news story, the last paragraph includes the least important information. In a feature, however, the conclusion may be the most important moment of the story; a feature's conclusion may have important dramatic value. Unlike in a straight news story, the conclusion in a feature provides a sense of closure.

Feature Organizational Strategies. You can organize a feature many different ways. Features almost always begin with a lead (one or two paragraphs) that entertains and hooks readers. Feature leads don't reveal the full subject, or topic, of the story. That's the job of the "nut graf" or "nut paragraph." A nut graf isn't a feature story's first paragraph, but it does come early in the story—usually right after the lead paragraph or paragraphs. The nut graf tells what the story is really about. It links the lead to the big idea, the main point, of the story. A nut graf is sometimes called a "swing graf" because it swings the lead into the true focus of the story. A nut graf comes early in a feature because you don't want readers wondering about the exact subject of the story.

In short features, consisting of only a few paragraphs, the nut graf is sometimes part of the lead paragraph. A first sentence or two hooks readers; the first paragraph then declares more precisely what the story is about.

After the lead and nut graf comes the body of the feature story, which delivers most of the *who, what, where, when, why* and *how* information in an entertaining or dramatic manner.

The conclusion of a feature often is just one or two paragraphs. Unlike the conclusion of an inverted pyramid news story, which can be cut for space, a feature conclusion is indispensable. It may be the most dramatic moment of a story. Feature conclusions, often quotations, generally sum up the story, dramatically noting what it all means or what has been learned. Sections on feature leads and conclusions appear below.

Seven good organizational strategies for features follow.

1. **The Gold Coin Theory.** Developed by two great journalists, Roy Peter Clark and Donald Fry, the gold coin theory asks you to imagine that readers fear your feature story is a dusty, uninviting path that they must walk. Tempt your readers by frequently dropping gold coins onto the path. Gold coins are bits of entertainment; they are fascinating anecdotes, great quotations, incredible facts, something that makes readers laugh or cry—anything that rewards the readers for reading. Ideally, your readers will think, "I just got rewarded for reading this far. I think I'll keep reading to find more rewards." Sprinkle gold coins throughout your feature. Gold coins must exist in the feature's lead and its conclusion.

2. **The *Wall Street Journal* Style #1.** Many *WSJ* features, particularly on page one, begin with a tightly focused anecdote. Then comes the nut graf. More anec-

dotes then lead to more information—or more information is followed by illustrative anecdotes—or both. The feature often closes with a quotation or an anecdote that memorably sums up the story's main point.

3. **The *Wall Street Journal* Style #2.** Many *WSJ* features begin with snappy, one-sentence leads. That one sentence gets its own paragraph. The sentence doesn't explain the story. Instead, the sentence usually teases readers; it's a little mysterious. Readers keep reading to solve the mystery of the lead.

Immediately after that snappy sentence comes the nut graf, which announces the focus of the story. From this point on, the organization matches the organization that follows the nut graf in *WSJ* Style #1.

The difference between these two *Wall Street Journal* styles is the lead's length and snappiness. The long stories on page one of the *WSJ* offer great examples of feature-story organization.

4. **The *People* Magazine Personality Profile.** Personality profiles in *People* magazine generally begin with an anecdote that tantalizes readers. The anecdote often is a key dramatic point in the person's life. Frequently, the anecdote describes a crisis that becomes a turning point in the person's life. The goal of the anecdote is to make readers ask, "How in the world did she get into this situation? What's the story behind this? And what will happen next? How will she solve this?"

Next comes the nut graf, which gives quick background on the main character and her situation. After reading the nut graf, readers know who the story is about and why her story matters.

Next comes the relevant history of the central character. The history helps explain the opening anecdote. It often includes comments from the central character. This history also can include comments from other knowledgeable people. The history moves through time until it reaches the moment described in the opening anecdote. At this point, the central character often comments on the events described in the opening. The history then describes the resolution of the opening anecdote, often with comments from the central character and others.

The conclusion returns to the present and shows readers what the central character is doing now. If the opening anecdote hasn't been completely resolved, the final resolution is presented here. The feature often ends with a dramatic, moving, funny or revealing quotation from the central character. The quotation provides a sense of closure.

5. **The Epic Poetry Strategy.** *People* magazine personality profiles are based on the epic poetry organizational scheme (remember *The Iliad* and *The Odyssey*?). Epic poetry begins *in medias res*—"in the middle of things," usually at an exciting moment. This leads readers to ask two questions: "How did we get here?" and "What will happen next?"

The epic then flashes back to the beginning of the hero's story, takes us to the middle (which we already know) and reveals how the hero fared, then moves to a dramatic conclusion.

6. **The Bookend Strategy.** The story begins with a strong, appropriate, compelling image that captures the reader's interest. The story later closes with the same image—but with a twist. The image operates as a set of bookends—those matched props that keep a row of books from falling to the right or left—with one bookend at the beginning of the story and the other bookend, with a twist, at the end.

7. **The Theme Strategy.** The theme strategy resembles the bookend scheme, but instead of just appearing twice, the image is woven throughout the story, including the introduction and conclusion. For example, if you were to compare someone to a fairy-tale princess (which probably would be a little trite), a unifying element throughout the story could be references to fairy-tale images: handsome princes, dragons, fairy godmothers, witches and so on. Such a technique also is called an extended metaphor. The theme strategy works best with short features; it can get annoying in long stories.

The theme strategy also resembles the gold coin theory, except that in the theme strategy the gold coins all are thematically related to one another.

Feature Lead Strategies.   Feature leads should hook readers, gaining their attention and interest. Several traditional hooking strategies exist:

- A snappy, one-sentence teaser that creates a mystery

  Example: "Night after night, the danger came." (What danger? Who was affected? Why did it happen at night? Why did it happen night after night? How dangerous was it?) Readers will continue, wanting to solve these mysteries.

- A short, fascinating anecdote that illustrates the story's main point

  Example: "When Mary Smith felt the jagged granite atop Mount McPherson, she knew that she had conquered more than a killer mountain. She had conquered her blindness."

- A fascinating quotation from someone involved in the story

  Example: "'If Mark Edwards walked through that door again,' Tisha Bertram says, 'I don't know whether I'd kiss him or kick him.'"

- An impressive fact (be sure it's truly impressive and interesting)

  Example: "Mark Edwards can eat 17 and a half extra-large pepperoni pizzas in 20 minutes."

- A striking image

  Example: "The machine squats in a dark corner, wheezing and lurching like a has-been sumo wrestler seeking glory one last time."

- A thought-provoking question that can't be answered with a simple yes or no

  Example: "If you couldn't be yourself, who would you want to be?"

Again, feature leads are not as direct as the leads of straight news stories. Because a feature lead doesn't have to directly announce the story's subject, it can develop a hook that compels readers to keep reading.

In feature leads, avoid clichés such as "Little did she know . . . "

Don't allow the headline of a feature story (or any story) to function as your first sentence. Your feature story should be complete without the headline.

Feature Conclusion Strategies.   Many features return to a tight focus in the conclusion. One good conclusion strategy is to return to the image, question or anecdote developed in the lead and put a new, appropriate twist on it. Readers thus see the lead in a new light and, ideally, understand it even more. Sometimes the conclusion supplies the end of an anecdote that began in the lead. Often, a quotation can supply a dramatic, summary conclusion.

Feature conclusions are dramatic. In the words of the gold coin theory, feature conclusions have a gold coin. The story's most important fact or most entertaining moment may appear in the conclusion. (Again, features do not use the inverted pyramid organization, in which the last paragraph is the least important moment in the story.)

Oddly, a "for more information" paragraph following a feature conclusion doesn't undercut the drama of the true conclusion. Be concise in such paragraphs: "For more information, contact the Center City Humane Society at 555-123-4567."

Hybrid Stories

A hybrid newsletter/magazine story is a compromise between the straight news story and the feature story. To hook readers, the hybrid begins with a featurelike lead. Then, to save space, it moves to a straight news lead, focusing on the important aspects of *who, what, when, where, why* and *how*. After the featurelike lead, hybrids become inverted pyramids (page 34). Hybrids lack the strong, dramatic conclusions that characterize feature stories. The hybrid story can be a good short form for newsletters.

Hybrid stories generally have a traditional news headline (page 34), but they can have a feature-style headline (page 77).

TIPS

1. Be guided by a clear understanding of audience and purpose. Know who your audience is and what its interests in this situation are. Be able to define for yourself the story's strategic (goal-oriented) purpose in one clear sentence.
2. Do rigorous research. Gather more information than will ultimately appear in the story. The extra information will give you options and help you see what should be in the story. Trying to write a story, or any document, without enough research is painful and frustrating.
3. Read many newsletters and magazines. Analyze what works and what doesn't.
4. Use specifics, not generalities.
5. Show readers; don't merely tell them. Don't say that a person is busy. Instead, show that she's busy. Let readers draw the conclusion that she's busy.

6. Quotation attributions in feature stories usually are in present tense. In straight news stories, they usually are in past tense. In a quotation of more than one sentence, place the attribution after the first sentence. For example, "I rarely speak about this," she says. "It's far too embarrassing."

7. Feature-story organization can be used for so-called success stories, or case studies, which agencies sometimes use to describe successful communication campaigns. Success stories can appear in brochures, as inserts in folders or on a Web site.

Going Online

Newsletters can easily be distributed via e-mail attachments and Web site entries. National newsletters often have Web sites with archived stories. Magazines also often have Web sites with archived stories and teasers about stories in the current issue.

FEATURE STORY EXAMPLE

Nobody kicks Palmquist's grass

Injuries and penalties are nothing new to football, but several Palmquist University students were caught off guard, so to speak, when campus police cited them for unnecessary roughness to grass. On the defensive are eight Palmquist students who scrimmaged last October on the rain-soaked lawn in front of Rogers Hall. Fifteen yards and a loss of down apparently won't suffice: The undergraduate sodbusters will tackle the local legal system this month, and the misdemeanor charge of tearing up turf carries the possibility of both a fine and a jail sentence.

An official of the City Municipal Court recently said that although the Palmquist Eight had walked all over the rights of the grass, he doubted that they faced a stint in jail. If found guilty, he said, the students may have to pay their debt to society through a specified amount of community service.

Meanwhile, the alleged victim has made no comment, and a grassroots support movement for the defendants continues to grow.

###

STRAIGHT NEWS STORY EXAMPLE

Palmquist students arrested for property damage

Eight Palmquist University students were arrested Saturday for damaging grass in front of Rogers Hall. The misdemeanor charge could result in fines and a jail sentence.

"The students were incredibly irresponsible," said Charles Poole, clerk of the City Municipal Court. "Campus police say that the grass is badly damaged. But I doubt that they'll pay a fine or go to jail if they're guilty. In cases like this, people usually get sentenced to a certain amount of community service."

The eight students, all from Central City, are Barrett Fulton, 19; Dunc Brown, 20; Tobin Brown, 18; Jocelyn Snyder, 21; Kendra Snyder, 18; Mona Smith, 20; Gillian Williams, 21; and Emily Davidson, 20.

HYBRID STORY EXAMPLE

Palmquist students arrested for damaging grass

Injuries and penalties are nothing new to football, but several Palmquist University students were caught off guard, so to speak, when campus police cited them for unnecessary roughness to grass. Eight students were arrested Saturday for damaging grass in front of Rogers Hall. The misdemeanor charge could result in fines and a jail sentence.

"The students were incredibly irresponsible," said Charles Poole, clerk of the City Municipal Court. "Campus police say that the grass is badly damaged. But I doubt that they'll pay a fine or go to jail if they're guilty. In cases like this, people usually get sentenced to a certain amount of community service."

The eight students, all from Central City, are Barrett Fulton, 19; Dunc Brown, 20; Tobin Brown, 18; Jocelyn Snyder, 21; Kendra Snyder, 18; Mona Smith, 20; Gillian Williams, 21; and Emily Davidson, 20.

###

Annual Reports

Purpose, Audience and Media

In the United States, the federal Securities and Exchange Commission and most stock markets, such as the New York Stock Exchange, require companies that sell stock to issue an annual financial report to their stockholders. Annual reports must feature recent financial information, a year-to-year comparison of financial figures, a description of the organization's upper-level management and a discussion of the company's goals.

Earlier, in The Law and Strategic Writing (pages 23–25), we discussed disclosure law. Publicly owned companies (that is, companies that sell stock) rely heavily on annual reports to meet their legal obligation to disclose financial information. Annual reports, therefore, are serious, fact-laden documents. They may have a glossy, glitzy appearance—many do—but they stick to the facts. The concept of puffery—acceptable exaggeration (pages 24–25)—doesn't apply to annual reports.

Some nonprofit organizations issue annual reports to inform current donors and attract potential donors. However, the law does not require such reports. (Nonprofit organizations do report to the U.S. Internal Revenue Service through Tax Form 990.)

The legally specified audience for an annual report is a company's stockholders. However, the larger audience includes potential investors, investment analysts, employees, potential employees and government regulators. Thus, annual reports sometimes appear to have a split personality: a formal no-frills side and a flashier, friendlier side.

The traditional medium for an annual report remains paper. Most annual reports look like glossy magazines. However, some annual reports are published as CDs, DVDs and videotapes. Sometimes, these newer multimedia formats accompany the paper annual report. In addition to distributing paper annual reports, companies often publish their annual reports on their Web sites.

■ **Key to Success:** Annual reports should have a clear theme. They should not hide bad news. They should be specific and present information in a variety of ways, including charts, enlarged quotations and photographs with captions.

Format/Design

The format of an annual report defies concise description. Most annual reports have the format and appearance of a glossy magazine: an attractive cover, a table of contents, sections with titles and dozens of pages with type, photographs and charts.

Often, the mandatory sections on finance and operations are set in smaller type than the less technical sections. These sections also often appear on different paper from the rest of the report. These differences set the sections apart, helping them to seem more serious and technical than the rest of the report.

In long sections, use internal headlines to clarify content and increase readability.

Content and Organization

Annual reports often have five sections, each of which is discussed below. But in general, an annual report should discuss your organization's strategies and performance. The annual report should describe, in terms of fulfilling goals, where your organization is, where it has been and where it plans to be. Be specific. Cite specific goals and precise measurements of performance. Use numbers to show how close to your short-term and long-term goals you are.

Discuss any bad news openly, and show specifically how you're correcting the problem.

If possible, unite all this information with a theme, either implicit or explicit. A theme can help organize the report's information and keep it directed toward a specific message. In other words, ensure that your annual report is on-strategy: Understand what clear message the report should send, and direct all your writing toward the fulfillment of that message and theme. But don't forget that split personality: Even as you try to develop an engaging theme, remember that this is a legal document. You must scrupulously stick to the facts.

The cover title of an annual report traditionally is the name of your organization plus the words "annual report" and the year. Some annual reports also print the explicit theme on the cover.

Work with your company's legal and financial teams to ensure that the annual report complies with federal, state and stock-market laws and regulations.

Following are the traditional sections of an annual report:

Opening Charts and Graphs: Basic Financial Information

These financial charts—such as bar graphs and pie charts—should be clearly labeled and reader-friendly. Often, the charts have no captions, just clear titles. This short section is typically just one page and often is on the inside front cover. Usually, your role will be to edit the few words that accompany these charts. Financial personnel and the annual report's designer, or art director, prepare the charts. Most word-processing programs offer user-friendly ways of creating and inserting charts and graphs.

Message from the CEO

This message—sometimes called a letter—focuses on the achievements of the past year and thanks employees, stockholders and other groups that have helped the company work toward its goals. The leader of the company, generally the chief executive officer, writes this section (though, often, a member of her public relations staff actually writes the section with guidance from the CEO). The CEO's message should clearly reflect her personality. If the annual report has a theme, skillfully integrate that theme into this section.

Within the first few sentences, the CEO should say how the company performed during the past year. Were profits up or down? Why? If profits were down or were disappointing, the CEO should acknowledge that, explain why and discuss what's being done to improve the situation. Investors appreciate—and expect—candor.

The CEO often signs this section—again, just as if it were a long, informative letter.

Longer Section on the Company

This section resembles a long feature story in a magazine: lively, engaging, well organized, informative and specific. This section is one of your best chances to use the annual report to present your company as an attractive investment opportunity. Use smaller, inset articles (called sidebars) and charts and graphs to highlight key information. Photographs with captions also can enliven this section. Not all annual reports include this long section, though most do; sometimes information that would go here can be included in the other sections. And as you've read many times in this section, stick to the facts. Don't exaggerate in this legal document.

Management's Analysis of Financial Data

This section presents financial charts accompanied by long, technical explanations. Financial personnel from your company usually will prepare this section, and it will be verified by an outside accounting agency. You probably won't write this section, but you might help edit those long explanations. Be sure to confirm your edits with your company's legal and financial teams. Some of the financial jargon may seem boring and needlessly complex, but that language often protects your company by complying with laws and other financial reporting guidelines. Casual investors may flip through this section with a yawn, but investment analysts will study it carefully.

Who's Who in the Company

Most annual reports close with information about the board of directors and other high-ranking company officials. Often, this section simply lists names and titles under individual photographs. This "lite" approach can disappoint readers who want to evaluate the men and women who will implement company strategies. Instead of presenting such limited information, consider including more details in this section. State how long the officials have been with the company and where they were before. List any college degrees they've earned. List the individuals' specific duties, especially as those duties relate to the fulfillment of company goals. Consider quoting the officials on their personal priorities for the organization. Include a group photograph or a photo of each individual—or both.

TIPS

1. Get started early. Evaluate the previous annual report. What worked well? What didn't? Experts say that you should begin planning seven to eight months before the new report's mailing date. Federal regulations require distribution of the annual report to stockholders at least 15 days before the corporate annual meeting.

2. Use the annual report to promote your organization as a good investment opportunity. Besides informing stockholders and meeting legal requirements, use your annual report to attract investors and boost stock prices.

3. Select a design that enhances your words. Work with the best designer available, one who will use photos, charts and other illustrations to help tell the story. Be sure that the designer has read the current draft of the annual report and knows the overall theme. Some designers forget that their mission is to make the report's message clear and accessible; they become more interested in fascinating design that looks great but doesn't tell the story. The design of your annual report *should* look great—but first, the design must be functional: The design must work with, not against, the words that tell the story.

Going Online

Many companies place their annual reports on their Web sites, which allow enhanced annual reports, with features such as a video message from the CEO and interactive charts. Companies also can use their Web sites to store past annual reports, creating an archive of promises and performance. Some independent Web sites store dozens of annual reports. For example, see www.reportgallery.com.

Speeches

Purpose, Audience and Media

In strategic writing, a speech is a scripted monologue designed to be performed in front of an audience. A speech generally contains a main point, and it elaborates on that main point.

Speeches can challenge strategic writers because they add a new element to the usual "purpose, audience, media" analysis. Speeches have a speaker—and that speaker often is not the speechwriter. In other words, the speeches you write often will be delivered by someone else. Therefore, besides studying the purpose of the speech and the audience for the speech, you also must study the speaker. Your script must sound like the speaker at her best—not like you at your best. You must consider her communication abilities, not your own. In a speech, a human being is the medium.

The audience of a speech generally is a group that has something that the speaker needs. A presidential candidate addressing a campaign needs votes and money. A corporate leader addressing stockholders needs their support. The CEO of a nonprofit organization addressing potential volunteers needs volunteers. Members of the audience usually are united by a common interest. In the above examples, the audiences, in order, are people interested in politics; stockholders; and potential volunteers for a nonprofit organization.

Most speeches still are printed out onto paper for the speaker. However, some speeches are delivered, via computer, to transparent screens (called TelePromTers) from which the speaker can read the speech. Some speakers prefer to speak from outlines or from note cards.

> ■ **Key to Success:** Effective speeches are short, well-organized and focused on the audience's self-interest.

Format/Design

Format guidelines for speeches focus on making the pages easy for the speaker to read so that she can maintain frequent eye contact with members of the audience.

In a paper copy of a speech, triple- or quadruple-space between the lines. Use large type and wide margins.

Type only on the upper two-thirds of each page so that the speaker's chin doesn't dip too low as she reads.

Number the pages in the upper-right corner. (That placement will help the speaker avoid accidentally reading the page number aloud.) Put "-more-" at the bottom of each appropriate page. Put "-end-" below the last line of the speech.

Don't staple the speech—the pages must turn easily and quietly. Learn what kind of binding the speaker prefers. Some will want the pages clamped together; they will remove the clamp only when they reach the lectern. Others prefer that the speech be three-hole punched and clipped into a narrow three-ring binder. Different lectern sizes may influence the binding of the speech.

If you use visual aids, such as PowerPoint slides, note in the text where each new slide occurs so that the speaker can pause and, perhaps, gesture at the screen. Visual aids can be indicated in the text of the speech by highlighting relevant passages with a colored highlighter; or by placing indicators in the margins; or by inserting parenthetical, capital-letter notes into the text. Again, learn what the speaker is comfortable with.

Include "stage directions" in the speech in parentheses and, usually, in capital letters. For example, suggest a dramatic pause at a particular point by writing "(PAUSE HERE)" in the text of the speech. You also can suggest gestures.

Content and Organization

Begin by analyzing five things:

1. **The purpose.** After discussing the speech's purpose with the speaker, write, in one sentence, the main point of the speech. Then write a brief description of what the speech should include. Create a working title. Have the speaker review this, and get her input.

2. **The audience.** Who are its members? What is their common background? What is their strong self-interest in the situation that has prompted the speech? What topics, sure to draw a response, can the speaker discuss? What do audience members expect from the speech? They will be attentive if the speech focuses on their self-interests. Most audience members hope to be informed and, if appropriate, entertained.

3. **The speaker.** Be sure to write *her* speech—not yours. Again, the speech should sound like the speaker at her best—not you at yours. Spend as much time as possible with the speaker to learn any phrases, gestures and speaking styles.

4. **The time frame.** Has a time length been specified? If not, consider the subject, purpose, audience and speaker in determining how long the speech should be. Whenever possible, limit the speech to 20 minutes or less.

5. **The setting.** Where will the speech be given? Will the location be inside or outside? What is the size of the room? Will there be a lectern and a microphone? Will audiovisual systems be available if needed? Will a glass and a pitcher of water be available?

Organize the Speech Logically and Gracefully

The content of a speech can be organized in many ways. Almost all speeches have an introduction, a body and a conclusion—much like a feature story for a newsletter or a magazine (see pages 77–81).

Most business speeches have a *what* and a *why*: The *what* announces the main point, and the *why* explains or justifies that main point. The *what* and the *why* are the foundations for the following two traditional ways to organize the contents of a speech.

Emphasizing *What*.   Use this organizational strategy when the *what* of the speech is more important than the *why*—that is, when the announcement is more important than the explanation or the justification of the news. Use this strategy when you want audience members to be able to repeat the main point to themselves and others.

■ **Introduction.** Build up to the main point (the *what*) and announce it. If the *what* is something positive that you want to emphasize, make it the last words of the introduction and pause after it.

You can build up to the main point by thanking the audience members for attending and very briefly providing the reasons for the *what*. You could complete this build-up in two or three sentences. If that seems too abrupt, provide a few general comments that provide a transition from the thanks to the reasons.

■ **Body.** Expand on the *what*. One of the best ways to flesh out the main point is to explain what it means to the audience.

Another way to develop the *what* is to discuss the *who, what, when, where, why* and *how* of the main point.

However you choose to elaborate on the main point, if you have more than one elaboration to make, the subject-restriction-information technique can work well for each new paragraph. This technique shows the relationship of each new elaboration to the main point. For an explanation of subject-restriction-information, see page 231.

■ **Conclusion.** Reiterate the *what* once again and put a dramatic or memorable spin on it.

One effective variation of the *what* organizational strategy is to create a "theme" speech, in which a strong theme is announced in the introduction, along with the *what*. The theme is clearly intertwined throughout the elaboration of the *what* in the body and then dramatically reasserted in the conclusion.

For example, a speech in which an executive announced the retirement of a valued colleague might review the colleague's career and compare it to a year. The theme could include references to spring, summer and autumn. The theme also could include references to planting and harvesting, storms and holidays. It could close by borrowing from a Frank Sinatra song: "It was a very good year."

Emphasizing *Why*.   Use this organizational strategy when the *why* is just as important as the *what*. Use the *why* organization when you want the audience to understand why something has happened or is about to happen. Use it when you want members of your audience to be able to explain and justify the main point to themselves and others.

Also use the *why* strategy when your main point involves bad news. Just as in the bad-news business letter, the *why* organization allows you to give the explanation for the bad news before you actually announce it. Ideally, if audience members understand the *why*, they will better accept the *what*.

The *why* organizational strategy consists of five parts:

1. **Introduction.** Often, the introduction contains only a greeting. Do not mention the main point of the speech—the *what*—in this brief section. The introduction can be something as simple as "Good afternoon, and thank you for that warm reception."

2. **Explanation.** The body of the speech begins here. Discuss the *why* in this section. Cover the relevant points that explain or justify the main point, even though that main point has not yet been spoken. Basically, establish a cause–effect relationship. This explanation section describes the causes, discussing all the reasons that justify the main point to come. When the speaker then delivers the main point, the audience is prepared to accept it. The listeners already have heard and considered the logic that supports the main point.

3. **Main point.** The body of the speech continues, and the speaker delivers the main point, the *what*. This section usually is brief. Sometimes it consists of only one sentence.

   Note again the sequence of parts: The speaker logically builds up to the main point. The main point is not mentioned until the third section of the speech.

4. **Remarks.** As the body of the speech continues, the speaker develops the main point. For example, what are its consequences? What does it mean to audience members?

5. **Conclusion.** The speaker can repeat the main point here, though such repetition often is unnecessary. The conclusion usually is concise. The speaker often appeals to audience members' emotions. Recall how many presidential speeches end with "God bless the United States of America," a powerful appeal to the emotions.

Each part of the above five-part *why* speech should lead logically and gracefully to the next.

Write for the Ear, Not the Eye

Audience members can't scan back up the page or hit rewind to clarify meaning. Therefore, consider the following:

■ Have a clear beginning, middle and end. However, avoid overworked, boring transitions such as "My next point" and "In conclusion." Use the subject-restriction-information method to avoid "My next point." Use the expanded focus of the conclusion (a clear return to a more general tone and to the big picture) to avoid "In conclusion."

■ Keep sentences short. However, vary sentence rhythms in accordance with meaning. For example, deliver blunt ideas in short, blunt sentences. Deliver relaxing ideas in longer (though not long), flowing sentences. Avoid using conjunctions such as *and* to unite two sentences into one. Use two sentences.

■ Don't use big, pretentious words. Remember the advertising maxim "Big ideas in small words." It can be done: Recall Hamlet's "To be or not to be—that is the question." He's discussing whether to live or die, and he's using mostly one-syllable words.

■ Avoid technical terms unless you're certain that your audience knows and understands them.

■ Spell out big numbers for the speaker. Consider phonetically spelling tough words or tough names. Learn what she is comfortable with.

■ Don't expect the audience to remember more than two or three key ideas.

■ Review the tips for broadcast-style writing on pages 10–12.

TIPS

1. Give the speech a title, even if that title is known only to you and the speaker. A title can help you stay focused on the main point.

2. Consider an opening hook. Instead of saying, "Thank you. I'm glad to be here" (or immediately thereafter), wake up the audience with a provocative question, an outrageous statement or a short, entertaining anecdote.

3. Many speechwriters recommend that you avoid jokes, especially jokes with punch lines. If the speaker misspeaks the line or if the joke isn't funny—or worse, if it's inappropriate—the speech and the speaker are damaged.

4. Be specific. Be innovative in how you present facts. For example: "We use four tons of paper a day. That's enough to bury this room eight feet deep every working day of the year. Eight feet deep!"

5. Address the self-interest of audience members. Talk to listeners about themselves.

6. Use simple visual aids, especially computer-generated, if appropriate and available. Remember that what is both heard and seen is often more memorable than what is just heard or seen. If you use visual aids, make the images simple. Use few words. If audience members have to interpret images or read long passages, they're not listening to the speaker. Proofread all such materials, and have others do so. Test any related equipment. Know what backup systems are available and be prepared to switch to them. Don't feel compelled to use visuals. In a short, well-written speech, words alone suffice.

7. Act out the speech for yourself or a critical listener before giving it to the speaker. Get feedback. Then act out the speech for the speaker. Use the delivery you hope she will use. Ask for her feedback. (It's not always possible to get this much time from busy executives. And it's not always advisable if the executive is a polished, experienced speaker.)

8. When possible, have the speaker practice the speech in front of you and others she trusts. Coach her delivery and get feedback from others. In some cases, the speaker may be too busy or too embarrassed to rehearse

in front of you. If she's embarrassed, consider tactfully pointing out that it's better to get negative feedback from you than from the real audience.

9. Be sure to have more than one copy of the speech in the room where the speaker delivers the speech—just in case the main copy gets lost.

10. Scout the location for the speaker. She'll be grateful to learn about the lectern, a glass of water, room size, audiovisual equipment and so on. She'll appreciate your extra effort, and you may learn things that help you write a great speech.

11. See Appendix E, Tips for Oral Presentations.

Going Online

Speeches generally are delivered in person, but they can appear online as streamed video or as a live feed. Often, organizations use their Web sites to offer copies of important speeches delivered by their executives.

SPEECH MANUSCRIPT

Gettysburg Speech—Page 1

Fourscore and seven years ago, our

fathers brought forth upon this continent

a new nation, conceived in liberty and

dedicated to the proposition that <u>all</u> men

are created equal.

Now we are engaged in a great civil

war, testing whether that nation, or <u>any</u>

nation so conceived and so dedicated,

can long endure.

We are met on a great battlefield of

that war. We have come to dedicate a

portion of that field as a final resting-place

for those who here gave their lives that

-more-

Web Writing

Purpose, Audience and Media

Web sites are today's means of distributing information quickly and to a diverse audience. They can inform, market goods and services, share opinions and entertain. Anyone and everyone can have a Web site.

No other audience is potentially as diverse as the Web audience. Your viewer could be the person next door or someone in Algeria. However, that doesn't mean that the Web is a typical mass medium. Think of it as one-to-one communication. After all, people don't surf the Web in groups. When writing or designing a Web site, think of a specific user. Give him a name; list his needs, desires and goals. Put yourself in his shoes. Ask yourself these questions:

- To what category of users does he belong? (Student, parent or alumni, for example)
- How old is he?
- What are his interests?
- What language(s) does he speak?
- What does he want to accomplish at the site?
- What are his needs and expectations?
- How technically proficient is he?
- What type of Internet connection does he have?
- How did he get to the site?
- At what time of day will he visit the site?
- How long might he stay at the site?
- From what page(s) might he enter and leave the site?
- What will make him return to the site?

Web surfers, from novices to power surfers, do share some distinguishable characteristics. They are busy people who want information quickly. They are impatient. They move through pages randomly and make snap decisions. They don't just read or look at information—they interact with it; they manipulate it.

- **Key to success:** Web sites must provide current content-driven information in an easy-to-navigate format that is relevant to the user's needs.

Content and Organization

Studies show that people read information on a computer screen 25 percent slower than information in print. In fact, we know they don't read every word. They skip and scan and move through the page looking for things that interest them. In a Stanford and Poynter Institute study that tracked eye movement on Web sites, readers found text more important than graphics: Participants first scanned for headlines, article summaries and captions. Readers in this study kept multiple browsers or windows open, switching among multiple Web sites.

Writing for the World Wide Web differs from writing for print media. Knowing a Web user's habits helps us create documents for the user who clicks and scans, spending only a few seconds at the site before he moves to the next.

Split content into information bites. To attract and hold such a user, make text short with one idea per sentence. Keep paragraphs short—two to five sentences in length. Put key information in the first sentence of each paragraph. Include only fact-filled sentences that provide objective information. This doesn't mean that you dumb down your copy. Organize it so that the reader can choose how in-depth he wants to go.

Use hypertext links to interior pages to provide more in-depth coverage or background information. Think in terms of layers. The top layer is the outer skin of your Web site and as you go deeper inside, you reach the meat. Use internal links also to appeal to specific audiences. Let the audience decide what to download.

For in-depth sites, use the bite-snack-meal approach developed by Marilynne Rudick and Leslie O'Flahavan. The headline serves as the bite and is a hypertext link to the full article (the meal), which appears on an interior page. The snack is a two- or three-sentence summary of the article beneath the headline. This allows the reader to choose what level of detail he wants.

Use a modified inverted pyramid style (page 34). The opening paragraph summarizes the content. The next paragraphs give the most interesting and supportive information. Then come details about each important point, followed by background.

Write headlines and subheadlines that summarize content. Make every word in a headline meaningful. Don't be cute. Don't be promotional. Web site users seek information, not humor or sizzle. The headline should clearly explain what information follows.

Use fewer, smaller and simpler words. Web writing should use about half as many words as conventional prose. Edit. Then edit again. Consult the 10 Tips to Writing Better Sentences on pages 3–5.

Be objective. Avoid overpromotion. Excessive sales writing muddies the water and requires too much time to decipher fact from fluff. Work to earn trust and credibility. Use hypertext links to other sources to support your data.

Use bullets (•) for lists. Bullets slow down the eye and bring attention to information. Use bullets when the sequence doesn't matter; use numbers when it does. In Web sites, bulleted information should be one or two words in length. Using sentences or long phrases defeats the purpose of delivering information quickly.

Highlight text for emphasis. Put key words in bold or colored text. Avoid blue and purple, however. The default settings on most computers are blue for unvisited sites and purple for visited sites. Don't use italics or underlining for emphasis. Italic type is hard to read on a computer screen, and underlining may be confused with hypertext links. Think in terms of eyebites—two or maybe three emphasized words—and use about three times as many highlights as you would in print.

Integrate graphics within text. Caption all graphics clearly. Remember, unlike print, Web readers view text first and then graphics. Clear captions also assist the understanding of visually impaired viewers whose specialized computers may not display the graphics.

CONTENT AND ORGANIZATION TIPS

1. Write concisely. Use simple, short sentence structure when possible. Use subject-verb-object order (see page 11). Use present tense (*are*) or present-perfect tense (*have been*). Use short, familiar words and strong verbs. Write conversationally, using personal pronouns such as *you, we* and *I*. Avoid technical jargon (see page 227).

2. Avoid puns and figurative or colloquial language. Remember that you're writing for an international audience. To a Brit, packing a boot means putting something in the trunk of the car. To an American, it might mean something quite different. Date conversions can be confusing as well. To an American 3/8/05 means March 8, 2005. In other countries, it means 3 August 2005.

3. Check spelling and grammar. Don't ruin your credibility by being careless. Proofread your Web site, and then proof it again. Better yet, print it out and have at least two other editors proof it. Errors are more difficult to catch on the screen than in print.

4. Update. Update. Update. The Web is a fluid medium. To be credible you must frequently update statistics, dates, numbers and documents. For example, one week your site might include a story about an upcoming board meeting. The next week it should report on that meeting.

5. Respond to e-mail inquiries. The Web is an interactive medium. If your site includes a "Contact Us" page, you are obligated to read incoming messages and respond in a timely manner.

6. In headlines and text, especially near the top of the page, use words that visitors might type into a search engine when looking for an organization like yours. This will make your Web site rank high in search engine searches.

Format/Design

Writing and designing a successful Web site must be a collaborative effort. Design must enhance readability and not distract from content. The success of the site depends upon how well the viewer can navigate the site to find specific information. Navigation problems cause users to give up. Users rarely think about site structure. They simply go forward or backward—or they quit in frustration. Studies show that readers prefer to navigate with hyperlinks to interior pages.

Much debate exists among designers about whether scrolling for information inhibits users. One theory is to keep important information above the fold. That's a term borrowed from the newspaper industry that means placing the most important news on the upper half of the paper. On the computer, above the fold means above the scroll line. However, this may mean creating numerous internal pages that take time and effort to load. You may lose an impatient user or confuse a novice if your site has multiple layers of pages. Therefore, creating fewer and longer pages with numerous hypertext links may be preferable. The audience and content should dictate your choice.

Graphics should be included only if they amplify the message. Animated and "cute" graphics distract the reader and frustrate comprehension. Animated graphics can attract attention, but if they take too long to download or if they detract from the message, you've lost your reader.

Your Web site should have a separate and distinguishable home page. It should function as a front door that welcomes the user inside. The home page is where audiences can be split into different interest groups and guided to specific information. For example, a Web site for your university might have links for current students, prospective students, faculty, parents and alumni. Clicking on the appropriate link would send a user to a unique page that addresses his specific interests.

FORMAT/DESIGN TIPS

1. Make each page capable of standing alone. Your Web site is like a house with many rooms. Each room has a door through which people can enter and leave. Be sure to tell the user his arrival point and how it relates to the other pages. Each page should contain

   - The organization's name or logo, usually in the upper-left corner
   - A tag line that summarizes the organization's purpose
   - A link to the home page
   - An advanced search tool, usually in the upper-right corner
   - A headline that summarizes the page content
   - Content-driven copy with hypertext links
   - Navigation bars
   - Copyright information
   - The date the page was created or revised
   - A URL address

2. Make table of contents frames visible at all times. Users prefer navigation links at the top and bottom of the page to side navigation links, which usually require scrolling.

3. Keep line length short. The normal reading distance the eyes can span is only three inches wide or approximately 12 words. Use columns, tables and graphics to narrow the line length. Fonts with exaggerated x-heights are easier to read (x-height refers to the height of a lowercase x within a typeface). Consider using the Georgia typeface for body type and the Veranda typeface for headlines.

4. Create a new browser window with each hypertext link so that returning to the original page is easy. However, too many hypertext links within text can be distracting. If your copy is too cluttered with links, consider grouping them at the end of the page.

5. Test for dead links frequently.

6. Assume readers will print hard copies of long, detailed materials. Provide print-friendly versions.

7. Label buttons clearly to tell the reader where the link leads. For example, *About Us* is more descriptive than *Overview*.

8. Use mouseover tooltips to provide short definitions for unfamiliar terms. A mouseover is a small popup window that appears when the cursor scrolls over a highlighted word.

The definition of that word then appears in the window.

9. Use pull quotes—quotes set larger as graphic elements—to repeat important information.

10. Avoid using too much white space. Unlike printed materials, white space doesn't enhance readability. It slows down the person scanning the page.

WEB SITE HOME PAGE

Back Forward Stop Refresh Home AutoFill Print Mail

Address:

Live Home Page @ Apple @ Apple Support @ Apple Store @ iTools @ Mac OS X @ Microsoft MacTopia @ Office for Macintosh @ MSN

Favorites History Search Scrapbook Page Holder

RIVERVIEW
COMMUNITY MEDICAL CENTER

About Riverview

Services

Physician Directory

Calendar

Health Resources

Employment

Volunteer

Endowment

Contact Us

Copyright © 2005
Revised 3/5/05
www.riverviewusa.org

For more than half a century, Riverview Community Medical Center has served the people of Gleason County, USA. Licensed for 150 acute care beds, 10 rehab and 21 skilled nursing facility beds, Riverview offers top-quality care to all who need services regardless of ability to pay. Riverview, a not-for-profit hospital, receives no tax support from the city or county.

Riverview Community Medical Center
123 Riverview Lane
Riverview, USA 12345
Tel. 555 843-2111
Fax 555 843-2115

Accredited by the Joint Commission on Accreditation of Healthcare Organizations (JCAHO)

Search

What's Happening at Riverview

View Newborns

Health Tips

News Releases

Riverview Renovates Pediatrics

A fantasy land comes to life on the walls of the Pediatrics Unit, thanks to a $35,000 grant from the Riverview Arts Commission.

First in State to Perform New Prostate Laser Procedure

Riverview Medical Center is the first site in the state to perform a new, minimally invasive laser treatment for enlarged prostate known as Niagara PVP.

Section III
Strategic Writing in Advertising

Objectives

In Section III: Strategic Writing in Advertising, you will learn to write these documents:

- Strategic message planners
- Print advertisements
- Radio advertisements
- Television advertisements

- Radio and TV promotions
- Radio and TV public service announcements

Advertising consists of persuasive messages that identified sponsors send to consumers through controlled media.

That standard definition just doesn't convey the excitement of advertising. Few things in strategic writing beat the satisfaction of writing a successful ad. Don't you wish you were the creative genius behind MasterCard's "Priceless" campaign or Nike's "Just Do It" slogan? Still, let's examine our definition of advertising a little more. By *identified sponsor,* we mean your client or product. By *persuasive message,* we mean a message that gets a consumer to act—usually to buy your product. And by *controlled media,* we mean media (such as television or magazines) in which you can control exactly what your message is, how often you send it and the medium or media you use. Controlled media aren't free, however. As an advertiser, you pay not only to create your persuasive messages but also to place them in the media.

Advertising faces severe challenges in the 21st century. We're bombarded by ads in print media, broadcast media, the Web—on buses, billboards, airline-ticket covers—even, sometimes, in restrooms. Ads are everywhere. And you expect your message to be noticed in that avalanche of persuasion? A successful ad must cut through that clutter. To win a consumer's attention, you must conduct extensive research on the client, product, competition and target audience. And you must be creative: Everyone can be creative—some just have to try harder. Professors Sandra Moriarty and Bruce Vanden Bergh note that advertising may be the only profession in which people actually have the word *creative* in their job titles. Perhaps your personal career goal is to become an advertising agency's creative director.

But creativity alone can't guarantee a successful ad. In fact, creativity probably matters less than the research you conduct. Your research should lead you to the development of one clear message for your ad. (If your ad has several messages or even one unclear message, how can it hope to fight its way through the clutter of competing ads?) We call this one clear message a strategic message. The one clear message is strategic because it focuses on the precise goal of the advertisement. As we've said before, strategic means goal oriented.

The first document you'll encounter in this section on advertising is called a strategic message planner. Different advertising professionals have different names for the document, including copy platform, creative work plan and strategy statement. No matter what we call it, a strategic message planner helps you organize your research to create your ad's one clear message: the strategic message.

A strategic message usually focuses on a unique benefit that your product offers to the target audience. The late David Ogilvy, an advertising genius of the 20th century, said that the most important sentence in his book *Ogilvy on Advertising* was this: "Advertising which promises no benefit to the consumer does not sell, yet the majority of campaigns contain no promise whatsoever" (page 160).

Only members of your target audience can truly identify the benefits of your product. Benefits derive from product features. Benefits are good things that members of your target audience believe your product will do for them. So your toothpaste creates whiter teeth? That's just a product feature. But to your target audience, that feature means sex appeal—a benefit. So your lawn fertilizer guarantees no weeds? Another product feature. But to your target audience, that feature means freedom on the weekends—no more digging up dandelions.

Not all product features generate benefits. A product feature that appeals to you may have no value whatsoever to your ad's target audience. Only careful research can tell you which features can create benefits—and which benefit is so important that it belongs in your strategic message.

Benefits can build brands. A brand is a consumer's image of a product, a product line or a company. As advertisers, we certainly have our own definition of our brand—but the consumer's opinion is all that really matters. Brands help differentiate competitors. A brand gives your product a position in a consumer's mental map of a market. For example, which do you prefer: Coke or Pepsi? Nike or Reebok? Burger King or McDonald's? Why? What is your image of each of those products? For you, that image is the brand.

Although benefits usually are essential to successful advertising, they occasionally play only a small role—or no apparent role at all—in so-called image advertising. Generally, image advertising—also known as identity advertising and reminder advertising—promotes a brand whose benefits are so familiar that they don't need to be restated in the ad. Instead, the ad simply reminds consumers that the product exists. Consumers then automatically supply the positive brand image. Products that flourish with image advertising include market leaders in the soft-drink and athletic shoe industries. Also, announcement ads—those stressing only product names and prices—fill newspapers every day. In this book, however, we'll focus more on the challenge of creating ads with benefits-related strategic messages.

Once you know the strategic message of your ad, you can begin thinking of images, sounds, headlines, slogans—all the aspects of creativity that make advertising so much fun. We think that you'll find strategic messages planners so valuable that you'll soon consider them fun as well.

Strategic Message Planners

Purpose, Audience and Media

The strategic message planner helps create the one, clear strategic message that is the heart of a successful advertisement. A strategic message planner helps you summarize and study your research in order to discover an idea that will motivate the target audience of an advertisement. Before strategic writers begin to think of an ad's visuals or jingles or slogans or headlines, they first conduct research and complete a strategic message planner. Why? Because all the creative elements of a successful ad must support a core theme—a strategic message—that unites each element of the ad. Experienced advertising copywriters know that they waste time and money if they try to create an ad before they have conducted extensive research and specified the strategic (goal-oriented) message of the ad. A strategic message planner helps create that core message.

Strategic message planners also are called copy platforms, creative work plans and strategy statements. No matter what you call it, a strategic message planner helps you create your ad's one clear messge—the strategic message—by enabling you to organize and study your research.

Consumers, or target audiences, do not see the strategic message planner. Instead, this document stays within the team that creates the ad. The team probably will show a finished strategic message planner to a client to ensure that the client agrees with the strategic message. However, unlike the finished ad, few people will see or hear the strategic message planner.

Strategic message planners exist either on paper or as online documents that easily can be transferred among members of an advertising team.

> ■ **Key to Success:** You must complete a strategic message planner before you begin to consider the more creative aspects of an ad. If you begin to plan the ad before you develop the ad's strategic message, your creative ideas may distort your vision of what the strategic message truly should be.

Content and Organization

A strategic message planner should be concise but highly detailed and specific. Before completing a strategic message planner, an advertising copywriter should conduct extensive research in several areas: client, product, target audience and competition. Completing a strategic message planner involves summarizing your research or drawing conclusions in 10 areas:

1. Client and product
2. Target audience

3. Product benefits
4. Current brand image
5. Desired brand image
6. Direct competitors and brand images
7. Indirect competitors and brand images
8. Advertising goal
9. Strategic message
10. Supporting benefits

Each of these subheadings should be a concise, labeled section of your strategic message planner. Let's look at each section in more detail.

1. Client and Product

Completing this section involves more than just writing the names of your product and the organization that produces or offers it. Include important details of both the company and the product. Advertising copywriters suggest that you answer the following 13 questions in order to supply information for this section. You probably won't include all your client/product research in the strategic message planner, but answering these 13 questions may lead to discoveries that can help you create a successful strategic message:

What Is the Product?
  i. To what product category does this product belong? (Product categories can include areas such as soft drinks and athletic shoes.)
 ii. What are the features of the product, particularly those that distinguish it from other products in the category?
iii. What attributes of the product are discernible through the senses: seeing, hearing, touching, tasting, smelling?

What Is the Product Made of?
 iv. What are the materials, the ingredients, of the product?
  v. Do those materials, or ingredients, have their own ingredients?
 vi. For services, are there intangible ingredients (such as a particular kind of workout routine at a health club)?

Who and What Made the Product?
 vii. What organization created the product? What are the features of that organization, especially features that distinguish it from competitors?
viii. What specific individuals created the product? What are the features of those people, especially features that distinguish them from others in their profession?
 ix. What vendors supplied materials for the product? What are the features of those vendors, especially features that distinguish them from competitors?
  x. What processes did the organization use to create the product? What are the features of those processes, especially features that distinguish them from others?

xi. What equipment did the organization use to create the product? What are the attributes of that equipment, especially features that distinguish it from other equipment?

What Is the Purpose of the Product?

xii. Why did the organization create the product (besides making money)?

xiii. What unintended uses for the product have been discovered?

2. Target Audience

Your client or your boss often will specify the target audience for the upcoming ad or ad campaign. However, you still must dedicate yourself to understanding the members—the human beings—of that target audience.

Don't equate the target market of the product with the target audience for the specific ad you plan to create. In other words, don't try to create one ad that will appeal to all the different groups that might purchase your product. For example, the target market for milk can include babies, senior citizens and everyone in between. No ad could successfully appeal to everyone in such a broad target market. Instead, your ad might focus on mothers who buy milk for their teenaged children. You can try to reach the other markets (except, perhaps, for babies) with different ads.

To define and understand a target audience, you should seek both demographic and psychographic information. Demographic information is "nonattitudinal" information—things such as age, gender, race, income and education level. Demographic information can even include how often members of the target audience buy or use your product. Psychographic information is "attitudinal" information—things such as religious, political and social beliefs.

Your client or your own organization may be able to supply research on the target audience. However, if you gather your own research (generally a good idea), you should begin by seeking secondary research, which is data gathered by others. Good sources of secondary research include the U.S. Census Bureau, online at www.census.gov, and the Gallup Organization, online at www.Gallup.com. Companies such as SRI Consulting Business Intelligence, with its VALS analyses (values and lifestyles) can, for a fee, provide target audience research. You also may need to gather primary research, which is original research that you conduct yourself. Basic primary research methods include in-depth interviews, focus groups and surveys. A good textbook on marketing research can steer you to reliable secondary sources and teach you how to conduct your own primary research. Just asking questions of people who produce or use your product can lead to important research discoveries.

3. Product Benefits

A benefit is a product feature that appeals to the ad's target audience. In the previous two sections, you studied the features of your product and the characteristics of your target audience. You're now equipped to combine your research and determine which features will appeal to members of your target audience. If you list more than one benefit, which benefit would your target audience see as most important? Probably, you will introduce some or all of those benefits in your finished ad.

The one underlying concern of all consumers is "What's in it for me?"—also known as the WIIFM philosophy. Advertising works because consumers seek solutions to three main needs:

- The need for control
- The need for companionship
- The need for confidence

As you search for the benefits of your product, consider the consumer's need for control, companionship or confidence.

Products that appeal to the need for control will

- Save time
- Save money
- Simplify a task
- Be easy to use
- Eliminate unpleasant tasks or consequences (escape pain)
- Alleviate guilt
- Alleviate fear

Products that appeal to the need for companionship will

- Improve appearance
- Increase sexual attraction
- Increase acceptance and belonging
- Be fashionable
- Improve family relationships

Products that appeal to the need for confidence will

- Lead to praise and accomplishments
- Improve skills and knowledge
- Lead to personal advancement
- Be dependable
- Improve status and protect reputation
- Give pride of ownership
- Give special privileges and recognition

4. Current Brand Image

Brand image is your target audience's impression of your product. For example, what do you think of when you hear the name Coca-Cola? Nike? MTV? Your quick mental definitions of those brands are their brand images.

In describing current brand image, be sure to avoid wishful thinking. Don't describe what you wish your target audience believed. Instead, describe brand image as your target audience would. Your research should allow you to do so.

Often, the current brand image presents a problem. Organizations generally advertise because consumers don't know or don't understand their product. Your advertisement will try to improve the current brand image and solve the problem.

Sometimes, however, the current brand image is exactly what an organization desires. In that case, your advertisement will try to reinforce the current brand image rather than change it. Reinforcing ads often are called image, identity or reminder ads (see page 102).

Your entry in this section of the strategic message planner should be brief—a sentence or two. Most consumers don't spend time expressing lengthy, highly detailed brand images.

5. Desired Brand Image

Your client usually will have specific ideas for you regarding desired brand image. Desired brand image is the impression that you *wish* the target audience had of your product. If your ad is successful, desired brand image would be your target audience's new and enduring impression of the product.

Desired brand image isn't necessarily a slogan. Instead, desired brand image is a description. It's how you wish a member of your target audience would, in his own informal words, briefly describe his impression of your product.

Like the previous section, your entry for this section should be brief—ideally one sentence. You can't expect your target audience to remember a lengthy, highly detailed brand image.

6. Direct Competitors and Brand Images

Earlier, when you conducted product research, you placed your product in a product category. To identify direct competitors, name the leading products in that category. For example, if your client is Coca-Cola, you certainly would mention Pepsi. If your client is Burger King, you certainly would mention McDonald's. For each direct competitor you name, include a concise description of that product's current brand image with your target audience. One goal of the strategic message planner is to help you design a brand image that will distinguish your product from its direct competitors.

7. Indirect Competitors and Brand Images

Completing an entry for this section can be more challenging than describing direct competitors. Indirect competitors are in a different product category from your product. However, they are things that could keep your target audience from buying your product. For example, if your product is a new breakfast cereal, indirect competitors could be frozen waffles, restaurants and even diets. Specifying brand images for indirect competitors can be vague and challenging, though you still should make the effort. For example, if you list fast-food restaurants as an indirect competitor of your breakfast cereal, how would your target audience describe the brand image of such restaurants? The brand image of diets might be even more challenging. Remember that brand image is your target audience's impression of a product or even a product category, such as fast-food restaurants.

8. Advertising Goal

According to your client, what is the goal of the soon-to-be-created ad? Of course, the ultimate goal usually will be "to make a lot more money." For this section, avoid an easy answer like that. It won't help you. Instead, focus on *how* the ad will generate those additional profits. For example, the advertising goal for your new breakfast cereal might be "To get middle-aged women to view AsparFlakes as the best natural source of calcium, which fights bone loss." If your ad reaches that goal, the final goal—to make a lot more money—should be realized.

Your entry for this section should be very brief—ideally, just one sentence or sentence fragment. Your entry may be similar to your entry for the section on desired brand image. It certainly shouldn't contradict it.

9. Strategic Message

Your entry in this section is very important. The words you write here will be the one, clear message of the ad—the theme of the ad. In this section, you clearly state the strategic message that will help generate all the creative elements of the ad. In the book *Creating the Advertising Message,* Jim Albright says that one of the best ways to concisely state the strategic message is to finish this sentence: "Target audience, you should buy this product because _____" (page 26). The words that follow *because* are the ad's strategic message.

You won't pluck your strategic message out of thin air. Instead, these important words will come from your analysis of the previous eight sections. For example, the strategic message will, ideally, move the target audience from the current brand image to the desired brand image.

Your strategic message is not necessarily a slogan. In fact, your strategic message may never appear word-for-word in your ad. Instead, it may be powerfully implicit, just as the theme of a short story may be absolutely clear though it is not directly stated.

A good strategic message gives your product a unique and positive position in the target audience's mind. A good strategic message makes a beneficial claim that no other competing product can make.

To guarantee the strength of your strategic message, you must test it against the previous eight sections by asking these questions:

i. Will the strategic message satisfy the advertising goal?
ii. Will the strategic message set my product apart from the brand images of the direct competitors? Could any of the direct competitors send this same message? (If so, the strategic message needs revision.)
iii. Will the strategic message set my product apart from the brand images of the indirect competitors? Could any of the indirect competitors send this same message? (If so, the strategic message needs revision.)
iv. Will the strategic message help create the desired brand image?
v. Will the strategic message help eliminate a negative current brand image (or reinforce a positive current brand image)?

vi. Does the strategic message focus on an important benefit?

vii. Is the strategic message consistent with the demographic and psychographic characteristics of the target audience?

viii. Is the strategic message consistent with the features of the client and the product?

Notice that in answering these questions, you are moving backward through the strategic message planner. This backward movement can help show you that the only way to create a successful strategic message is to study your entries to the first eight sections.

Your strategic message should be brief—ideally, one sentence.

10. Supporting Benefits

Supporting benefits are also called selling points. Supporting benefits are the bits of information you could include in the ad itself to support the claim made in your strategic message. Remember that a benefit is a product feature that appeals to your target audience.

A good strategic message (from the previous section) is brief. It usually doesn't include evidence. The supporting benefits supply the evidence. And, again, the supporting benefits can give you a good idea of what product benefits to present in your ad.

For example, the strategy statement for your breakfast cereal product might be "AsparFlakes is the only asparagus-flavored breakfast cereal that helps build stronger bones." Your supporting benefits for this strategy would involve the details of *how* AsparFlakes builds strong bones. In most cases, your ad would avoid presenting other benefits, such as low price or prizes inside the box. Discussion of those benefits would weaken the focus on your one, clear strategic message: AsparFlakes is the only asparagus-flavored breakfast cereal that helps build stronger bones.

Our imaginary cereal also points out a reality of all advertising: Over time, an ad is only as good as the product. Your ad may get the target audience to buy AsparFlakes once—but if they don't like it, your cereal ads are toast.

Format/Design

The format of a strategic message planner is simple. It is titled Strategic Message Planner. It is single-spaced, and it has 10 subheadlines for the 10 sections described above. Generally, there is a blank line (a double-space) before each new section.

Strategic message planners are concise. They do not include all your research regarding the client, product, target audience and competition. Instead, they include only the relevant highlights. Strategic message planners generally are two to three pages long.

Because strategic message planners often are shown to clients, they generally are produced on an organization's stationery and are typed neatly. A good heading for a second page is "Product Name SMP–2."

TIPS

1. Always complete a strategic message planner before you begin an ad. (The powerful temptation will be to rush to the design or copywriting aspects.) If you begin to think about images and headlines or music, you reduce your ability to develop an effective strategic message. You may inadvertently develop a strategic message that fits only your creative ideas for the ad.

2. Specify just one well-defined target audience for your ad. Don't try to create an ad that will appeal both to college students and to young married professionals. Those two different groups may be target markets for your product—but it's unlikely that one ad can appeal to them both.

3. Ensure that your strategic message is unique. The strategic message should make a claim for your product that no competing product could make.

4. Realize that when you advertise the same product to a different target audience, the strategic message will change. However, the strategic messages in a coordinated campaign to different target audiences should complement—and certainly not contradict—one another.

Going Online

Strategic message planners are confidential documents, discussed only among a client and the members of the advertising team. A strategic message planner may go online as an e-mail message. However, it would not be posted on a Web site. An advertising team would not share its strategic ideas with competitors.

Strategic Message Planner: AsparFlakes

Client and Product

AsparPower Mills Inc. of Asparagus City, Mich., makes AsparFlakes breakfast cereal. Michael Campion founded AsparPower Mills in 1903. The company's primary products are asparagus bread, asparagus dinner rolls, asparagus breadsticks and asparagus juice. AsparPower Mills primarily sells its products to health-food stores in the United States and Canada. Total revenues in 2005 were $13 million.

AsparPower Mills has produced AsparFlakes, an all-natural breakfast cereal, since 2004. The ingredients of AsparFlakes are dried organic tofu, ground whole wheat, ground whole oats and ground dried asparagus. AsparFlakes appears in 16-ounce boxes at a suggested retail price of $4.75.

STRATEGIC MESSAGE PLANNER

STRATEGIC MESSAGE PLANNER

AsparFlakes is baked in brick ovens. Its ingredients are supplied by certified organic farms in Michigan.

AsparFlakes tastes and smells like dried asparagus. With skim milk, one bowl provides 1,000 milligrams of calcium, the recommended daily allowance for adults.

AsparPower Mills created AsparFlakes to provide a high-calcium, tasty, organic breakfast cereal for America's health-conscious consumers. Early testers of the product report that they also enjoy AsparFlakes as a dry snack food.

Target Audience
The target audience for this ad is middle-aged (ages 40 to 60), health-conscious women in the United States and Canada. They are college-educated professionals. They are married with children. Their family income averages $90,000 per year.

These women shop in health-food stores at least twice a week. They buy healthy, organic foods for three meals a day, not just for the evening meal. Though they are not vegetarians, they prefer foods made from all-natural fruits, vegetables and grains. Because of their shopping habits, they are familiar with the traditional products from AsparPower Mills. However, they are not familiar with AsparFlakes, a new product.

Ingredients and production processes are important to this target audience. They prefer all-natural, organic ingredients. They like old-fashioned, natural production processes.

Members of this target audience see their physicians at least once a year. Osteoporosis, a disease in which bones become porous and brittle, is a primary health concern for this target. Postmenopausal women are the highest-risk group for osteoporosis, and our target knows that. Physicians often recommend high daily doses of calcium to prevent osteoporosis.

Product Benefits
AsparFlakes helps prevent osteoporosis by supplying the recommended daily allowance of calcium. Being all-natural, it is healthy and nature-friendly.

Current Brand Image
AsparPower Mills is known and respected by the target audience. However, the target has not heard of AsparFlakes all-natural breakfast cereal. The target has no brand image of AsparFlakes.

Desired Brand Image
Ideally, the target will view AsparFlakes as a tasty, healthy, environmentally responsible source of calcium, needed to help prevent osteoporosis.

STRATEGIC MESSAGE PLANNER

AsparFlakes SMP–3

Direct Competitors and Brand Images

AsparCrunch cereal, produced by the AsparCrunch Company, holds 70 percent of the market for asparagus-flavored breakfast cereals. It is an all-natural cereal. Because it lacks tofu, however, it is not high in calcium. Our target audience views AsparCrunch only as a tasty, asparagus-flavored all-natural cereal.

The closest competitor to AsparCrunch is Aunt Martha's Asparagus Cereal, produced by Aunt Martha's World Conglomerate. This cereal holds approximately 20 percent of the market for asparagus-flavored breakfast cereals. Aunt Martha's is not an all-natural cereal. It includes chemical preservatives. It lacks tofu and is not high in calcium. Our target views Aunt Martha's Asparagus Cereal as a cheaper, less healthy alternative to AsparCrunch, the market leader.

Indirect Competitors and Brand Images

Indirect competitors include all-natural nonasparagus breakfast cereals. The best selling all-natural nonasparagus breakfast cereal is NaturoBreakfast Solution. Our target likes it for its taste and its calcium content. However, it delivers only 50 percent of the recommended daily allowance of calcium.

Other indirect competitors are diets and breakfast cereals that are not all-natural. Our target audience usually avoids both, believing them to be unhealthy.

Advertising Goal

To get target audience members to view AsparFlakes as the healthiest all-natural asparagus-flavored breakfast cereal because it fights osteoporosis.

Strategic Message

All-natural AsparFlakes fights osteoporosis because it's an excellent source of calcium.

Supporting Benefits

Feature	Benefit
All-natural	Healthy
100 percent of recommended daily allowance of calcium	Fights bone disease
Made in old-fashioned brick ovens by AsparPower Mills	A name you know and trust; a process that represents old-fashioned, wholesome values

Strategic Message Planner: Riverview Community Medical Center

Client and Product

Riverview Community Medical Center is a 190-bed community hospital owned by the city of Riverview. It serves Gleason County (pop. 150,000). The medical center is licensed for 150 acute care beds, 10 rehabilitation beds and 21 skilled nursing facility beds. It is accredited by the Joint Commission on the Accreditation of Healthcare Organizations. Located in the Midwest, Riverview is a growing community about 45 minutes from Metropolitis (pop. 1.2 million). Medical centers in Metropolitis provide competition for Riverview Community Medical Center.

Riverview, a not-for-profit hospital, receives no tax support from the city or county and serves the community's health care needs regardless of individuals' ability to pay.

Riverview Rehab & Sports Therapy Services and the Center for Joint Replacement are new services offered by the medical center. Under the direction of Dr. John Hamp, the Rehab Center is staffed by registered physical and occupational therapists and provides postsurgical rehab, nutrition management and sports medicine. Dr. Susan Gear's specialty at the Center for Joint Replacement is knee and hip replacement surgery.

Target Audience

The target audience for this ad is middle-aged (ages 40 to 60), health-conscious residents of Gleason County. They are unaware of the sports medicine services offered at Riverview Medical Center. The average age of the target audience is 45. Its members have a median household income of $78,000. They are college graduates, and most hold professional positions: They are managers, teachers, engineers and lawyers.

Members of the target audience are proud of their ability to stay in shape and look younger than their age. They exercise at least three times a week for a minimum of 45 minutes per workout. Most exercise alone so that they can concentrate on their workouts. Many change activities, alternating between jogging on Riverview's riverside trails and workouts in a gym. However, they are beginning to experience joint pain, particularly in the knees, a common affliction of this age group. They believe that this is just part of aging, so they tend to fight it with over-the-counter pain medications and just "toughing it out."

Members of the target audience don't like to discuss their joint-pain problems because they think it's a sign of advancing age. They believe they just have to cope with the pain; they're not aware of solutions.

Product Benefits

New treatments and preventive therapies that will help eliminate joint pain. No need to travel 45 minutes to Metropolitis for such treatments.

STRATEGIC MESSAGE PLANNER

Riverview SMP–2

Current Brand Image
The target audience sees Riverview as a hospital where sick people are treated. Little awareness exists about the new Rehab & Sports Therapy Services and the Center for Joint Replacement. Members of the target audience believe that they would have to travel to Metropolis for special services like sports medicine.

Desired Brand Image
Riverview Community Medical Center, the Rehab & Sports Therapy Services and the Center for Joint Replacement want to be viewed as a local solution to joint pain.

Direct Competitors and Brand Images
Because Riverview is located near Metropolis, members of the target audience sometimes bypass Riverview Community Medical Center and seek treatment in larger medical centers—especially for special needs, such as cosmetic surgery and sports medicine. The target audience sees bigger as better. Metropolis has three major medical centers, all offering sports medicine services. However, none of the three is particularly known for its sports medicine services.

- St. John's Medical Center: The target audience knows it best for its heart-treatment facilities.
- Metropolis Regional Health Center: The target audience knows it best for its maternity facilities.
- Palmquist University Medical Center: The target audience knows it best for its cancer treatments and as a teaching hospital for university students.

Other competitors include chiropractors and physical therapists. City Chiropractic Clinic is Riverview's largest group of chiropractors. The target audience views it as being helpful for pulled muscles but not for joint pain or sports medicine. Armstrong Physical Therapy is the city's largest group of physical therapists. The target audience views it as a facility for accident victims or senior citizens.

Indirect Competitors and Brand Images
Indirect competitors include over-the-counter pain medications, such as Extra-Strength Tylenol, which the target audience views as a temporary solution, not satisfactory for the long term. Other indirect competitors are a lack of time (the target audience doesn't want to seek treatment in Metropolis) and apathy (some members of the target audience think joint pain is just a part of aging).

Advertising Goal
To get target audience members to know of Riverview Rehab & Sports Therapy Services and the Center for Joint Replacement—and to get them to attend the upcoming free seminar.

STRATEGIC MESSAGE PLANNER

Riverview SMP–3

Strategic Message
You can live with less joint pain. Come to our seminar.

Supporting Benefits

Feature	Benefit
Free	No cost
Local	Convenient
Two sessions	Convenient
Led by physicians	Can talk one-on-one with experts
New treatments, like ultrasound and electrostimulation	High-tech; cutting edge

STRATEGIC MESSAGE PLANNER

Strategic Message Planner: SlimWhims

Client and Product
SlimWhims is a new prepackaged diet program. To lose weight, dieters use SlimWhims to follow a prescribed eating regimen and manage calorie intake.

SlimWhims was founded by two gourmet chefs who believe that low-calorie food can taste good. They use only the freshest, natural ingredients and combine spices and herbs to give each SlimWhims meal a distinctive, delicious flavor. SlimWhims meals contain approximately 300 calories and feature 24 different entrées for breakfast, lunch and dinner. The meals contain all of the vitamins and minerals needed for a healthy diet.

Each SlimWhims meal is vacuum sealed in a pouch and can be heated easily in a microwave. A special processing technique keeps vegetables crisp and tender. SlimWhims meals are moderately priced. They sell for approximately $7 apiece.

Target Audience
The target audience for this ad is women ages 24 to 34 who are concerned about their appearance, particularly their weight. They typically are five to 50 pounds overweight and

SlimWhims SMP–2

have tried numerous diet programs without lasting success. If they're not on a diet right now, they're about to start a new one.

The average age of the target audience is 27. Its members have a median household income of $67,000. Many are first-time homeowners. Most are married and have, on average, two young children. They are high school graduates, and approximately 40 percent are college graduates.

Many are young mothers who have not been able to lose all the weight gained during pregnancy. These women are more concerned with convenience than cost. Most have children and careers, and they are devoted to both. They attend their children's school events and tend to enroll their children in a variety of programs, ranging from music lessons to swimming lessons. They're too busy to coordinate an elaborate, complicated diet.

Members of the target audience live busy lives and don't have time for elaborate cooking. However, they truly enjoy good food. They refuse to consider a diet of unpleasant drinks or what they call "rabbit food." For them, gourmet food is one of the finer things in life that they aspire to. They enjoy their rare evenings at fancy restaurants. They are more than willing to prepare one meal for family members and a separate meal for themselves—if the low-cal meal is part of a successful diet plan and if it doesn't take too long.

The target audience doesn't expect a three-week miracle. Its members are willing to invest long-term in a diet that satisfies their desire for good food and for results. They're educated, and they understand that a diet requires an investment of time. Unfortunately, boring, bland diets—or complicated, time-consuming diets—make it impossible for them to go the distance.

Product Benefits
SlimWhims entrées are so delicious that you won't feel deprived. They're quick and effective, meaning you save time and lose weight.

Current Brand Image
SlimWhims is new to the market and has little brand image. If anything, it is perceived as just another fad diet.

Desired Brand Image
SlimWhims meals are gourmet experiences that really help you lose weight.

Direct Competitors and Brand Images
Direct competitors are store-bought diet foods:

- Ms. Svelte Model Diet Meals: The target audience has a positive image of this leading brand. However, members of the target audience wish the meals tasted better and offered more than seven different entrées.

STRATEGIC MESSAGE PLANNER

SlimWhims SMP–3

- WeightBusters Diet Liquids: The target audience views these drinks as effective but tasteless and unsatisfying.
- Card-a-Day Weight Loss Foods: The target audience views this system, which involves charts and calorie counting, as too complicated and time-consuming.

Indirect Competitors and Brand Images

Indirect competitors include do-it-yourself diets, desire to save money, frustration with unsuccessful diets and a desire to eat fattening foods. Members of the target audience doubt their ability to sustain a do-it-yourself diet, such as just eating vegetables. Saving money is important—but they would spend moderately for a truly successful diet. They are frustrated with unsuccessful diets, but they are willing to try new diets that sound promising. They fear their desire for fattening foods; they'd like to combat that desire with a truly good-tasting diet.

Advertising Goal

To get members of the target audience to believe that SlimWhims is the easy, tasty and effective diet they've been searching for.

Strategic Message

You should buy this product because it satisfies your desires for good food and losing weight.

Supporting Benefits

Feature	Benefit
Only fresh, natural ingredients	Tastes like a gourmet meal
Natural spices and herbs	
Recipes by chefs	
Special processing techniques	
Prepackaged	Convenient, no hassle, no guesswork
Guaranteed results	Weight loss!
24 entrées	Provides choices
300 calories per meal	Weight loss!
All required vitamins and minerals	Health

Print Advertisements

Purpose, Audience and Media

Print advertisements are persuasive messages that appear in newspapers, magazines or other controlled media. Their goal is to get a specific audience to take a specified action—for example, to buy a product (a good or a service), make an inquiry, fill out and mail a coupon, call a phone number, visit a Web site or adopt a new image of the product. Print ads often are part of a larger advertising campaign that may include radio, television, direct mail, outdoor and promotional advertising.

Print ads fall into three categories: announcement ads, image ads (also known as identity or reminder ads) and product ads. Announcement ads fill the pages of newspapers every day. They are the grocery store ads, the one-day-only ads and the Presidents' Day sale ads. They contain very little copy except for the names and prices of the items for sale. They must be timely and direct to be effective. Image ads remind the consumer of a product or brand. They create consumer awareness and depend on a larger marketing campaign to deliver the real product message. Industry leaders such as Nike or Absolut Vodka use image advertising. Product ads, our focus in this segment, persuade the consumer to take an action or change a behavior. Although there is no definitive right or wrong way to create an effective ad, there are some basic guidelines that will help you be successful.

The audience for a print ad should be precisely defined in the strategic message planner that you complete before creating your ad (page 106). The audience for a print ad is *not* everyone who might purchase the product. Amusement parks, for example, have different advertising strategies for parents and children. Usually, the target audience is a well-defined segment of the total potential market for the product.

The medium for a print ad is paper, usually in a newspaper or magazine.

■ **Key to Success:** Effective print ads capture the consumer's attention, interest him in the product and create a desire for him to take action.

Content and Organization

Effective print ads deliver a clear strategic message. To fine-tune your message, begin with a strategic message planner (pages 104–118). The more time and effort you put into researching your product and developing the SMP, the easier your copywriting job will be.

One of the oldest advertising copywriting formulas is AIDA: Attention-Interest-Desire-Action. First you must get your reader's attention; then you must interest him in your product. Finally, you must create a desire for him to take a specified action, such as purchasing the product.

Let's look at each part of an ad and see how the AIDA formula works. The basic parts of an ad are

- Visual
- Headline
- Subheadlines (optional)
- Swing line
- Body copy
- Zinger
- Call to action
- Logo/slogan/tagline
- Mandatories

Visuals

Research shows that two-thirds of print ad viewers see the visual first. That makes it your best opportunity to get noticed. Photographs of people in situations that the reader can identify with have a stronger appeal than illustrations or all text. Your visual must direct the consumer's attention to the ad's message. It must create a mood, establish a theme or tell a story that appeals to the consumer. The visual leads the consumer to the headline and body copy.

Headlines

The headline, which is read by approximately a third of a print ad's viewers, must capture the ad's key message and direct the consumer's attention to the body copy. That's a pretty tall order for a line of type containing approximately eight words. That's right, eight words. You want to write short, direct headlines that command the consumer's attention.

An effective headline contains a key benefit. It shows the consumer why this product will meet a basic need. Look at the list of basic needs described on page 107. Which of these needs does your product fulfill? Look at the list of product benefits you made for your SMP. Which of these is the key benefit for your target audience? The answer to these questions is the message your headline must deliver. The headline answers the question "What's in it for me, the consumer?"

Remember AsparFlakes breakfast cereal from the previous segment (who could forget)? Let's say AsparFlakes fulfills the need for confidence by making you healthier. You see that one of its features is that it contains calcium. The resulting benefit is that eating AsparFlakes daily builds strong bones and fights osteoporosis. If your target audience is middle-aged or senior women, then that's a key benefit. Your resulting headline might be *Build strong bones with AsparFlakes*.

A successful headline is not about how great the product is; it's about how great the product can make you, the consumer. Always appeal to the consumer's self-interest.

An effective headline usually will

- Stop the reader and get his attention
- Target the primary audience
- Identify the product
- Fulfill a need
- Offer a benefit
- Summarize the selling message
- Speak directly to the consumer. Imperative mood works well for this.
- Stimulate interest by using strong verbs
- Lure the consumer into the copy
- Be short and avoid unnecessary words

An effective headline might

- Ask a question
- Make a claim
- Put a new twist on an old phrase
- Tell a story
- Invite the consumer to do something
- Appeal to emotions and desires

Subheadlines

Subheadlines are optional secondary headlines. They clarify the main headline or divide longer copy blocks into manageable chunks. They can expand on the key benefit, add information or provide the second part of a one-two punch. When they clarify the main headline, they generally are longer than that headline.

Body Copy: Swing Lines, Benefits, Zingers and Calls to Action

The body copy begins with a swing line. This opening sentence moves—or swings—the reader from the headline into the body copy. It coaxes the reader to continue. It explains the headline, connecting it logically to the body copy. The body copy is the heart of the ad. It's where the reader is rewarded with specific information about the product or service. Only one in seven viewers will make it this far, so your sales pitch better be worth it.

Body copy has a clear beginning, middle and end. Here you'll use research from your strategic message planner to explain the important features and benefits to the consumer. Begin with your strongest selling point. Emphasize the key benefits in a way that makes an emotional connection, not just a logical one. Dramatize the feeling your customers will get from your product. Paint pictures with words or tell real-life stories. Testimonials from satisfied customers work well if there is space. The ending should create a sense of urgency and make the final sales pitch.

The zinger is the last or second to last sentence of the body copy. It focuses on the strategic message. The zinger is snappy, clever and memorable—it zings. The zinger often is a sentence fragment. It might restate a key benefit or answer a question. It might ask a question or leave the consumer with one parting thought. The zinger often is followed by a call to action. This line asks for the sale and tells the consumer specifically what to do next—for example, call, stop by or visit a Web site.

Body Copy Guidelines
- Be conversational. Write to the average person in your target audience.
- Be positive, not negative.
- Focus on the reader. Use *you*.
- Emphasize the benefits of your product.
- Support facts with evidence. Be specific.
- Overcome objections.
- Use present tense and active voice (pages 3–4).
- Avoid vague words and clichés.
- Avoid *-ing* words.
- Use transition words like *but, and, however*.
- Use *italics* for emphasis. Don't underline or use all caps.
- Vary the length and structure of your sentences and paragraphs.
- Create copy with action, rhythm and excitement.
- Use metaphors, alliteration, assonance, rhyme, meter.
- Be convincing. Prove your product is what you claim.
- Ask for the sale!

Sixteen words that sell:

benefit	guarantee	money	results
easy	health	new	safe
free	how to	now	save
fun	love	proven	you/your

Logos, Slogans and Taglines
A logo generally is a visual identifier, such as Nike's swoosh or Ford Motor Co.'s blue oval. A logo may be a graphic, or it may be words in a distinct type face—or it may be both.

A slogan, or tagline, usually appears near the bottom of the ad, just above or below the logo. A slogan is a phrase that consumers closely identify with your client. Avis uses "We Try Harder," and Chevy trucks use "Like a Rock."

Mandatories
Mandatories include items that are required by law, such as copyright symbols, registration marks and fairness statements, such as *Equal opportunity employer* or *Member FDIC*. Agencies have specific usage guidelines concerning size of logos and exact phrasing of words.

Format/Design

Good design attracts and holds the consumer's attention. It amplifies the message and provides direction and order. Since the visual is seen first by 70 percent of the viewers, its placement is crucial to effective advertising. Five principles of design will help you create visually appealing ads. They are balance, proportion, sequence, unity and emphasis.

Balance

Balance means equalizing the weight on one side of a centered vertical axis with the weight on the other side. Elements in an ad have visual weight. For example, a photograph is heavier than a headline, which is heavier than body copy. The heavier the element, the more your eye is drawn to it. You can create symmetrical or asymmetrical balance. Symmetrical balance centers elements along the vertical axis and creates a more conservative, formal look. Asymmetrical balance places elements off center and creates a sense of tension and movement.

Proportion

Proportion deals with how one element relates to another in terms of size, weight, shape, color and location. The dominant element is where the eye naturally goes first. Every ad should have one and only one dominant element. A one-third/two-thirds division of space is more dramatic than dividing space in half. Elements that are placed closer to the center have less visual weight than elements in the corners.

Sequence

Sequence refers to the visual path your eye takes. Good design directs the eye in the desired sequence. Typically the eye enters the page at the top left corner and moves across to the right, then diagonally down the page to the lower left corner and then off the page in the lower right corner. For this reason, place your logo in the lower right corner of the ad. It will be the last thing on the page that the consumer sees.

Unity

Unity brings order to your design. Related elements should be close to each other. Headlines and subheadlines should be directly over their copy blocks or visually connected in some way. Often, you should be able to mentally trace a rectangle or square around related elements.

Emphasis

Emphasis creates a point that acts as a bull's eye for the viewer. It compels the viewer to look there first. This can be done by isolating an element with white space, creating imbalance or making one element disproportionate to another.

Here are some basic ad layout templates:

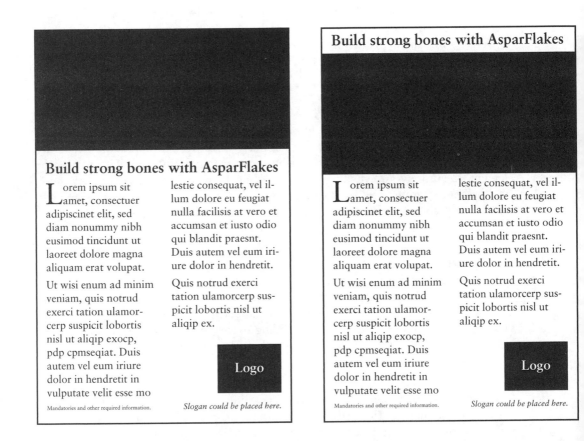

Build strong bones with AsparFlakes

Lorem ipsum sit amet, consectuer adipiscinet elit, sed diam nonummy nibh eusimod tincidunt ut laoreet dolore magna aliquam erat volupat.

Ut wisi enum ad minim veniam, quis notrud exerci tation ulamorcerp suspicit lobortis nisl ut aliqip exocp, pdp cpmseqiat. Duis autem vel eum iriure dolor in hendretit in vulputate velit esse mo

lestie consequat, vel illum dolore eu feugiat nulla facilisis at vero et accumsan et iusto odio qui blandit praesnt. Duis autem vel eum iriure dolor in hendretit.

Quis notrud exerci tation ulamorcerp suspicit lobortis nisl ut aliqip ex.

Logo

Mandatories and other required information.   *Slogan could be placed here.*

Build strong bones with AsparFlakes

Lorem ipsum sit amet, consectuer adipiscinet elit, sed diam nonummy nibh eusimod tincidunt ut laoreet dolore magna aliquam erat volupat.

Ut wisi enum ad minim veniam, quis notrud exerci tation ulamorcerp suspicit lobortis nisl ut aliqip exocp, pdp cpmseqiat. Duis autem vel eum iriure dolor in hendretit in vulputate velit esse mo

lestie consequat, vel illum dolore eu feugiat nulla facilisis at vero et accumsan et iusto odio qui blandit praesnt. Duis autem vel eum iriure dolor in hendretit.

Quis notrud exerci tation ulamorcerp suspicit lobortis nisl ut aliqip ex.

Logo

Mandatories and other required information.   *Slogan could be placed here.*

TIPS

1. Stay on message! Be creative, but don't let a fun idea for a great visual or clever headline pull you away from the strategic message you developed in your strategic message planner.

2. Be conversational—even if that means being ungrammatical. Sentence fragments—if clearly done for style—work well in ads.

3. Don't repeat yourself in the headline, the zinger and the slogan. Each of those elements should develop your strategic message, but each should be unique. Your zinger, for ex-ample, will lose impact if your reader already has encountered that idea in your headline.

4. Edit. Proofread. Follow the procedures recommended in The Writing Process (pages 6–9) and The ACT Agenda (Appendix D). Even one small error can damage your credibility with your supervisor or your client.

5. Study magazine ads. Analyze what works and what doesn't work. If you like an ad, tear it out (if you own the magazine). Your ads need to be original, but it helps to have a collection of ideas that work.

PRINT ADVERTISEMENT

Greet each morning – pain free

RIVERVIEW
COMMUNITY MEDICAL CENTER

Tired of waking up with stiff, painful joints? Think it's just old age? Think again. Discover what you can do to relieve hip, knee and foot pain. Find out how the latest treatments, including ultrasound and electrostimulation, may offer dramatic relief. Learn about new medicines, therapies, nutrition and exercises that can help you live pain free. It's good news for bad joints.

Dr. John Hamp and Dr. Susan Gear will be your hosts at this **FREE** seminar sponsored by Riverview Rehab & Sports Therapy Services and the Center for Joint Replacement.

March 5
1 PM & 7 PM
Riverview Education Center
123 Riverview Lane
Riverview, USA 12345

Call **555-2111** for reservations. Seating is limited.

Accredited by the Joint Commission on Accreditation of Healthcare Organizations (JCAHO).

When was the last time you weren't on a diet?

Been awhile, huh? Now *SlimWhims* makes dieting a thing of the past. Eat three delicious meals daily and lose weight at a natural, healthy pace. No more weighing portions or starving yourself. With *SlimWhims*, you'll know exactly what to eat and when to eat it. In just four short months, you'll discover a slimmer, healthier you. Guaranteed.

SlimWhims contains only the finest ingredients, specially prepared by our chefs and seasoned to please the most discriminating palate — yours. With more than 20 entrées to select from, you'll find dining a delectable experience. So bring back the good ol' days. Treat yourself to a new you with *SlimWhims*.

Radio Advertisements

Purpose, Audience and Media

The purpose of a radio advertisement—also known as a *radio spot*—is to motivate the listener to take a desired action. That action could be to buy a product, encourage or change a behavior or adjust the way one looks at the world. Because of its geographic flexibility and relative low cost, radio advertising often is used to complement advertising messages delivered in other media.

The demographic and psychographic makeup of the audience of a particular radio station is based on the station's geographic location and programming format. To put it simply, different radio stations appeal to different audiences in much the same way that different magazines appeal to different readers. For this reason, products often have customized commercials for different radio stations. An organization's media planner and buyer will determine the stations on which a particular advertisement will appear. The job of the advertising account manager and the creative team is to choose and craft a message that is most suitable for a particular target audience. Using a strategic message planner (pages 104–118), the creative team must determine the strategic message before making any creative decisions.

Radio is an aural medium, which means it engages the sense of hearing. It is also a linear medium, which means that its messages are fleeting: The listener can't replay or re-read them. The strength of radio as a medium is that it is portable. Radio spots reach listeners in places traditionally unreachable by other media, such as the car, the bathroom or the beach. The major weakness of radio messages is that they engage only one of the five senses (unless, of course, the radio volume is so loud as to physically hurt the listener). As a result, radio listeners can be distracted easily. Your challenge as a strategic writer is to develop a message that grabs—and keeps— the listener's attention.

> ■ **Key to Success:** An effective radio commercial has a simple message and a clear call to action. It takes advantage of the possibilities of voice, music and sound effects.

Format/Design

Because time is to radio what space is to print media, precision is important. Radio spots are written in standard time lengths: typically 10, 15, 20, 30 or 60 seconds. (There is no such thing as a 30-second radio spot that runs 33 seconds!) In the upper left corner, radio scripts include so-called traffic information: the title of the spot (keeping in mind that there may be several versions of the advertising message), the client/sponsor of the message, the length of the spot and the dates the spot is scheduled for broadcast. Traffic information is necessary to ensure that the paperwork is routed at the right time to the right place and people.

Radio scripts generally take two forms: announcer continuity and a production script.

Announcer Continuity

This is the simpler of the two formats, containing only the words the announcer will read live—or in real time—on the air. Take this approach in connection with live broadcast events or when you want to associate the product with a strong, popular radio personality. Therefore, design the script for the convenience of the announcer. It is often placed in a ring binder on a stand in front of the microphone. Write the copy in a large, easy-to-read typeface. Double-space it, and limit it to one page. Do not divide words or key phrases on different lines of copy. Within parentheses, provide the announcer with a pronunciation guide—also known as a *pronouncer*—for unusual or difficult words and names. For example, the city of Newark, N.J., is pronounced "NEW-ark." The Delaware community with the same name is pronounced "new-ARK." (If you don't think it makes a difference, just ask the people of Newark!)

Production Script

This is for prerecorded spots. Prerecording provides a consistent presentation of the message and takes advantage of a variety of voices, music and sound effects. A production script provides a roadmap for how the radio spot is to be produced. For that reason, it uses a more complex, two-column format. The left column contains production instructions for the use of voice, music and sound effects. The right column contains the script that announcers or actors follow. Write the copy that will be read in a large, easy-to-read typeface. Double-space it. Because of the two-column format, you often will need more than one page. For that reason, do not divide words or key phrases on different lines of copy or on different pages. And, as is the case with announcer continuity, provide a pronouncer for difficult words and names.

Content and Organization

The content and organization of each radio spot are driven by a strategic message developed in the strategic message planner (pages 104–118). Therefore, the content and organization of radio spots vary widely. However, even with those differences, common elements still exist. In writing your script, be sure to follow the broadcast writing guidelines on pages 10–12.

In your script, grab the audience's attention. Your spot needs to stand out from the crowd. There's probably a lot going on around your listeners. You want the audience's undivided attention.

Keep attention. Now that the audience is listening, can you keep its attention? Thirty seconds is a lifetime in this microwave, fast-food, instant-gratification world. Do the unexpected. Make the audience want to stick around until the end.

Reinforce key information through repetition. Key information depends on what you're trying to accomplish. If the ad's purpose is to generate business, be sure to repeat the name and location of the store. If the purpose is to get people to telephone, repeat the telephone number. If your ad focuses on a product, mention the product's name at least three times in a 30-second ad. Do the same if the ad focuses on a client, such as a store. For added emphasis, the key points should be among the first and last things the listener hears.

Be explicit. Write in concrete terms easily understood by the audience. For example, the audience more easily relates to a "going out of business sale" than it does to a "stock liquidation sale." The audience also understands better if you say a store is "located next to the Old Post Office on Main Street" than if you give just the street address.

Use the medium effectively. When used to its fullest advantage, radio can create mental images that make even Hollywood special effects gurus jealous. Voice, music and sound effects can transport the listener into a time, place, environment and mood of your choosing. Like TV commercials, most radio spots include background music. In fact, they can sound empty without it.

But don't overdo it. Beginning scriptwriters have a tendency to go overboard with sound effects and music. Every element in the production should complement the strategic message instead of detracting from it. That's why it's better to use instrumental versions of songs than versions with vocals. You don't want the message to compete with the singer for the listener's attention. Never have an announcer try to speak over song lyrics.

Finally, don't forget to sell. The bottom line *is* the bottom line. Your ad must include a call for action, such as "Get down to John Doe's Used Cars today! At John Doe's, we're itching to make you a great deal!" And the ad must include enough information for the audience to take that action.

TIPS

1. Be anonymous. There's no personal style in copy writing. The copy should reflect the characteristics of the product, not the person writing about it.

2. Be honest. The listener may believe you once. But is once enough? Honest copy that delivers what it promises upholds the product's credibility. It encourages repeat purchases. It also keeps you out of court.

3. Write the way the target audience talks. Speak the language of your audience. Write conversationally, using familiar words and phrases. This ain't English literature. It's persuasive communication!

4. Write to just one person. The size of the audience shouldn't distract you. Your copy should speak to each member of that audience, one person at a time. For example, "Hello. How are you?" is much better than "Hello, everyone. How is everyone doing?"

5. Consider using story-telling skills to capture the listener's attention. Several of the organizational strategies discussed earlier in Newsletter and Magazine Stories can be effective (pages 77–81).

6. Read the copy aloud to yourself. You may look silly to others. Maybe you are shy and self-conscious. Get over it. (We had to.) Broadcast copy is written to be read aloud. It may look good on the page. But the only true test of quality is whether it sounds good. Sound it out!

7. Review the guidelines and vocabulary for broadcast writing, pages 10–12.

Going Online

Thanks to satellite technology and the Internet, a radio broadcast is no longer limited to a specific geographic region. Although a message may be intended for a specific public, it now may be exposed to a much broader audience. But don't water down the strategic message in an attempt to be all things to all people—after all, radio advertising is targeted communication. However, you should always be sensitive to how any message will be received and interpreted by others.

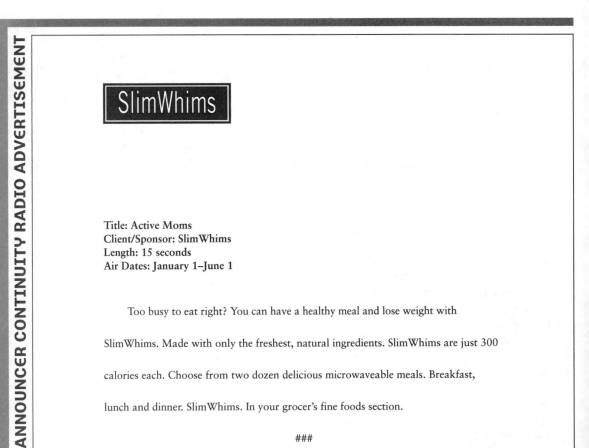

ANNOUNCER CONTINUITY RADIO ADVERTISEMENT

SlimWhims

Title: Active Moms
Client/Sponsor: SlimWhims
Length: 15 seconds
Air Dates: January 1–June 1

Too busy to eat right? You can have a healthy meal and lose weight with

SlimWhims. Made with only the freshest, natural ingredients. SlimWhims are just 300

calories each. Choose from two dozen delicious microwaveable meals. Breakfast,

lunch and dinner. SlimWhims. In your grocer's fine foods section.

###

RADIO ADVERTISEMENT PRODUCTION SCRIPT

Title: Game On!
Client/Sponsor: Riverview Community Medical Center
Length: 30 seconds
Air Dates: June 1–September 1

SFX: Sounds of people playing softball (Establish, then fade)	
ANNOUNCER:	It used to be your favorite time of year. But you're banged up and on the bench. It's time for you to step up to the plate!
SFX: Sounds of a softball being hit off a metal bat with people cheering.	
MUSIC: Upbeat (Establish, then under)	
ANNOUNCER:	It's time to visit Rehab and Sports Therapy at Riverview Community Medical Center. Why go for treatment out-of-town when you can get personal attention from people you know? With Riverview Community Medical Center's team of trained therapists, you'll be back in action before you know it.
ANNOUNCER:	Ask your family doctor about Rehab and Sports Therapy at Riverview Community Medical Center.
SFX: Sounds of a softball being hit off a metal bat with people cheering. (Establish, then fade)	
ANNOUNCER:	Get back in the game!
MUSIC: (Fade, out at :29)	

# # #

Television Advertisements

Purpose, Audience and Media

The purpose of television advertisements—also known as *television commercials*—is to motivate the viewer to take a desired action, usually in the form of a marketplace transaction. Because of its sight and sound dynamics, television is considered a prestigious medium and seen as particularly effective in building and maintaining a corporate or product image. Its reach is unsurpassed: More than 99 percent of U.S. homes have televisions. In terms of costs—for both commercial production and advertising placement—television is also the most expensive medium.

Three major classifications of television advertising exist. The first is local (or *spot*) advertising generated by individual stations or cable companies. National advertising is distributed to individual affiliate stations from nationwide network programming services, such as ABC, NBC, CBS and Fox. Syndicated advertising comes to individual stations/outlets in connection with contracted programming, such as *Oprah* or *Wheel of Fortune*. As is the case with radio, the media planner and buyer decide which television outlets to use. For a television commercial, a strategic writer crafts a message based on a predetermined strategy and designed to reach a particular target audience (see Strategic Message Planners, pages 104–118).

With the explosive growth of the cable television industry during the past two decades, the television audience has become increasingly segmented. Because it has become more difficult to reach a large audience with just one commercial, successful television commercials target well-defined segments of consumers. At the time your parents were growing up, they were lucky if their televisions received over-the-air signals from three or four stations. Today, via cable or direct satellite, many homes receive more than 100 different stations or cable outlets. Unlike specifically formatted radio stations, where advertisers usually purchase placement in certain day parts, such as morning or afternoon "drive time," television advertisers purchase time in specific programs based on the demographic and psychographic nature of the audience each program attracts.

Television is the most powerful and widely used of the advertising media. Since the introduction of commercial television to the United States in 1947, many commercial messages have become cultural icons. Television's integration of sound, pictures and motion leaves strong impressions on viewers. Like its cousin radio, television is a linear medium with fleeting messages. Also like radio, technical advances have made television sets more affordable and portable. However, television requires more of an audience's attention than does radio—a good thing for advertisers but a bad thing if you are driving a car. While advertising messages in all media strive to grab the audience's attention, the clutter of competing messages on television provides the commercial writer with a significant challenge.

> ■ **Key to Success:** An effective television commercial stays on strategy. It uses both sight and sound to rise above the clutter of media messages. It grabs and holds the attention of viewers.

Format/Design

Because of the considerable investment of time and money in television commercial production, several steps usually precede production. As is the case with all advertising, the first step involves developing the strategic message. Beyond that, producers often develop a treatment, a detailed narrative of what the commercial will look like, where and how it will be photographed and other logistical/technical requirements. Scripting is the next step. Television commercial lengths vary, but the most common lengths are 10, 30 and 60 seconds. Depending on how the client and/or producer wishes to proceed, the script can be one of two—and sometimes both—forms:

Written Script

Some similarities exist between this script format and the one used for radio production. Both provide instructions for bringing together the various production elements. Both include traffic information (see page 127) at the top to ensure that the paperwork goes when and where it is needed. Both also use a two-column format. However, here the similarities end. Because of television's added visual dimension, the left column of a TV script describes visual information. This includes descriptions, lengths, widths and sometimes angles of camera shots, as well as descriptions of any special effects or graphic information. The right column details audio information. Write the copy in a large, easy-to-read typeface and double-space the lines. Because of the two-column format, you often will need more than one page. Number and label each page. Do not divide words or key phrases on different lines of copy or on different pages. And, as is the case with radio advertising scripts, provide a pronouncer for difficult words and names.

Storyboard

The storyboard is a more visual demonstration to a client or an account executive of how the words and pictures will be married into a single persuasive message. In a storyboard, drawings for each camera shot depict the sequence of action, camera angles, widths, settings, special effects and graphics to be used. Depending on the writer's skills, these drawings may be as simple as sketches using stick figures. However, in some large agencies, storyboards often appear to be works of art. Accompanying each drawing is the relevant audio information. The obvious advantage of the storyboard approach is that it forces the writer to think visually when creating a television commercial.

Content and Organization

In terms of content and organization, practically everything discussed in the radio advertising section (pages 128–129) holds true for television. But television has the added dimension of visual communication. To suggest that television advertising is radio advertising with pictures is a poor use of the medium. While a goal of an integrated advertising campaign (pages 13–14) is to have messages in different media that reinforce one another, that doesn't mean you *have* to use the exact same words in all media. In radio, words carry most of the burden of delivering the message. In television, pictures and graphics share that burden.

In writing your script, be sure to follow the broadcast writing guidelines on pages 10–12—particularly the passage on so-called "hit and run writing." Marry images and words so that the two complement each other.

In the left column of your script, describe each shot concisely but thoroughly. A shot is a camera placement. When the camera physically moves to a different location, a new shot begins. For each shot, specify the length (how many seconds the shot will last) and the width (wide shot, medium shot or close-up). With storyboards, you also can indicate the angle of each shot.

A series of shots that convey a single action within the same setting is called a sequence. If you think of a single shot as a sentence, then think of a sequence as the video equivalent of a paragraph. Just like a paragraph in print, each sequence has a topic sentence, which is the establishing shot—usually a wide shot that sets the scene. The establishing shot provides context for shots that follow.

To carry our paragraph analogy a little further, good writers like to vary sentence length to avoid boring, predictable patterns. They want to maintain their readers' interest. This is also true in the world of television and film. For each new shot within a sequence, change the width, the length and the angle. For example, if we have a six-second medium shot of a woman at a desk, our next shot might be a three-second close-up of her face. The angle of our first shot might be straight ahead. The angle of our second shot, for variety and movement, might be about 45 degrees to the left. Remember that television is an active visual medium: Viewers expect movement and variety.

The terms *wide, medium* and *close-up* are relative, flexible terms. Commonly, a wide shot might show a room with people in it. Again, wide shots are the most common form of establishing shots. A related medium shot could be two people talking, shown from their waists up. A related close-up could be a person's face. However, in a commercial for contact lenses, a wide shot might be a man shown from the waist up. A related medium shot could be his face, and a related close-up could be his eyes.

Generally, begin your script with a wide shot—an establishing shot. Avoid putting two wide shots or two medium shots back-to-back. The lack of detail and variety becomes boring. Again, remember that TV viewers expect movement and variety. Close-up shots can follow one another, especially if the visual element changes. For example, we might go from a close-up of a woman's face to a close-up of her hand tapping a desktop.

In a standard 30-second commercial, shots generally range from two seconds to eight seconds in length. Again, variety is important. A series of five-second shots will bore viewers.

TIPS

1. Remember the tips for radio advertisements: All of the guidelines discussed for radio on pages 127–131 hold true for writing television advertisements.

2. But also remember that television is not radio with pictures. Think visually. Work toward marrying pictures, graphics, words and music into a cohesive and effective message.

3. Tell a story that relates to both the reality and dreams of the target audience. In successful commercials, viewers project themselves into the situations being portrayed. That means that the advertisement must be in touch with reality—either the reality of the audience's current situation or that to which it aspires.

4. Entertainment is a strategy, not a goal. It's fine to use entertainment to raise a commercial above the clutter of competing media messages. But if the viewer doesn't remember the purpose for the commercial—the strategic message about the client's product—the ad is a waste of money.

5. Test your message. This isn't bad advice for any advertising message. But it's especially true for television advertising because of its cost. It's a lot easier to fine-tune the message during the preproduction stage than it is after the ad is—using the jargon of the business—"in the can." Large agencies and companies will first produce several versions of a commercial and conduct private audience tests before public release.

6. Respect the audience. Remember that the viewers have most of the power in this relationship. If they don't like you or think you don't like them, the ad will be a wasted effort. Earn viewers' respect by talking to—not at—them. And because of the size of the television audience, many who see your message may be outside your target audience. They deserve—and will demand—equal respect.

Going Online

More and more, television advertising is designed to draw the viewer to a Web site. In essence, the commercial whets the appetite, encouraging the audience to surf the Internet for more detailed information and to close the sale. As the speed and capacity of computers improve, online video will increasingly complement message elements in other media. Some video productions, such as a series of U.S. Army features that took Web surfers through the phases of boot camp, are created exclusively for online use.

Title: Riverview Image Ad
Client/Sponsor: Riverview Community Medical Center
Length: 60 seconds
Air Dates: June 1–September 1

WS—Riverview Community Medical Center front entrance exterior (:07)	MUSIC:
	(Light, bouncy mood music. Establish, then under)
	ANNOUNCER:
	For more than 60 years, Riverview Community Medical Center has been your hometown health care provider.
MS—Doctor and nurse looking at a child's tonsils with Mom watching (:05)	Hometown professionals.
CU—Mom's face, smiling at the scene (:03)	The best care.
MS—The doctor handing the child a lollipop (:02)	Neighbor to neighbor.
WS—Family members visiting a new mom in her room (:05)	We have been there . . .
MS—Nurse comes into the room with a newborn baby and hands the infant to Mom with Dad watching (:04)	. . . in good times and bad . . .
CU—Mom, Dad and baby (:03)	. . . from generation to generation.
WS—Entrance to Rehab & Sports Therapy Services (:05)	For the health of our community, we have added two new services.
MS—Therapist working with a patient (:06)	Rehab and Sports Therapy . . . and the Center for Joint Replacement.

-more-

Riverview Image Ad
Page 2

CU—Therapist and patient at work (:06)	Just two more examples of how we meet the needs of the people of Gleason County.
MS—Small congregation of a cross-section of RCMC staff, doctors and nurses (:05)	Riverview Community Medical Center. . . . . . . your hometown health care team.
CHYRON (centered in the lower-third of the frame): Riverview Community Medical Center/555-1983 (:08)	
	MUSIC:
FADE TO BLACK AT :59	(Up and then fade out at :59)
RT—:59	

# # #

TELEVISION ADVERTISEMENT PRODUCTION SCRIPT

TELEVISION ADVERTISEMENT STORYBOARD

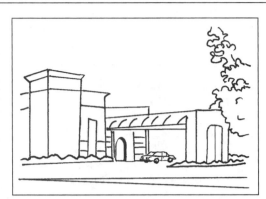

For more than 60 years, Riverview Community Medical Center has been your hometown health care provider.

Hometown professionals.

The best care.

Neighbor to neighbor.

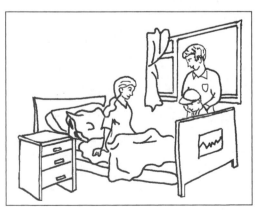

We have been there . . .

. . . in good times and bad . . .

TELEVISION ADVERTISEMENT STORYBOARD

For the health of our community, we have added two new services.

Rehab and Sports Therapy . . . and the Center for Joint Replacement.

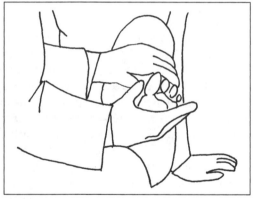

Just two more examples of how we meet the needs of the people of Gleason County.

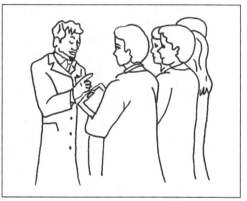

Riverview Community Medical Center. . . .

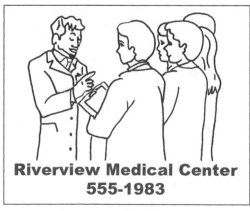

. . . your hometown health care team.

Radio and TV Promotions

Purpose, Audience and Media

The most effective and efficient means for radio and television outlets to promote programming and establish brand image is on-air promotional announcements using their own stations or channels. These announcements—commonly referred to as *promos*—are often tied to advertising, public relations and promotional efforts in other media. The purpose of promos is to build and maintain a desired audience. Strategic writers can design these announcements either to attract an audience to a particular program or to nurture the relationship between the audience and the station or channel. The latter is particularly true for broadcast (as opposed to cable) stations, which are required to demonstrate that they operate in the public interest as part of government licensing requirements.

Radio and TV promotion is particularly important in this era of media convergence, in which companies may own mass communication outlets in a variety of media. The use of integrated promotional announcements in multiple media—a practice known as *cross-promotion*—is common. Promos are used to support individual programs or entire channels, stations and networks (syndicated, regional and national).

The purpose of a promo dictates its target audience. Program promotions target audiences of specific programs. For example, fishing shows tend to attract a predominantly male audience, whereas soap opera audiences are predominantly female. Image promotion, on the other hand, helps create a desired brand image, or position, for an entire station, channel or network, which generally has a more diverse audience. Highlighting a media outlet's competitive edge over its competition is the key to successful image promotion. Image promos also help attract viewers and listeners to programming geared to a more diverse audience, such as the evening news.

Promos help people remember where they watch and hear their favorite programs. This is important because their responses to audience measurement surveys determine ratings and, in turn, each station's or channel's advertising rates.

Broadcast and cable promotion became a significant element of programming strategy starting in the 1970s because of a combination of factors. The Federal Communications Commission required national television networks to open the first hour of prime viewing time to local programming. Hollywood and programming syndicates seized the opportunity by providing original and previously broadcast programs for local use. Technological advances made it easier to produce and distribute programming. With the growth of cable and satellite television, competition dramatically increased as the audience was dispersed. These factors led to increased promotional activity designed to attract an audience to improve ratings and to defer escalating programming costs.

■ **Key to Success:** Through crisp writing and effective repetition, a successful promo delivers an unambiguous message, often about program name, time and station. It closes with a clear call to action.

Format/Design

On-air broadcast/cable promotions follow the same script formats used in radio advertising (pages 127–128) and television advertising (page 133). This should not be surprising, since the only major difference between an advertisement and promotional announcement is the client.

Content and Organization

Promos follow the same preliminary research and planning process used in advertising. In other words, complete a strategic message planner (pages 104–118) for your promo. The segments on radio and television advertising also include advice that can apply to successful promos.

Besides basic image promos, there are two kinds of on-air broadcast/cable promos: topical and generic. A topical promo provides information about a specific program airing at a particular time. Examples include a promo teasing the story line of an upcoming entertainment program. Just like that last piece of pizza in your refrigerator, topical promos have a limited shelf life. Once the program featured in a topical promo has aired, the promo is of no further use.

Contrast topical promos with generic promos: A generic promo is designed for broadcast at anytime. Rather than promoting a specific episode of a program, a generic promo reminds viewers and listeners of when and where a favorite program airs. Generic promos often are referred to as evergreen promos because they are always fresh and never out-of-date. An example is the promo that reminds viewers to "Watch Eyewitness Action News (insert TV channel here) every night at six." That promo is good as long as Eyewitness Action News Whatever sticks to that same program schedule.

As we've mentioned, repetition of key information is important in promo writing. (Notice how we cleverly used repetition to reinforce this point!) In radio and television, your message competes with a variety of distractions for the audience's attention. Remember to include the key information the audience needs to know:

■ The name of the program
■ The time and day it is broadcast
■ The station/channel/network on which it is broadcast. Don't assume that just because people watch a program they know which station they are watching. Through "channel surfing," they may be a part of your audience by chance rather than choice. The goal of a promo is to have viewers and listeners remember your station when they make a programming choice—*and* when they fill out ratings surveys.

It is not enough to tell viewers or listeners the *when* and *where* of your program just once—they may have missed it. During a 30-second promo, you should repeat key information visually or aurally three times—in the opening sentence of the promo, once in the middle and at the very end for closing emphasis. This is easier to do in television, where visual images complement the words.

In writing your promo scripts, be sure to follow the guidelines for broadcast writing on pages 10–12.

TIPS

1. Think before you write. Is the promo image, generic or topical? Have a clear understanding of this before you do anything else.
2. TDT: Tease; don't tell. You want to pique interest—not give the plot away. Who would want to watch a murder mystery if the promo announced who done it?
3. Transition, transition, transition. In topical promos that use sound or video clips, the announcer should create smooth transitions from clip to clip.
4. Don't promise what you can't deliver. Remember that the goal is a relationship, not just a one-time audience. If you make a promise—such as a special appearance by a popular celebrity—but don't deliver on it, you will lose credibility. Hyperbole is fine. But if you go too far, you will lose the audience.
5. Take some liberty with the language. Write the way people talk. Sentence fragments and questions are fine. You also can stretch the rules of grammar—just as long as doing so makes sense to the audience and doesn't detract from the message.
6. Target the promo to a specific audience with clearly defined demographic and psychographic characteristics.
7. Repeat yourself. Did we mention this one? Identify the program, time and station *at least three times*. Be sure to close with this information and a call to action.
8. Write "light, tight and bright." In the clutter of today's media, the goal of any promo is to be remembered. Your listeners and viewers value creativity—as long as it doesn't come at the expense of giving them the key information. Get the audience's attention and keep it.
9. Follow the tips presented for radio and television advertising—they apply to promos as well.

Going Online

Programs, stations and networks often strengthen their relationships with their audiences through Internet promotions. Media outlet Web sites typically include program synopses, biographies of performers, contests and opportunities to purchase promotional items branded to the program or media outlet. The sites often encourage Web surfers to download on-air promotional announcements for their private viewing. On-air promos also encourage the audience to visit these sites. This integrated marketing approach focuses on making the program or media outlet an integral part of how the audience defines itself.

Title: Health Beat
Client/Sponsor: Station promo
Length: 20 seconds
Air Dates: Until further notice

Want the latest news in health and medicine? Join Riverview Radio weekday

mornings at 7-15 for Health Beat with Doctor Marco Podestra (pah-DESS-trah).

Weight loss tips. The warning signs of cancer. Skin care. We cover it all.

Health Beat is brought to you as a public service of this station and the

Riverview Community Medical Center. That's Health Beat with

Doctor Marco Podestra. Weekday mornings at 7-15 on Riverview Radio.

# # #

RADIO PROMOTION PRODUCTION SCRIPT

Title: Don't Skip a Beat
Client/Sponsor: Station Promo
Length: 30 seconds
Air Dates: November 8–14

SFX: Sound of a human heartbeat, with the rate gradually increasing (Establish, then under)

ANNOUNCER: 60 times a minute. 36-hundred times an hour. 86-thousand times a day. More than 30-million times a year. It is easy to take your heart for granted. . . .

SFX: Heartbeat stops. Flat line tone replaces heartbeats. (Establish, then fade)

ANNOUNCER: . . . until it stops.

MUSIC: Action News Six Theme (Establish, then under)

ANNOUNCER: This week on Action News Six at Six. Join medical beat reporter Melissa Cochran for her special health series "Don't Skip a Beat."

ANNOUNCER: Melissa will bring you the information you need to keep your loved ones safe. And we will have heart specialists from Riverview Community Medical Center standing by to answer your questions.

MUSIC: (Fade)

SFX: (Re-establish sound of heartbeat)

MELISSA COCHRAN: I'm Melissa Cochran. Join me every night this week for life-saving information. That's "Don't Skip a Beat." Every night this week on Action News Six.

SFX: (Heartbeat stops abruptly)

MELISSA COCHRAN: This is one series you can't afford to skip!

# # #

TELEVISION PROMOTION PRODUCTION SCRIPT

Title: 11:00 News Promo
Client/Sponsor: Station promo
Length: 29 seconds
Air Date: Until 11:00 p.m., Tuesday

ESTABLISHING SHOT: Paul Rodgers, evening news anchor, at news set.

MUSIC:

News theme. (Establish, then under)

PAUL RODGERS:

Tonight at 11 on Action News Six.

VO/SOT: Pictures of police working a crime scene.

Just how safe is it to live in Riverview? Our Michelle Masters has the latest crime statistics. Get them in her special report "Mean Streets."

REPORTER STAND-UP: Medical beat reporter Melissa Cochran in front of the emergency room at Riverview Community Medical Center.

MELISSA COCHRAN:

I'm Action News Six Medical Beat Reporter Melissa Cochran. Did you know that one in four Americans suffers from heart-related illness? What do you need to know to protect your family? Watch my special report, "Don't Skip a Beat."

MS—Rodgers at news desk

PAUL RODGERS:

Biff has the latest in college hoops. Bev has your weekend forecast. That's tonight at 11 on Action News Six!

FADE TO BLACK AT :29

MUSIC:

(Fade at :29)

# # #

Radio and TV Public Service Announcements

Purpose, Audience and Media

Public service announcements are persuasive messages carried without charge by radio and television outlets on behalf of nonprofit and social-cause organizations. Broadcast stations carry PSAs to fulfill federal licensing requirements that those outlets serve the public interest. PSAs look and sound like commercial announcements. They are targeted communications that contain a call for action. However, two major differences separate PSAs from commercials. The first has to do with control. Commercial announcements use controlled media. Advertisers pay for the right to choose the form, timing and placement of messages. However, PSAs use uncontrolled media. With PSAs, media outlets—and not the message provider—make decisions about whether and when to use a PSA. The second major difference is that commercial announcements tend to promote marketplace transactions, whereas PSAs more often promote social causes and behavior change. Paid commercial announcements promoting social causes and behavior are not PSAs. Neither are network or station promotional announcements designed to sound like PSAs (such as NBC-TV's "The More You Know" campaign).

Like all persuasive messages, PSAs target specific audiences. However, because they are not guaranteed airtime, they also target the media preferred by the desired audience. For example, it would not make sense for the Future Farmers of America to send a PSA to an urban radio station that plays rap music. It seems unlikely that the FFA's desired audience listens to that station. A better fit might be rural country music stations. Similarly, organizations often create PSAs with a station's format in mind, such as a PSA featuring a hip-hop music artist for broadcast exclusively on hip-hop music stations. Conversely, television stations affiliated with one network may not wish to show PSAs featuring stars from another network. Local media outlets are more likely to carry messages of local interest, and national media outlets are more likely to carry messages that are relevant to a national audience. Although CBS-TV is not likely to broadcast a PSA for a local blood drive, the local CBS affiliate might.

As mentioned above, in the United States the federal government licenses broadcast stations, and, as a part of the licensing agreement, those stations must serve the public interest. Although cable television outlets do not face the same requirement, they may have to carry PSAs as part of a local franchising agreement. However, even without these requirements, media outlets are often willing to use PSAs in an effort to build mutually beneficial relationships with their service areas. As one might expect, these outlets are inundated with requests for free airtime. A media outlet chooses which PSAs to broadcast based on its strategic and logistical needs. It will select messages compatible with the audience it wants to attract.

Conversely, it will shy away from controversial material that may alienate an audience. Because PSAs do not directly add to the media's bottom line, those that require the least amount of prebroadcast preparation are most likely to be accepted. With that in mind, it is not unusual for organizations seeking public service airtime to provide a package of PSA materials that give media outlets maximum flexibility, especially in terms of message length. These packages typically include 10-second, 15-second, 20-second, 30-second and 60-second versions of the same announcement.

> ■ **Key to Success:** It's not enough to consider the needs of the target audience. You must also consider the needs of the media outlet through which you hope to reach that audience.

Format/Design

Public service announcements follow the same script formats used in radio advertising (pages 127–128) and television advertising (page 133). This should not be surprising because of the aforementioned similarity to commercial announcements.

Content and Organization

PSAs follow the same preliminary research and planning process used for advertising. Yes, for the one-millionth time, we're telling you to complete a strategic message planner (pages 104–118) before you begin to write a persuasive message.

In terms of content and organization, virtually everything discussed for radio advertising (pages 128–129) and television advertising (pages 133–134) holds true for PSAs. Because of the nature of the persuasive messages delivered by PSAs—often for social causes or to create changes in behavior—it's especially important for a PSA to reflect the values of the sponsoring organization. Advocates of particular perspectives are often held to a high standard of conduct.

A PSA package sent to a media outlet contains

- ■ **A cover letter.** This is written like a one-page sales letter (see pages 171–175). Your challenge is to show why this message is relevant to the media outlet's audience and/or its strategic interests.
- ■ **A list of enclosed materials.** You may have only a few moments to win over a program director or public service director. This list makes her job easier, and, therefore, she may be more likely to spend time reviewing the package.
- ■ **Scripts of recorded messages and/or announcer continuity** (page 128). Include these to ease the work of the program director or public service director.
- ■ **Recorded messages in a variety of versions and lengths.** People like having options. Program directors and public service directors are no different.

Be sure to follow the guidelines for broadcast writing on pages 10–12.

TIPS

1. Beggars can't be choosers. Supply media outlets with materials that do not require prebroadcast preparation. The easier you make it for the broadcaster to use your PSA, the more likely it is to be accepted. Multiple versions of the message increase a media outlet's options.

2. Remember each media outlet's audience. Its audience should be the same as your desired audience. Media target programming to attract specific audiences. When seeking public service airtime, identify the media that reach the desired audience.

3. Don't expect a free lunch. Because media outlets are in the business of making money, they rarely accept PSAs for which space or time has been purchased in other media.

4. Remember: You can't always get what you want. Because PSAs use uncontrolled media, don't expect to see or hear them during prime programming hours. The media charge the highest advertising rates for the times they have the largest audiences. It is not likely they will give this time away. (If you're wondering about those United Way spots during the Super Bowl, the National Football League requires their broadcast as part of its contractual agreement with the networks.)

5. Don't pinch pennies. Although media outlets do supply airtime without cost, don't assume that PSAs are inexpensive. PSAs often cost as much to produce as any commercial announcement. This shouldn't be surprising: PSAs, like commercial announcements, need to rise above the clutter to gain and maintain an audience's attention.

6. Remember who you are. PSAs must reflect an organization's values and mission. Typically, nonprofit and social organizations use PSAs as a tactic in their strategic communications. These organizations are especially sensitive to the opinions of key stakeholders. Therefore, all messages delivered on their behalf are viewed with a critical eye.

Going Online

As is the case with radio and television advertising, there's a growing trend toward directing audiences to Web sites for more detailed information. As the speed and capacity of computers improve, online audio and video will increasingly complement message elements in other media.

Title: Project Graduation
Client/Sponsor: Riverview PTA
Length: 30 seconds
Air Dates: May 20–June 4

MUSIC: "Pomp and Circumstance"
(Establish, then under)

ANNOUNCER: You have finally made it. The big day has

                                     arrived. You have graduated! It's time to

                                     celebrate.

SFX: Pop-top on a can of beer

ANNOUNCER: But the <u>way</u> you celebrate may affect <u>how</u>

                                     <u>long</u> you celebrate.

SFX: Turning key on a car ignition

ANNOUNCER: As you celebrate graduation, please remember

                                     that drinking and driving do not mix.

MUSIC: (Ends abruptly)

SFX: Car crash sounds

ANNOUNCER (after short pause):   Don't make this a day that your family and

                                      friends will remember for all the wrong rea-

                                      sons. Celebrate safely. A reminder from the

                                      Riverview P-T-A.

# # #

TELEVISION PSA PRODUCTION SCRIPT

Title: Take a Hike
Client/Sponsor: Riverview Medical Association
Length: 30 seconds
Air Dates: until 9:00 a.m., September 15.

VO—Scenes from last year's cancer walk (:06)	<u>MUSIC:</u> "Hit the Road, Jack" by Ray Charles. (Establish opening chorus, cut to instrumental music, then under) <u>ANNOUNCER:</u>
CHYRON—Tell Cancer to Take a Hike/ 9:00 a.m. Saturday, September 15 (:08)	Join your friends and neighbors on Saturday, September 15th, as they tell cancer to "take a hike." You can run, walk or ride the short course while raising money for cancer research.
CHYRON—555-0000 (:07)	If your company or organization would like to participate, call 555-0000 or sign up at the start line in City Park.
CHYRON—Riverview Medical Association/www.riverviewmedassoc.org (:08)	Tell cancer to take a hike. Saturday, September 15th, at City Park. Brought to you by the Riverview Medical Association.
FADE TO BLACK AT :29	<u>MUSIC:</u> (Fade at :29)

# # #

Section IV
Strategic Writing in Sales and Marketing

Objectives

*In Section IV: Strategic Writing in Sales and Marketing,
you will learn to write these documents:*

- Proposals
- Brochures
- Sales letters
- Direct-mail packages
- Fund-raising letters
- Collection letters

Marketing is the process of researching, creating, refining and promoting a product—and distributing that product to target consumers. Strategic writers participate in every stage of marketing. For example, in the research stage they research and write proposals and business reports. The creating and refining stages include package design and more reports. The promotion stage usually demands the most writing: proposals, advertisements, news releases, direct-mail packages and more. Can overworked strategic writers finally relax during the distribution stage? Of course not. Distribution can require sales-support materials and, yes, more reports.

One part of marketing involves directly asking consumers to buy the product. When that's done interactively—face-to-face or through a Web site or some other device that allows consumers to respond—it's called sales. Even when the sales process involves a face-to-face meeting, which is called personal selling, strategic writing can play an important role: Sales people often use brochures or other written material—so-called product literature—to help explain and promote the product. Strategic writers who prepare written materials for a sales force work in area often called sales support.

Tension sometimes exists between an organization's sales force and its marketing team. Often, the source of that tension is poor communication. Members of a sales force sometimes believe that the marketing team is out-of-touch with consumers and the realities of trying to sell the product. On the other hand, the marketing team sometimes believes that the sales force will say or do anything to sell the product. However, an organization should speak with one clear voice when trying to sell a product. In other words, the sales force and the marketing team—plus the product literature, the advertisements and the news releases—should all focus on the same strategic message when addressing a target audience. This "one clear voice" philosophy is part of integrated marketing communications, discussed earlier in Section I (pages 13–14). Ideally, an integrated, strategic message provides a consistent, beneficial image for a product—and that clear image leads to sales. Communication between the sales force and the marketing team before, during and after a sale is an important part of strategic communication.

Because marketing is product-oriented, it can include advertising and some parts of public relations. And with all those reports, marketing definitely includes parts of business communication. All this inclusion means that the dividing lines among marketing, advertising, public relations and business communication can be blurry. Some documents included in other sections of this book also can be part of sales and marketing. For example, a news release that announces the launch of a newsworthy product fulfills a marketing function. A good-news business letter written to a customer can fulfill a marketing function.

Even professionals and professors sometimes disagree among themselves about the dividing lines that separate marketing, advertising, public relations and business communication. To some, it's all marketing. Others say that because public relations and business communication often focus on groups other than customers, those professions are not entirely part of marketing. The authors of this book will let you debate that issue with your professors and fellow students. We believe that it's more important for you to focus on the strategic purpose of each document you write. We believe you should focus on a document's goal-oriented reason for existence rather than wondering whether that document is part of marketing or public relations or nuclear physics. We believe that a well-trained strategic writer should be ready to tackle any situation that requires the power of good writing to help achieve a goal.

We also believe in short segments, so let's close this one with a final bit of advice: For all sales and marketing documents, be sure to do your research. For class projects and for real-world assignments, make it your business to know everything possible about your product, your competitors and your target audience. Consider using the strategic message planner (pages 104–118) for sales and marketing documents. In sales and marketing—like all areas of strategic writing—knowledge is power.

Proposals

Purpose, Audience and Media

A proposal is a reportlike document that promotes and describes a plan—for a new magazine, a new departmental structure, a public relations campaign and so on. Proposals also describe the need for or the advantages of action.

The audience for a proposal is the person or people with the power to approve and implement the plan.

The primary medium for proposals continues to be paper. Proposals must be studied; therefore, they generally appear as bound documents. However, formal oral presentations of proposals often include multimedia elements such as PowerPoint presentations and videos.

■ **Key to Success:** Through clear organization, a successful proposal shows how a specific plan solves a well-defined problem or seizes a well-defined opportunity.

Format/Design

Write proposals on standard-sized (8.5- by 11-inch) paper. Single-space the text. Double-space between paragraphs, and don't indent paragraphs. Number the pages of the proposal, starting not with the table of contents but with the executive summary. The formats of proposals often include the following features:

- Bold, larger-than-ordinary type for the title on the title page (18-point Times is a standard size for report titles)
- Section titles and subheadlines in boldfaced type
- Margins of at least one inch
- White space (extra spacing) between sections; in long reports, new sections often begin on a new page
- Colorful charts and graphs, when appropriate, to reinforce and clarify meaning. Most word-processing programs offer user-friendly ways to create and insert charts and graphs.

Content and Organization

A formal proposal contains, in order, the following sections, each of which often begins on a new page. (Less formal proposals can discard some of the following sections.)

Tailor your proposal to the specific situation, but in general your proposal should contain the following sections. The order of presentation below reflects the order of a traditional proposal.

Memo or Letter of Transmittal

With a paper clip, attach a brief memo or letter addressed to your audience to the cover or title page of your proposal. The memo or letter essentially says, "This proposal presents an idea to solve the problem of . . . " [or "to seize the opportunity of . . . "]. It can close with an implicit or explicit request for action, such as "I'm available to discuss this at your convenience." A "Thank you for your time and consideration" can follow the request.

Use a memo for proposals submitted to internal audiences (groups within your organization). Use a business letter for proposals submitted to external audiences (groups outside your organization).

Title Page

The title page often is the cover of the proposal. It includes a title; a descriptive subtitle, if necessary; the name(s) of the author(s); and the date. Your title should be compelling, positive and descriptive. Often, a snappy, teasing title—much like a slogan—is effective. If your proposal introduces a promotional campaign that has a theme, consider using that theme as your title. A descriptive subtitle can make it clear that the document is a proposal. The subtitle generally includes the word *proposal*. For example,

Partners for Progress
A Proposal to Gain Local Consent
for the Expansion
of the Portland Headquarters

Table of Contents

A table of contents lists each section, in order, and its starting page. (Do not list the span of pages for each section; just list the starting page.) In the table of contents, do not include the memo/letter of transmittal, the title page or the table of contents itself. With a headline, clearly label this page as the table of contents.

Table of Charts and Graphs

This optional section lists the names and page numbers of the charts and graphs in the proposal. This section generally is not listed in the previous table of contents. It generally does not have a page number.

Executive Summary

An executive summary is a concise, one-page (if possible) overview of the proposal's highlights. In general, include an executive summary if the report is formal and will take more than 15 minutes to read. In proposals, an executive summary normally summarizes the following sections: situation analysis; target audiences; and tactics. Each of these sections is described below.

Do not use your executive summary as an introduction to your proposal. A reader may skip the executive summary. Everything in your executive summary must appear elsewhere in the proposal. You can avoid this error by writing the executive summary last.

Situation Analysis (the Problem or Opportunity)

The situation analysis describes, in detail, the status quo—the way things are right now. However, the situation presents the status quo in such a way that it fills readers with the desire to act to solve a problem or seize an opportunity. Don't discuss any kind of response to the situation. Let your readers, as they study the facts, realize that the situation demands a response.

In the situation analysis, *do not* mention the solution (the plan) that the proposal will present. Keep the focus solely upon the problem or opportunity.

Ideally, the situation analysis describes the status of an important organizational goal. Readers familiar with the written goals of your organization should immediately see the relevance of the situation analysis.

Statement of Purpose

This brief section announces the purpose of the proposal. Having just finished the situation analysis, your readers ideally are saying, "We need to act. We need to address this situation." The statement of purpose reassures readers by simply stating, "This proposal presents a plan to win citywide acceptance for the expansion of the Portland headquarters" (or whatever the situation analysis described).

The statement of purpose often can be one clear, determined sentence.

Target Audiences

As we note in Section I, much of your work as a strategic writer involves creating productive relationships with specific audiences. Proposals for public relations, advertising, sales and marketing, and business communications generally involve plans designed to affect relationships. Thus, proposals usually specify target audiences.

A section on target audiences generally begins with a brief explanatory paragraph. This first paragraph explains that the forthcoming plan focuses on a clear target audience or a set of target audiences. This first paragraph can be as short as one sentence: "The forthcoming plan targets five distinct audiences: the City Commission, neighborhood committees, city religious organizations, city business leaders and the local news media."

After presenting this brief explanation, describe each target audience. Descriptions should include demographic information (nonattitudinal information such as age range, gender, income, race and education) and psychographic information (attitudinal information such as political philosophy, religious beliefs and other important values). Descriptions also should include the desired resources that each public controls.

Use internal headlines to provide a new subsection for each new target audience.

The Plan (Goals, Objectives and Tactics)

Plans usually exist in an outline form. They usually begin with a goal. A goal is a general statement of the outcome you hope your plan will achieve. Goals often begin with infinitives, such as "To improve" or "To increase." By beginning your plan with a verb, you place an immediate focus on action. For example, a goal might be "To win citywide acceptance for the expansion of the Portland headquarters." The goal often echoes the earlier statement of purpose.

Some plans have more than one goal. In such plans, each goal would have its own set of objectives.

After the goal come the objectives. Unlike goals, objectives are specific. Objectives clarify the exact things you must achieve in order to reach a goal. Objectives are like specific mini-goals.

How many objectives should your plan have? In a plan with more than one target audience, consider presenting one objective for every target public. Each objective would specify what outcome you plan for each public. For example, an objective related to the above goal might be "To gain approval from the City Commission by June 15."

Like goals, objectives usually begin with an infinitive. Objectives also are measurable; that is, they establish a clear line between success and failure. Finally, objectives include a deadline. Number your objectives.

Tactics are the actions you recommend to achieve each objective. List and describe tactics under the appropriate objective. Unlike goals and objectives, tactics don't begin with infinitives. Tactics begin with active verbs; they're commands. For each tactic, include the following information: brief description, deadline, budget, special requirements, supervisor and evaluation. Number the tactics under each objective, beginning with "Tactic #1" for each new objective.

The beginning of a plan, therefore, looks something like this:

Goal: To win citywide acceptance for the expansion of the Portland headquarters.

> **Objective #1:** To gain approval from the City Commission by June 15
>
>> **Tactic #1:** Send personal letter from CEO Sarah Jones to each city commissioner
>>
>>> *Brief description:* Ms. Jones will send each commissioner a personal letter announcing the proposed expansion of the Portland headquarters. The letter will emphasize the benefits to the city.
>>>
>>> *Deadline:* March 31
>>>
>>> *Budget:* $12 for stationery and postage
>>>
>>> *Special requirements:* City Commissioner Dennis Jackson is blind. He prefers to receive correspondence via e-mail. His computer has audio-reader software.
>>>
>>> *Supervisor:* Communications Specialist Kris Palmer
>>>
>>> *Evaluation:* The success of this tactic will be measured by whether the City Commission is already familiar with our key points when we make our formal presentation.

Ideally, the plan leaves readers with no questions about the details. Specify sizes, colors, dates, places, prices and so on. If the description of tactics becomes too detailed and begins to clutter the plan, consider including samples or sketches in a Supplements section. If you include supplements, direct the readers' attention to that section at appropriate moments in your description of each tactic.

Timetable

This section is optional because the plan already includes proposed deadlines. As a separate section, however, a timetable can be a useful chart. Organize the timetable in chronological order, with the first action first and the last action last. Place the date in a left-hand column and the related action in a right-hand column:

March 31:   Mail CEO letters to city commissioners.
April 1:   Mail news releases to city news media.
April 4:   Send open-house invitations to neighborhood committees.

Budget

Although you already have specified the cost of each tactic, include a "line-item" budget in your proposal. In a two-column format, list each expense and the projected cost. In a detailed, lengthy budget, consider including a "contingency line" for unforeseen expenses. To include a contingency line, total all the expenses and label the resulting sum as a subtotal. Next, determine what 10 percent of the subtotal would be and list that amount in your contingency line. (Check with your supervisor or consult previous proposal budgets to determine an acceptable percentage of the subtotal for your contingency line.) The end of a detailed line-item budget would look like this:

Posters, 40 copies $100.00
Campaign buttons 50.00
Direct-mail letters/postage . . . . . <u>125.00</u>
    SUBTOTAL 947.00
    Contingency budget . . . . <u>95.00</u>
    TOTAL 1,042.00

Challenges

This optional (and generally rare) section presents and refutes challenges to the situation analysis and the proposed tactics. Consider including it when your proposal contains controversial material, and, therefore, obvious challenges exist. Clearly and concisely state the challenge and the refutation:

Challenge: The City Commission opposed the past four corporate building proposals.

Refutation: Those four proposals did not include an expanded work force. Our proposal includes more than 200 new jobs for the Portland area.

Additional Benefits

This optional section details the "add-on" benefits that your proposal would create—besides the basic benefit(s) of reaching the identified goal(s). For example, improving a relationship with a target public might have additional, future benefits. List those benefits as "Additional Benefit #1" and so on.

Conclusion

Proposal conclusions are brief. Summarize the need for action. State that the proposal offers a plan to address that need. Consider closing with specific recommendations for next steps, which might include dates and places for future discussions of the proposal and procedures for the formal acceptance of the proposal. Consider recommending a timetable for those actions.

Supplements

This section can include samples, dummy layouts, charts, graphs and articles—anything that the proposal calls for or that supports the clarity or integrity of the proposal. Include only materials cited earlier in the proposal.

TIPS

1. Be diplomatic! Don't present your proposal as the savior of a sinking ship or as the solution to stupid errors. Your proposal often will target an area managed by the very people who will evaluate the proposal. Don't hurt their feelings or make them defensive. Such diplomacy is particularly important in the situation analysis.

2. Proposals for advertising campaigns sometimes use first-person narratives instead of formal descriptions of target audiences. For example, in an ad-campaign proposal, a description of a target audience might begin "Hi! My name is Michael Khomsi, and I'm a 27-year-old Arab American. I grew up in Detroit. . . ." Such a description, though fictional, would be a highly detailed analysis of a representative target consumer.

3. If you are proposing a campaign that has a theme, include that theme in the Statement of Purpose section. You might even label that section Statement of Purpose and Theme.

4. In tactics, be sure to evaluate outcome rather than process or output. For example, the evaluation measure for a tactic on news releases should not address the number of news releases you distribute. Rather, the evaluation measure should address how many media outlets published or broadcast the main points of the news release—or, better, whether the media's audiences received and believed your message.

5. Appearances count. Consider working with an art director to create an attractive (though economical) proposal.

Going Online

You might distribute a proposal as an attached file in an e-mail message, but most proposals are paper documents. As noted earlier, however, you will often introduce your proposal to supervisors and/or clients in a formal presentation. Those presentations can be high-tech, multimedia events with videos, PowerPoint presentations and visits to relevant Web sites.

Brochures

Purpose, Audience and Media

Brochures, booklets and fliers are strategic communication messages printed once (although they may be reprinted) and distributed to a specific audience for a specific purpose. The three differ slightly in their formats. Brochures are typically a single piece of paper printed on both sides and folded into panels. They can use full color, spot color (accent color) or black ink only. Booklets, on the other hand, are printed in four-page increments and usually are saddle stitched (stapled down the middle, forming a mini-book). They typically are full color and are ideal for company annual reports or elaborate promotional pieces. Fliers are mini-posters, printed on one side of the page and intended for bulletin boards or hand delivery. They usually are quick-copied on colored paper. They are ideal for event announcements and one-page advertisements. Although this section will focus on writing and designing brochures, the basic principles also apply to booklets.

Brochures inform or persuade. They usually are part of a larger media mix that might include print ads, television commercials, radio spots, direct-mail packages or billboards. Because of their abbreviated length, brochures don't tell the whole story; they merely deliver highlights. They can be used as material on display racks, enclosures in direct-mail packages, handouts, leave-behind sales materials or stand-alone direct mailers. They might advertise a product, recruit volunteers, make people aware of an issue or announce a workshop, lecture, performance or conference.

When defining your target audience, answer these questions in addition to the typical demographic queries:

- How will your audience receive the brochure?
- Why is your audience reading this brochure?
- What does the audience already know about your product?
- What is the audience's current attitude (if any) toward your product?
- Where else will the audience encounter the message of the brochure?

As noted, brochures exist primarily on paper, though sales forces sometimes use brochures in CD formats.

- **Key to Success:** Effective brochures marry words and images to deliver a single message to a specified audience.

Content and Organization

Like any effective advertising message, a brochure begins with the completion of a strategic message planner (pages 104–118). Just as with the print ad, the SMP helps to define the audience and focus the message. The target audience determines the tone, vocabulary and type of appeal the message takes. The strategic message must be clear and specific. A brochure designed to speak to several audiences or accomplish several goals is doomed to fail. For example, a brochure designed to recruit volunteers for a hospital auxiliary won't work to invite new community members to use the hospital's outpatient services.

Brochures need a theme or unifying concept that amplifies the strategic message. The theme helps to interpret, define and present the message to the audience. The theme might take the familiar and give it a new twist. It might create a visual metaphor and show how two seemingly unrelated topics share many characteristics. It might create a distinct personality for the printed piece. For example, a brochure on financial services might be illustrated with images of a needle, thread and tape measure, all tools used by a tailor. The implication is that the same attention and personal service needed to make a custom suit will be given to building a client's financial portfolio. A brochure on pediatric services at a hospital might be illustrated with crayon drawings, giving it a feeling of youthful exuberance.

Sometimes themes are created with words, and other times they are created with graphic images. Often, both words and images develop a theme. A brochure might begin and end by telling a story. Another brochure might repeat graphics to link elements together. Both provide a unifying element.

Panels

Because brochures are typically folded into panels, the designer must create a clear roadmap to direct the reader into and through the piece. The size, shape and number of folds determine how the reader views the piece. The six-panel brochure, also called a tri-fold brochure, is the most common organizational structure. Other folds and designs are discussed later in this chapter. Subheadlines help keep passages short and keep the reader focused.

In the six-panel brochure the *front cover* invites the reader into the piece. It catches the eye and provides a visual focus. It hooks the reader with a provocative headline, a question or a compelling image. It may contain a teaser headline with a subheadline that explains the nature of the piece. Usually the cover contains an image, a headline and the company name and/or logo.

Panel 2 is the next most-likely panel to be read because of its position in the six-panel format. (You may understand this better if you take a sheet of paper, mark the front and back just as in Figure 1 and then fold the sheet.) Panel 2 typically presents a stand-alone message that summarizes the reason the customer should choose this product. It also may reinforce key points, begin a compelling story or present a testimonial. It often is written after the main copy message.

Panels 3, 4 and *5* present the main copy message and are viewed as one three-column unit. This copy clearly explains the product's features and benefits. The message has a distinct beginning, middle and end, much like an essay. This three-panel section often includes subheadlines.

| Panel 2 | Panel 6 | Cover |

| Panel 3 | Panel 4 | Panel 5 |

FIGURE 1

Panel 6 is the back cover. This is the panel people are least likely to read, so avoid continuing the copy message to this space. Use it for contact information such as the phone/fax number, Web site address, e-mail contacts and physical address. It often repeats the company name and logo. It also can be used for a recipient's address if you design the brochure to be mailed.

As mentioned above, brochure copy—particularly in the cover plus panels 3, 4 and 5—has a beginning, middle and end. Here are some copy approaches that help organize and deliver the message. Choose the one that best fits your audience.

The Beginning
- Ask a question: Questions invite conversation and break down barriers. They imply that an answer is forthcoming and that reading further might provide that answer.
- Pose a problem: Position your brochure as the answer to a problem. If the reader shares that problem or is interested in it, he will read further.
- Offer an opportunity: Many people can't resist the chance to experience new things, whether they are new products or new experiences.
- Set a mood or create an emotion: Emotions are powerful persuaders. Evoking nostalgia or empathy helps the reader identify with your cause.
- Tell a story: Hook your reader with an intriguing story. Get him to identify with a character or action.

The Middle
- Make key selling points: Describe your company's or organization's competitive advantages. Write in terms of features and benefits. Make one point per subheadline.
- Give the solution: If you presented a problem in the opening, now is the time to explain the solution.

- Arrange information from least important to most important: Sometimes it works best to save your strongest arguments for the end and build your argument gradually. Test different organizational strategies on sample, representative audiences if you're not certain about the best organization.
- Explain the steps in a process: If your information is sequential or requires elaborate explanations, break it down into manageable bits. Explain each step under a separate subheadline.

The End

- Summarize the main points: Repeat your key points. Leave the reader with a clear idea of why he should act now.
- Remind the reader of the importance of the topic: Make one more appeal for why your topic deserves consideration.
- Link the end with the story in the beginning: If you began by telling a story, finish it or give some indication of how it ends. The reader needs closure. Don't leave him hanging.
- Make a call to action: Tell the reader what he should do now. Leave no doubt in his mind what his next action should be: Call, give, buy, volunteer or return a coupon.

Format/Design

Good design provides the structure and form that hold the piece together. Good design works seamlessly with the copy to reinforce the message. A well-designed publication

- Enhances readability
- Amplifies the message
- Organizes the message
- Is practical
- Doesn't call attention to the design alone

The adage that you have only one chance to make a good first impression especially holds true for brochures. If a reader isn't attracted to the cover, chances are he won't pick up your brochure.

In designing a brochure, you must select the format, type, layout, color and paper.

Format

One of the first considerations in designing a brochure is deciding what size it needs to be. Ask yourself

- How will the piece be used?
- Does it need a return coupon?
- Should it be vertical or horizontal?

- How many panels will it need?
- How will it be distributed?
- Will it be mailed?

The standard six-panel brochure can be folded from an 8.5- × 11-inch piece of paper and easily fit into a #10 business envelope. If cost is a consideration, avoid running images to the edges, since that requires trimming an oversized sheet and adds expense. If cost is not your primary consideration, use a 9- × 12-inch piece of paper. It still will fit into a #10 envelope but gives you more space for your message. If your piece is a self-mailer, consult your local post office for standard mailing sizes and rates. Odd-sized pieces require additional postage. It's best to know before the piece is printed that it will cost more to mail it. It's always a good idea to talk with your local printer throughout the design stage, especially if you are creating an unusual piece. Often she can make suggestions that will save you money and time.

Type

A good basic rule is to use no more than two typefaces in a publication. For example, you might use Franklin Gothic (a sans-serif typeface) for headlines and Garamond (a serif typeface) for body copy. These typefaces provide good contrast in styles. Use consistent type styles for headlines and subheadlines. Avoid using tilted headlines or vertical type. Headlines set in all caps are difficult to read, so use them only for very short headlines. Likewise, italic type is difficult to read. Use it sparingly.

Layout

Keep your layout clean and balanced (see Figure 2). Use the basic principles of design: balance, proportion, sequence, emphasis and unity (see page 123). Use white

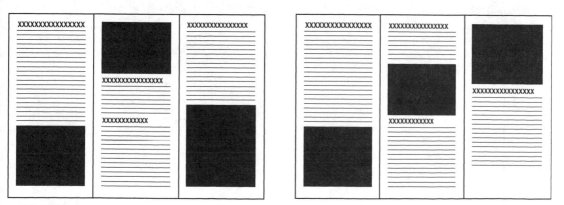

FIGURE 2

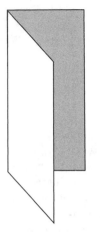

Parallel fold—Creates four panels that can be used vertically or horizontally.

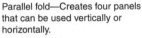

Letter fold—Creates six panels that can be used vertically or horizontally.

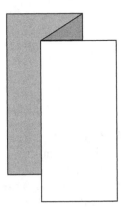

Accordion fold—Creates six panels. The reader views one side at a time.

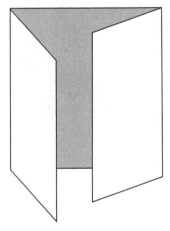

Gate fold—Creates panels that open like doors. The reader views the inside information at one time.

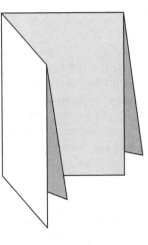

French fold—Creates a poster when completely opened and is ideal for large layouts.

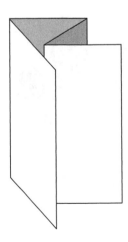

Double parallel fold—Creates eight panels. The first fold creates a double-page spread. The second fold opens to four full panels. This fold is ideal if the brochure needs a coupon or return card.

Barrel fold—Includes numerous panels that are unrolled slowly to continue the message.

FIGURE 3

space (blank space) to your advantage, and don't make your layout feel cluttered or too busy. Use generous leading (the space between lines of type—pronounced *ledding*) to enhance readability. Use short line lengths to make copy easier to read. And remember: Be consistent with your layout throughout your brochure.

Color

Color definitely enhances design. A full-color brochure printed on glossy paper jumps out and demands attention. However, color, especially full color (also called process color or four color) significantly increases your cost. The majority of the cost increase occurs in the prepress stage (preparing scans, film, plates and proofs). So the greater the quantity printed (press run), the less of an impact color has on the total cost. As a general rule four-color printing runs about 30 percent more than two-color printing. Color affects the design and production process from the beginning, so make this decision carefully and early. If your budget won't permit full color, you can use spot color or two-color printing. Use the additional color for headlines, subheadlines and graphics. Don't overdo the accent color, and consider carefully before you use it on photographs. Coloring people blue in photographs seldom works.

Paper

Paper adds texture to a publication. It makes it a three-dimensional experience. Always work with your printer when choosing paper. Often, she will have a house stock that will save you money. Ink performs differently on different papers, so ask lots of questions.

When choosing paper, consider the finish, weight and color. Paper is either coated or uncoated. Coated paper has a hard, enamel finish and comes in gloss, matte and dull. It is ideal for full-color pieces. Uncoated paper has a smooth, vellum or pattern finish, like linen or laid.

Paper is categorized by weight. It comes in text weight and cover weight. Either will work for a brochure. If you use cover weight, you may need to have the folds of your brochure scored to prevent cracking and tearing along the edges (see Figure 3). Also if you are mailing your piece, check with the post office concerning the weight restrictions.

Paper comes in thousands of shades and colors. As a general rule, full color photography works best on white or cream paper. An inexpensive way to add color to your brochure is to choose a colored paper stock and print in black ink.

Figure 4 shows an example of a six-panel brochure. Read the copy and study the layout. Study how the words and design work together.

TIPS FOR BROCHURE COPY

1. Use strong headlines and subheadlines that lead the reader into the text. These headings should make the reader curious or make him think he will learn something if he continues. A benefit-driven headline might be "How to grow award-winning roses."

Animal Haven
BARRY COUNTY HUMANE SOCIETY

The cover invites the reader into the piece.

The headline speaks directly to the reader and calls him to action.

The image adds interest and reinforces the headline.

Graphics build the theme using the circle design that mirrors the logo (see panel 6). Dots are used as a graphic element throughout the piece. The vertical bar creates contrast with the circle graphic and adds asymmetrical balance (see page 123).

The name of the organization appears on the cover.

ANIMAL HAVEN ... A COMMUNITY RESOURCE

Each year we care for more than 7,000 animal friends and serve the animal-related needs of approximately 100,000 people. The average cost of care for each animal is $250 during its stay.

As a nonprofit organization, Animal Haven relies on a Barry County government grant and on donations from you, our generous supporters.

MISSION STATEMENT: *Animal Haven acts as an advocate for all animals whether they are companion animals, wildlife, farm animals or animals in laboratories. We believe in the humane treatment of all living creatures. We believe that through compassion and caring we can make a difference in the lives of animals and in the lives of the people who love them.*

The image connects people and pets in an emotional way that encourages nostalgia.

Panel 2 stands alone. The copy introduces the organization and explains its purpose. The mission statement adds credibility.

FIGURE 4

Panel 3 begins the copy message with an opening that sets the tone. It metaphorically compares Animal Haven to relief programs for people.

Copy blocks are broken into manageable chunks under separate subheadlines. Notice the specific details included in the copy.

ANIMAL HAVEN ... A PLACE FOR LOVE

There is a place in our community where the hungry are fed, the homeless are sheltered, the abused are treated and the lost are returned. That place is Animal Haven, the Barry County Humane Society..

SHELTER AND ADOPTION SERVICES

As an Open Admissions shelter, we accept every animal that is brought to us, regardless of age, health, behavior or special needs. Our number one goal is finding responsible, caring homes for animals. Whether the animal is lost or abandoned, we find joy in uniting people and pets. Last year alone, 1,175 dogs and cats were returned to their owners and 3,546 were adopted.

We offer special programs to help you choose the right pet for your family. The initial adoption fee for dogs, cats and rabbits of $100 includes

- Professional health examination
- First vaccinations
- De-worming (for dogs and cats 4 months old)
- Microchip implant
- Access to an animal behaviorist
- Educational materials on the care of the animal
- Spaying/neutering at Animal Haven

Bullets are used to list points.

VACCINATION AND HEALTH SERVICES

Animal Haven provides health care for companion animals, sterilization surgery for dogs, cats and rabbits and microchip services. We have four licensed veterinarians on staff who care for animals of all ages. Open Monday-Friday 9 am to 7 pm, the clinic provides vaccinations, including rabies, distemper and bordatella, as well as de-worming, heartworm prevention, flea and tick control and laboratory testing services. We also provide emergency care for injured, lost and stray animals.

For a nominal fee, we implant a microchip in your pet that will help more than 12,000 shelters, like Animal Haven, identify you as the owner. There's no better way to instantly reunite you and your pet.

To help low-income families care for their pets, we offer the Prevent a Litter Assistance Program that subsidizes spaying or neutering services. The CARE discount program also helps families pay for emergency medical treatment.

COMMUNITY EDUCATION PROGRAMS

Animals teach all of us about compassion, empathy and unconditional love. Animal Haven brings animals and animal issues into the lives of schoolchildren throughout the county. Staff and volunteers lead discussions about pet care, local wildlife and other animal-related topics through

- Classroom visits with dogs, guinea pigs, rabbits and other living creatures.
- Dogtalk, attention-grabbing, interactive presentations about dog behavior and safety.
- Reptiletalk, discussions regarding ethical and practical issues of keeping reptiles as pets.
- Operation Pet Pals, a week-long curriculum designed for children K-6.

Panel 4 continues the message. Two more subheadlines explain key features as benefits.

Bullets are used to list points.

F I G U R E 4 (continued)

HELP US BUILD A NEW HAVEN

Founded in 1964, Animal Haven began as a mission to foster humane treatment of farm animals. The society purchased four acres of land and constructed a shelter on New Hope Road. Now 40 years later, we've outgrown our present facilities and plan to build a new complex on the adjoining six acres.

But building a new house for a friend won't be possible without your support. Help us continue to provide community education and animal rescue programs for Barry County. Help us build a safe haven for all creatures great and small. Help us be a place for love.

RSVP by sending your donation to Animal Haven
435 New Hope Road
Anywhere, USA 12345
(444) 777 2345

Closing copy provides more detail about the organization.

The final paragraph makes a call to action and links the closing with the opening copy theme.

The final call to action gives specific information about where to send a donation.

HOW YOU CAN HELP ANIMAL HAVEN

We rely on support from generous donors, like you, to provide comfort and care for unwanted animals. Here are ways you can help.

- Give to the Build a House for a Friend fund.
- Donate food, old blankets, towels or other needed supplies.
- Volunteer your time. Become a pet caregiver. Bathe and groom the animals. Walk dogs, or play with cats. Stuff envelopes for mailings, or help publicize an event.
- Find a special friend. Choose your next pet from Animal Haven, and give a dog or cat a good home.
- Be a responsible pet owner. Keep current identification on your dog or cat. Keep vaccinations current and have your pet spayed or neutered.
- Teach your children to be humane citizens. Set an example by treating all animals with compassion and kindness.

435 New Hope Road
Anywhere, USA 12345
(444) 777 2345
FAX (444) 777 3456

www.animalhavenusa.org

Panel 6 stands alone. Since this panel is the least likely to be read, non-essential information is placed here. Bullets are used to list points.

Logo and contact information appear at bottom of panel 6.

F I G U R E 4 (continued)

2. Good headlines should
   - Grab attention
   - Set the tone
   - Carry much of the message
   - Have a visual complement that supports the message
3. Use subheadlines to break up information into manageable chunks. Let the reader feel that he can read any section independently of the other sections. Subheadlines should flow from the main headline. Collectively, they should describe the page content. Label-style headlines work well for subheadlines. For a product, label-style headlines could be single words such as *Colors, Sizes* and *Prices*.
4. Speak directly to the reader in a casual, informal tone. Remember, *you* is the most important word in persuasion.
5. Use present tense and active voice (pages 3–4).
6. Choose a tone appropriate to your audience.
7. Use bullets to list information, and, of course, use parallel construction (see pages 245–246).
8. Put the emphasis on what the reader will gain: What's in it for me?

9. Keep copy short. Use short sentences of 15 words or less. Use short paragraphs of no more than 15 lines. Use sentence fragments and phrases if they are appropriate for the rhythm of the copy.
10. Use details, details and more details. Don't write in generalities. You must know your product or service thoroughly and tell the reader the details of its features.
11. Use imperative mood, just as this sentence does. Command your reader to action.
12. Choose short words rather than long words. For example,
    - *Achievement* can be replaced with *success*
    - *Advantageous* can be replaced with *good* or *cheap*
    - *Utilize* can be replaced with *use*
    - *Employment* can be replaced with *work*
13. Avoid puffery (see pages 24–25). Don't be melodramatic. Avoid clichés, buzzwords and unfamiliar acronyms. Make valid claims. Don't exaggerate your product or service. Double-check your facts.

TIPS FOR SAVING MONEY (AND GRIEF)

1. Get quotes from several printers. Don't assume that one printer always has the best prices for all jobs. Quantity, complexity of the job, scheduling and in-house equipment all affect prices.
2. See samples of the printer's work. Be wary of printers who have no samples to show you.
3. Remember, the greater the press run (such as 10,000 or more), the more economical four-color printing becomes.
4. Check and recheck your files before sending them to the printer. Avoid content and design changes after proofs are made.

5. Use standard-size pages, such as letter (8.5- × 11-inch) and tabloid (11- × 17-inch), whenever possible. This avoids paper waste.
6. Use house stock paper when possible. Don't order expensive paper if you don't need it. Brightness (or whiteness), weight and coating all affect paper costs. Generally the whiter, heavier and slicker the paper is the more it costs.
7. Avoid bleeds (ink that runs to the edge of the sheet). Bleeds require oversized paper that must be trimmed.
8. And finally, ask your printer for suggestions on how to reduce costs.

ANIMAL HAVEN ... A COMMUNITY RESOURCE

Each year we care for more than 7,000 animal friends and serve the animal-related needs of approximately 100,000 people. The average cost of care for each animal is $250 during its stay.

As a nonprofit organization, Animal Haven relies on a Barry County government grant and on donations from you, our generous supporters.

MISSION STATEMENT: *Animal Haven acts as an advocate for all animals whether they are companion animals, wildlife, farm animals or animals in laboratories. We believe in the humane treatment of all living creatures. We believe that through compassion and caring we can make a difference in the lives of animals and in the lives of the people who love them.*

HOW YOU CAN HELP ANIMAL HAVEN

We rely on support from generous donors, like you, to provide comfort and care for unwanted animals. Here are ways you can help.

- Give to the Build a House for a Friend fund.
- Donate food, old blankets, towels or other needed supplies.
- Volunteer your time. Become a pet caregiver. Bathe and groom the animals. Walk dogs, or play with cats. Stuff envelopes for mailings, or help publicize an event.
- Find a special friend. Choose your next pet from Animal Haven, and give a dog or cat a good home.
- Be a responsible pet owner. Keep current identification on your dog or cat. Keep vaccinations current and have your pet spayed or neutered.
- Teach your children to be humane citizens. Set an example by treating all animals with compassion and kindness.

Animal Haven
BARRY COUNTY HUMANE SOCIETY
435 New Hope Road
Anywhere, USA 12345
(444) 777 2345
FAX (444) 777 3456

www.animalhaven-usa.org

B U I L D
a house
for a friend

Animal Haven
BARRY COUNTY HUMANE SOCIETY

ANIMAL HAVEN ... A PLACE FOR LOVE

There is a place in our community where the hungry are fed, the homeless are sheltered, the abused are treated and the lost are returned. That place is Animal Haven, the Barry County Humane Society..

SHELTER AND ADOPTION SERVICES

As an Open Admissions shelter, we accept every animal that is brought to us, regardless of age, health, behavior or special needs. Our number one goal is finding responsible, caring homes for animals. Whether the animal is lost or abandoned, we find joy in uniting people and pets. Last year alone, 1,175 dogs and cats were returned to their owners and 3,546 were adopted.

We offer special programs to help you choose the right pet for your family. The initial adoption fee for dogs, cats and rabbits of $100 includes

- Professional health examination
- First vaccinations
- De-worming (for dogs and cats 4 months old)
- Microchip implant
- Access to an animal behaviorist
- Educational materials on the care of the animal
- Spaying/neutering at Animal Haven

VACCINATION AND HEALTH SERVICES

Animal Haven provides health care for companion animals, sterilization surgery for dogs, cats and rabbits and microchip services. We have four licensed veterinarians on staff who care for animals of all ages. Open Monday–Friday 9 am to 7 pm, the clinic provides vaccinations, including rabies, distemper and bordatella, as well as de-worming, heartworm prevention, flea and tick control and laboratory testing services. We also provide emergency care for injured, lost and stray animals.

For a nominal fee, we implant a microchip in your pet that will help more than 12,000 shelters, like Animal Haven, identify you as the owner. There's no better way to instantly reunite you and your pet.

To help low-income families care for their pets, we offer the Prevent a Litter Assistance Program that subsidizes spaying or neutering services. The CARE discount program also helps families pay for emergency medical treatment.

COMMUNITY EDUCATION PROGRAMS

Animals teach all of us about compassion, empathy and unconditional love. Animal Haven brings animals and animal issues into the lives of schoolchildren throughout the county. Staff and volunteers lead discussions about pet care, local wildlife and other animal-related topics through

- Classroom visits with dogs, guinea pigs, rabbits and other living creatures.
- Dogtalk, attention-grabbing, interactive presentations about dog behavior and safety.
- Reptiletalk, discussions regarding ethical and practical issues of keeping reptiles as pets.
- Operation Pet Pals, a week-long curriculum designed for children K–6.

HELP US BUILD A NEW HAVEN

Founded in 1964, Animal Haven began as a mission to foster humane treatment of farm animals. The society purchased four acres of land and constructed a shelter on New Hope Road. Now 40 years later, we've outgrown our present facilities and plan to build a new complex on the adjoining six acres.

But building a new house for a friend won't be possible without your support. Help us continue to provide community education and animal rescue programs for Barry County. Help us build a safe haven for all creatures great and small. Help us be a place for love.

RSVP by sending your donation to
Animal Haven
435 New Hope Road
Anywhere, USA 12345
(444) 777 2345

Sales Letters

Purpose, Audience and Media

The sales letter is a business letter that attempts to persuade the recipient to buy a product (a good or a service).

Sales letters can be challenging. Often, they're mass produced, as in a direct-mail campaign. However, that mass production shouldn't prevent you from including knowledge about the individual recipient. Some companies have detailed customer-information databases that allow them to send highly personalized sales letters. Organizations also can purchase detailed lists of potential customers or donors from list brokers.

The audience of a sales letter or fund-raising letter usually is one person. Again, even if you're mailing hundreds or thousands of similar letters, attempt to personalize the letter. Never send such a letter to "Dear Resident."

Organizations are increasingly sending sales and fund-raising letters as e-mail messages. However, the usual medium of such letters remains the traditional paper letter that you put in an envelope and place in the mail. Sales and fund-raising letters are often part of a larger direct-mail package (see pages 176–181).

> ■ **Key to Success:** The opening of a successful sales letter fills the recipient with a sense of need or desire. The letter returns to that scenario in the closing. A successful sales letter focuses on benefits to the target audience.

Format/Design

Follow the general guidelines for the business-letter format on pages 193–195. However, sales letters often delete the recipient information from the heading. They often lack the three lines that include the recipient's name, address and city, state and ZIP code. They do include the date.

Unlike most other business letters, sales letters highlight key passages with design elements such as boldface type, different-colored type, underlining, capital letters, subheadlines—and even handwritten sticky notes, prepared and attached to the letter by a machine.

The signature at the bottom of the letter often is overprinted in blue ink to make the letter seem hand signed. The P.S. also may be handwritten in blue ink.

Content and Organization

Sales letters can use a variety of organizational strategies. Sales letters generally are written by professionals with years of experience. Often, they exceed one page. (The theory is that if the letter delivers enough product-related benefits, the recipient will keep reading.)

Part 1 of 6: Begin with a Teaser Headline (Optional)

In sales letters, teaser headlines are optional. A teaser headline appears in the upper-left corner of the page, generally above the date and the salutation. (Remember that sales letters often delete the three lines in the heading that specify the recipient's name, address, and city, state and ZIP code). Teaser headlines usually use a different typeface—and often a different color—from the rest of the type. They are larger (usually 18-point or 24-point type), and they don't extend across the entire page. Instead, they split into two or three lines and remain in the upper left corner.

Unlike newspaper headlines, teaser headlines usually don't tell; instead, they tease. They ask a question, mention a problem, state an eye-popping statistic, refer to a solution or highlight words that sell. (For a list of words that sell, such as *free,* see Print Advertisements, page 122). The goal of a teaser headline is to capture the reader's attention and get her to read the letter in order to learn about the headline.

Part 2 of 6: Create a Sense of Need or Desire

Don't start by mentioning your product or by asking for the sale. Instead, create a sense of need or desire within the recipient. Often, this means creating a scenario that presents a familiar problem or desire to the recipient. The goal of this section is to remind the recipient that something in her life needs to be better. Don't mention your product yet. The recipient will view the product as a solution—and at this point, you want her to think only about her problem. Keep her focused only on her sense of need. By the time she reads the final sentence of this section, the recipient should be filled with a desire to improve some aspect of her life. Note that the sales letter (like the bad-news letter) does not follow the tradition of using the first paragraph to tell the recipient why she's reading the letter.

This section can be more than one paragraph. However, don't dwell too long on the problem; once the recipient realizes that the situation applies to her, she'll be seeking the solution you offer.

Part 3 of 6: Present Your Product as the Solution

Beginning with a new paragraph, satisfy the recipient by presenting a solution to her problem: your product. Be specific about how your product solves the problem and improves the recipient's life. Discuss the benefits of your product in detail. Remember that a benefit is a product characteristic—a feature—that creates something advantageous and desirable in the recipient's life.

The discussion of your product's benefits often exceeds one paragraph. As noted in the previous Format/Design segment, this portion often features design elements such as boldface type, different-colored type, underlining and capital letters. Consider using such elements to highlight particular benefits.

Part 4 of 6: Ask for the Sale

In a new paragraph, ask for the sale. Or demand it: "Order yours today! It's easy. Just . . . " Be sure to give all the details about how the recipient can acquire your product. In a short sales letter, this section usually is one paragraph.

If you're concerned that your product's price may dampen the reader's enthusiasm, consider these ideas from direct-mail expert George Duncan:

- Offer a guarantee or a free-trial period.
- Compare the product's price to the price of something familiar and desirable, such as dinner with friends or a cup of coffee every day for a month.
- Create a sense of urgency with a special benefit: "And if you respond within the next 30 days, we'll also send you a deluxe . . . "

Part 5 of 6: Re-evoke the Sense of Need or Desire and Again Ask for the Sale

In case the recipient has become too relaxed, in a new, final paragraph return to the idea you developed in the first paragraph: Something is missing in her life. After briefly re-evoking that sense of need, tell her to purchase your product today. Include a standard "Sincerely" sign-off.

Part 6 of 6: Add a P.S.

Almost all sales letters add a postscript, a P.S., below the sender's signature and title. (Include an extra space, just as if the P.S. were a new paragraph.) Some postscripts even appear to be handwritten, as if they were an urgent personal note from the sender to the recipient. The P.S. presents one final incentive to purchase the product. A sales-letter P.S. usually describes an additional benefit of the product or, more often, presents a bonus for purchasing soon: "Call now, and you'll also receive a . . . "

A P.S. is not signed. It appears at the bottom of a letter and is introduced simply by the initials *P.S.*

TIPS

1. Focus on the recipient's self-interest. She doesn't care what you think about the product. She wants to know what it can do for her. Any product features that you describe should be presented as benefits to her.

2. Avoid excessively negative scenarios in Parts 2 and 5. Don't threaten the recipient. If you successfully describe an unpleasant scenario, her imagination will supply the unfortunate consequences of inaction.

3. Some sales letters, especially those in direct-mail packages that contain brochures and other items (pages 176–181), are longer than one page. The theory is that if the recipient clearly sees how she benefits from your product, she'll continue to read for that length.

4. Like advertisements, sales letters should present a clear, concise, beneficial image of your product. Consider completing a strategic message planner (pages 104–118) before you write a sales letter.

Going Online

Sales letters can be delivered via e-mail. However, e-mail messages traditionally are shorter than sales letters and are often read in the recipient's office, where she may feel pressured for time. E-mail sales messages quickly describe a problem and just as quickly present the product's top problem-solving benefit—often in the same paragraph. Then, an e-mail sales message generally directs the recipient to a Web site where she can learn more about product benefits and purchasing information.

E-mail sales letters may be spam (unsolicited, mass-mailed messages) to your audience. To help your message avoid the smell of spam, use the e-mail screen's subject line wisely. If your target sees a benefit in the subject line, chances are good that she'll open the message.

Interactive Games
2010 Ridglea Drive
San Francisco, CA 55111
555·999·5555

*Hey, gamer!
So you think
you've seen it all?*

May 29, 2005

Dear Mr. Trip:

Great graphics? Hey, they're everywhere now. Cool sounds? What game doesn't have those? Hidden features and secrets? Big deal—nothing new there. Aren't there any surprises left for serious video game players?

Starklight Random is the new game from David Smith. You know David as the award-winning creator of *Night Terror* and *Are You Sleeping?* When you pop *Starklight Random* into your console for the first time, the graphics and sounds will dazzle you. But when you pop it in for the second time, they'll stun you: They're different. <u>Our unique randomizer technology creates a new game every time you play.</u> New graphics. New sounds. New challenges. Goodbye to the same-old, same-old: *Starklight Random* contains **MORE THAN ONE THOUSAND VARIATIONS.** No more waiting for the latest version of your favorite game.

Mr. Trip, we want you to be one of the first players of *Starklight Random*. In just one week, you could be playing the 1,000+ variations for <u>the special introductory price</u> of only $69.95. That's $20 off the store shelf-price—**half the cost of a new pair of basketball shoes.** Log on to MGSintgames.com or phone us at 1-800-555-5555. We accept all major credit cards, and we'll ship *Starklight Random* the day we receive your order.

OK, it's time to head back to the game console. Go play the old, familiar games. Or order *Starklight Random* today and play a new game every time you power up.

Sincerely,

Aaron Smith

Aaron Smith
Marketing Director

P.S. *Starklight Random* comes with a 100-percent money-back guarantee—not that you'll ever need it!

Direct-Mail Packages

Purpose, Audience and Media

A direct-mail package is an unsolicited persuasive message sent to consumers on a mailing list. It attempts to change attitudes, beliefs or actions. Direct mail can be used to raise money, expand membership, educate recipients, generate income, increase renewals or sell subscriptions or products.

Studies show that direct mail is opened by two-thirds of U.S. households. Direct mail differs from other forms of mass advertising in a number of ways. Direct mail

- Targets a specific audience
- Allows the message to be delivered directly rather than through intervening media
- Guarantees that the consumer will handle the envelope
- Can be personalized and, therefore, can speak directly to the consumer
- Can be timely
- Produces measurable results

Like sales letters, the usual medium for direct-mail packages remains traditional paper and the postal service. However, sales related e-mail messages with links to related Web sites can be considered direct-mail packages.

- **Key to Success:** A successful direct-mail package must have a targeted mailing list and deliver a highly persuasive, benefit-driven message directly to the target audience.

Content and Organization

Each part of a traditional direct-mail package has a specific function. The more pieces in the package, the greater the likelihood that the reader will look at one of them.

- Outer envelope—attracts attention with teaser copy and gets the package opened.
- Sales letter—explains the offer in detail, sells the benefits to the reader and asks for the sale.
- Brochure—restates the offer made in the sales letter in a visual presentation.
- Other teaser devices such as a lift letter (testimonial), product sample, free gift or coupon—attract attention and encourage the reader to spend time with the package.
- Reply card—asks for the sale and tells the reader how to respond.

Outer Envelope

The outer envelope is the storefront of the piece and will determine whether your customer walks inside. You have approximately three seconds to entice him to unseal the envelope and enter. When it comes to the outer envelope, size does matter. For a business-to-business piece or a letter to a top executive, a standard #10 envelope is fine. But for most consumer direct-mail packages, odd size pieces pull the best. Envelopes that are larger than a standard letter will stand out in a stack of mail. Likewise, illustrated envelopes or ones that contain colored type get more attention.

"Rocket" Ray Jutkins, an envelope designer, makes these observations about people and direct-mail envelopes:

- They look at their name first. So make sure you spell it correctly and that the envelope is personalized. Avoid using labels; use ink-jet addressing.
- They look at the teaser copy second, especially the copy that is close to their name.
- They look at who sent the mail. If your company has an artsy logo, you might consider using only the name and address so that the logo doesn't compete with the teaser copy located elsewhere on the envelope.
- They look at the type of postage used. Live stamps get more attention than metered mail. Bulk mail gets the least.
- Then they turn it over—three out of four people who touch a direct-mail envelope will look at both sides.

Teaser copy on the envelope—that is, printed on the envelope itself—begins the sales pitch. It must grab the customer's attention immediately and interest him in the product and offer inside. Use either an offer teaser or a benefit teaser. The offer teaser works best when you are sure that your market is interested in the product. A good offer will entice the customer to continue. A benefit teaser begins the sales pitch. It might mention a key benefit or ask a question to pique curiosity.

The Letter

The letter in a direct-mail package is a sales letter. For guidelines on writing a sales letter, see pages 171–175.

The Brochure

The brochure restates the benefits outlined in the letter and adds a visual element. The letter *tells* while the brochure *shows* why the consumer should act. The brochure and the letter must complement each other. A second reply form may be included in the brochure. Refer to the discussion on brochures (pages 159–170) for specific writing and design guidelines.

Other Teaser Enclosures

The more elements in a direct-mail package, the greater the chance that the consumer will look at and handle one of them. That's why some packages have stickers or tear-out coupons that must be affixed to the envelope. These are called involvement devices; they get the reader to do something. Other packages might contain a gift such as address labels or a small sample of the product. Still others might contain money. A dollar bill included in a package often makes a person feel that he should respond because he's being given something for his time.

Another teaser device is the lift letter. This is a short note from an authority or a testimonial written by a satisfied customer. It usually is on a note card in a different paper stock and gives one more reason why the consumer should act now.

The Reply Card

Make it easy for the consumer to respond. Tell him exactly what to do. Make writing spaces large, and repeat what the customer is purchasing. Whether you use a reply card or an envelope, make it postage paid. Don't give the customer any reason not to reply. The easiest response mechanism is a phone call to a toll-free number.

TIPS

1. Get the right target audience. The most crucial factor in producing a successful direct-mail campaign is the mailing list. According to the Direct Marketing Association (www.the-dma.org), the list accounts for more than 50 percent of the campaign's success. That means you must know your target audience and its buying habits. There are several ways to acquire a "good" list. Begin with your existing customers. They are the most likely to buy your new products. Second, add customer referrals. Third, acquire names from similar organizations or businesses. Finally, rent names from a list broker or mail house. More than 40,000 mailing lists are available for rental or purchase. Lists can be refined to include specific geographic areas, ages, incomes, buying habits and other characteristics. You can rent lists for one-time use, multiple use or unlimited use. The more restrictive you make the list, however, the higher the cost per 1,000 names. Seldom do you want to mail only once to a targeted list. Most experts recommend that you mail a minimum of three times to the same mailing list. And remember: You must keep the mailing list current.

2. Test your direct-mail package by sending it to a small sampling before undertaking a larger mailing. When testing different packages, introduce no more than two variables. Wes Martz of Martz Marketing Group LLC recommends testing these key elements: offer, product, creative approach, mail package format, seasonality and the list. He says that in one week you should receive 25 percent of your responses, within two weeks 50 percent and within four weeks 75 percent of your responses. The rest will filter in over the next month. Although there is no typical response rate, experts usually forecast a return of 2 percent or less.

3. Long direct-mail letters will get read, says direct-mail expert George Duncan. He recommends writing a two-page letter for business-to-business sales; a four-page letter for consumer sales; and a one- to two-page letter for fund-raising appeals. Print on both sides of the page and use 17- x 11-inch paper folded in booklet form for the four-page letter. End each page in the middle of a sentence to encourage the reader to continue to the next page.

4. After your direct-mail campaign, conduct a campaign review to evaluate the successes and failures of the mailing. This will help you and your organization determine what you can do differently next time to improve communication, efficiency, quality, cost controls and delivery requirements.

Going Online

Electronic direct mail is increasing while postal mail is declining, according to a study done by the Direct Marketing Association (www.the-dma.org/cgi/registered/ research/stateofpostalemailmarketing.shtml). Respondents reported the primary reason is economic. Regardless of which form of direct-mail you use, the mailing list remains critical to a successful campaign. The basics of the sales apply to e-mail correspondence—with one important difference: the subject line. You must begin your appeal there with an offer that will command attention. Your e-mail message can also contains links to related Web sites.

DIRECT-MAIL LETTER

January 2005

Vanish Stress Away
with a *Varma Vatten Spa!*

****

Dear Mr. and Mrs. Nelson:

Do your muscles ache at the end of the day and your feet feel twice their size?

Do you toss and turn each night trying to fall asleep only to wake in the morning still tired and troubled?

Do you long for a place where your worries simply fade away and you can relax?

Step out of your fast-paced world and into the peaceful surroundings of a *Varma Vatten Spa.* Within minutes the warm, soothing waters will relax tired nerves and muscles and rejuvenate your soul. Your stressful day will evaporate and leave you feeling serene and stress-free.

Sound intriguing? You can learn more by requesting our **FREE** video "**Vanish Stress Away with a *Varma Vatten Spa.***" It's yours without obligation. But wait. Listen to these ways a Varma Vatten Spa can change your life.

A *Varma Vatten Spa* is like no other spa on the market. It adds relaxation, romance, pleasure plus health and fitness to your life.

<u>Need a place to relax?</u> The *Varma Vatten Spa* is the answer. The warm waters and soothing massage reduce anxiety, relax your tense muscles and stimulate the release of endorphins, the body's natural "feel good" hormones. Countless studies have shown that warm-water therapy actually improves your state of mind and reduces stress.

<u>Need help falling asleep?</u> Tired of taking sleep aids or drinking too much to induce sleep? According to the National Sleep Foundation, 130 million Americans suffer from mild or chronic insomnia or other sleep disorders. Lack of sleep can have long-lasting health consequences. A recently released study from the scientific journal *Rest and Sleep News* says that relaxing in a hot tub 30 minutes before bedtime not only can help you fall asleep but also can provide a deeper, more peaceful sleep.

<u>Need to add some romance to your life?</u> What better place than in a *Varma Vatten Spa?* The old movie clips from the '60s and '70s show beautiful couples cuddling in bubbling hot tubs. Why not re-create a movie scene right in your own back yard? Whether you're just getting to know each other or have been married for years, the *Varma Vatten Spa* will add a new twist to your relationship.

> *"We find we spend more time just talking now that we own a Varma Vatten Spa. What better place to reconnect?"—B. Loving*

<u>Need a place for the whole family?</u> A *Varma Vatten Spa* isn't just for romance. It's great for family time. Kids love water, and you'll have hours of fun splashing and playing with your children or grandchildren. The convenient computer controls let you adjust the water temperature to make it just right for kids of all ages.

<u>Need a place for intense therapy?</u> The *Varma Vatten Spa* is a certified water-therapy spa. Use it before exercise to loosen muscles and enhance performance. Use it after your workout to relieve back pain, sports injuries, muscle pulls, spasms and soreness.

And if you have <u>specific therapy needs,</u> the *Varma Vatten Spa* can relieve chronic pain caused from injury or illness. Here's why. Just sitting in your spa alters your blood flow. Circulation improves as your blood vessels dilate. That brings more blood to your muscles and helps them recover. It actually increases your heart rate and lowers your blood pressure!

<u>And if you're diabetic</u> a *Varma Vatten Spa* may help you even more. Studies show that soaking in a hot tub gives you the same benefits as exercise without putting stress on your joints. In some studies it actually reduced blood sugar levels. One *Varma Vatten Spa* owner reports that he reduced the amount of insulin he takes by 20 percent!

> *"My doctor recommended I buy a Varma Vatten Spa to help my circulation. It's made a big difference in how I feel."—M. Bettor*

<u>What about painful arthritis?</u> Your *Varma Vatten Spa* will provide the warmth to relieve joint and muscle pain. In fact, doctors recommend water therapy for arthritis. It keeps your joints moving and helps you rebuild muscle strength. Here's a suggestion. Get in your *Varma Vatten Spa* first thing in the morning and again the last thing at night. We're betting the middle part of your day will be filled with less pain and discomfort. At least, that's what hundreds of satisfied *Varma Vatten Spa* owners tell us.

But aren't hot tubs expensive and difficult to maintain, you ask. Not a *Varma Vatten Spa.* With our 15-year warranty on the acrylic shell with its built-in UV inhibitor, you're assured that your tub will look just like new for years. As for cost, most customers tell us they run their tub for less than a penny a day including electricity and chemicals. What's more, a special filter system that comes standard on all *Varma Vatten Spas* lets you use fewer chemicals and still keep your spa looking and smelling clean every time you step in.

Varma Vatten Spas are built like no other spa on the market. They use a special material—XL 26—that has exceptionally high insulating value, keeping the warmth in your tub rather than letting it escape. We also triple wrap all components in R-20 equivalent insulation material. This added insulation makes your *Varma Vatten Spa* quiet and efficient to operate.

As for safety, *Varma Vatten Spas* has engineered special features to make operating your spa worry-free. For example, there are the safety locks on the cover, which discourage unwanted use by children; the automatic shut-off timer; the water temperature control lock; and many, many more you'll learn about on the free video. Every setting on the computer control panel can be custom set to meet your individual needs.

I could go on and on about *Varma Vatten Spas,* but you need to see for yourself why this is the spa for you. That's why we created a 20-minute video. It's yours absolutely free and without obligation. You'll see how *Varma Vatten Spas* are constructed and how we make sure your spa is custom-built to your specifications. If you want to learn even more, a customer service representative will come to your home and help you pick the spa that's right for you.

And if you act within the next 30 days, we'll include a certificate good for free installation, a month's worth of chemicals and a two-year warranty on the pump and motor. That's a $500 value!

Here's what you do. **Call toll free 555-123-1234** or simply fill out the enclosed reply coupon and mail it today. Within 10 days you'll receive your **free** video that you can watch in the privacy of your own home. No pressure. No sales call. Then if you're ready to learn more, call for an in-home appointment. It's that easy.

Before you know it, you'll be relaxing in your very own *Varma Vatten Spa.* No more neck pain or stress from a hard day. You'll join thousands of satisfied customers who wonder why they ever waited so long to own the industry leader—*Varma Vatten Spa.*

Best regards,

Gretta Von Haven

Gretta Von Haven
Owner of Varma Vatten Spas

P.S.

Act by March 30 and receive a coupon for a free neck jet in any tub you order—a $300 value. The neck jet is simply the best way to relieve stress at the end of the day. Happy hot tubbing!

Fund-Raising Letters

A fund-raising letter is an unsolicited business letter sent to potential donors on a mailing list. Nonprofit organizations use fund-raising letters to raise money, identify new donors, increase visibility, boost public relations, identify potential volunteers and publicize new programs.

Like traditional direct mail, fund-raising letters require a highly targeted mailing list. Organizations can build in-house lists from board members, volunteers and current donors and by trading names with similar organizations. They also can rent local lists from national organizations that support similar causes. A typical response rate from a donor acquisition mailing is between 0.5 and 2.5 percent. The response rate from resolicitation mailings is between 6 and 12 percent (www.nonprofits.org/npofaq/08/07.html).

> ■ **Key to Success:** A successful fund-raising letter delivers an emotional, benefit-driven message directly to the reader. It shows him that he can make a difference. Effective, ongoing fund-raising campaigns often include frequent mailings to the targeted audience.

Format/Design

Follow the general guidelines for the business-letter format on pages 193–195. However, like sales letters, fund-raising letters often delete the recipient information from the heading. They often lack the three lines that include the recipient's name, address and city, state and ZIP code. They do include the date.

Like sales letters, fund-raising letters often highlight key passages with design elements such as boldface type, different-colored type, underlining, capital letters, subheadlines—and even handwritten sticky notes, prepared and attached to the letter by a machine. However, fund-raising letters shouldn't seem excessively expensive (an apparent waste of donors' money) or too flashy (inappropriately frivolous for an important social need).

Content and Organization

A fund-raising letter can be part of a direct-mail package (see pages 176–181). A fund-raising package traditionally contains

- ■ An attention-grabbing outer envelope
- ■ A personalized fund-raising letter
- ■ A personalized reply form
- ■ A reply envelope
- ■ A brochure (optional)

Like a sales letter, a fund-raising letter traditionally consists of six sections.

Part 1 of 6: Begin with a Teaser Headline (Optional)

In fund-raising letters, teaser headlines are optional. A teaser headline appears in the upper-left corner of the page, generally above the date and the salutation. (Remember that fund-raising letters often delete the three lines in the heading that specify the recipient's name, address and city, state and ZIP code). Teaser headlines usually use a different typeface—and often a different color—from the rest of the type. They are larger (usually 18-point or 24-point type), and they don't extend across the entire page. Instead, they split into two or three lines and remain in the upper left corner.

Unlike newspaper headlines, teaser headlines usually don't tell; instead, they tease. They ask a question, mention a problem, state an eye-popping statistic or refer to a solution. The goal of a teaser headline is to capture the reader's attention and get him to read the letter in order to learn about the headline. Avoid any teasing strategies that seem frivolous or that seem to lessen the seriousness of the letter.

Part 2 of 6: Present an Emotional Description of the Need

Describe the social problem in specific, emotional terms. Grab the reader's attention and help him identify with the cause or issue. Begin with a piece of genuine news or a real-life story that evokes empathy. Your goal is to show the reader that something in life needs to be better. Use a personal salutation and, if possible, speak directly to the reader within the letter, calling him by name. Avoid first names, however. Use a courtesy title—Mr. or Ms.—and the reader's last name.

This section can exceed one paragraph, but don't let it dominate the letter. Don't overwhelm the reader with the scope of the problem. Show that the situation is serious—but not hopeless. At this point, keep the focus on the problem, not on the solution.

Part 3 of 6: Present Your Organization as a Solution to the Problem

In a new paragraph, present your organization as a solution to the problem. Concentrate on illustrating the benefits created by the organization. Show how your organization's good works have impacted society.

Part 3 can be several paragraphs. As noted in the Format/Design section, this portion often features design elements such as boldface type, different-colored type, underlining and capital letters. Consider using such elements to highlight particular strengths of your organization and its successes.

Part 4 of 6: Ask for a Donation

Wait until this section to ask for a donation. By this time you've built a case for why your organization can make a difference. Break the dollar amount into understandable figures—for example, "For only 50 cents a day you can provide a nutritious meal to a hungry child." Ask for a specific amount, or offer the reader several giving levels. Be sure to explain that the donation is tax deductible and that if the donation is $50 or more, the donor will receive a receipt. Create a sense of urgency by giving the reader a reason to respond now.

Part 5 of 6: Re-evoke the Sense of Need or Desire and Again Ask for a Donation

Close by re-evoking the sense of need. Remind the reader once more of the problem and how giving to your organization is the solution. One person should sign the letter, preferably in blue ink to make it appear personal. Include a standard "Sincerely" sign-off.

Part 6 of 6: Add a P.S.

Always include a P.S. It should reinforce your strongest reason for giving now. Place the P.S. below the sender's signature and title. (Include an extra space, just as if the P.S. were a new paragraph.) Some postscripts even appear to be handwritten, as if they were an urgent personal note from the sender to the recipient.

A P.S. is not signed. It appears at the bottom of a letter and usually is introduced simply by the initials *P.S.*

TIPS

1. Consider completing a strategic message planner (pages 104–118) before your write your fund-raising letter. The SMP will help you focus on your recipient's interests and help you deliver one, clear, goal-related message.

2. Review the discussions of sales letters (pages 171–175) and direct-mail packages (pages 176–181) for more information on writing successful fund-raising letters.

Going Online

E-mails are not the best approach for fund-raising appeals. Most people expect the personal contact that a personal letter delivers.

FUND-RAISING LETTER

Interactive Games
2010 Ridglea Drive
San Francisco, CA 55111
555·999·5555

Can a computer really save a kid's life?

May 29, 2005

Dear Ms. Shakur:

Henry Smith, age 12, is what society calls <u>a throw-away kid.</u> His dad left before Henry was born. His mom died four years ago from a drug overdose. Henry's grandmother is raising him. She does her best, but she can't keep up with an active sixth-grader. Henry has a criminal record—breaking and entering—and may be headed toward reform school. Six of his friends are there already, one of them for murder. Henry says he doesn't want to follow them. Henry says he wants a chance, any chance, to turn things around.

Ms. Shakur, I think Henry has found that chance: It's an after-school and weekend program called **Computers for California's Kids**—or just CCK. CCK provides computers and computer instruction for kids from kindergarten through 12th grade. CCK operates after school and during weekends. <u>So instead of getting into trouble, Henry and his friends are learning, developing job skills and having fun, all under adult supervision.</u> CCK operates in more than 1,000 public schools in California.

> *"My biggest interest in the world right now is computer graphics," Henry says. "When I grow up, I'm going to be a video-game designer. I'm going to buy the nicest house you ever saw for my grandma."*

Computers for California's Kids is sponsored by MGS Foundation of San Francisco. With your help, Ms. Shakur, we can buy enough computers for every precious child who wants to join CCK. Please phone us at 1-800-555-5555 or visit our Web site at *www.mgscck.org* and pledge $50, $75, $100 or more.

Henry Smith isn't a throw-away kid. Neither are the thousands of others who need Computers for California's Kids. Please help us provide the computers that save kids' lives.

Sincerely,

Mary Adams

Mary Adams
Foundation Director

<u>P.S. Governor John Jones just endorsed Computers for California's Kids. He called it "the best program I've ever seen for turning at-risk kids into great citizens."</u>

Collection Letters

Purpose, Audience and Media

A collection letter is a one-page business letter that strives to maintain goodwill with a customer while collecting money that is past due. The Federal Trade Commission's Fair Debt Collection Practices Act of 1978 restricts what debt-collection actions a business owner may take (www.ftc.gov/os/statutes/fdcpa/fdcpact.htm). A business owner may not

- Falsely imply that a lawsuit has been filed
- Contact the debtor's employer or relatives about the debt
- Communicate with others about the debt
- Harass the debtor
- Use abusive, obscene or defamatory language
- Intentionally cause mental or physical distress
- Threaten violence
- Communicate by postcard rather than sealed envelope
- Send anonymous COD (cash-on-delivery) communications
- Misrepresent the legal status of the debt
- Give false impressions by mislabeling the envelope

The recipient of a collection letter is someone who has failed to pay for a product (a good or service) he has received. Generally, you will have specific information about this person—certainly name, address and purchase date. Despite his nonpayment, this is someone you may wish to keep as a future customer.

The usual medium for a collection letter remains the traditional paper business letter. Business letters have a degree of formality that e-mail messages and phone calls lack. Business letters also are easier to present as court documents should legal action become necessary.

■ **Key to Success:** A successful collection letter is direct and to the point. It offers the recipient a way to eliminate his debt and restore his good credit. Frequently, more than one letter is necessary.

Format/Design

Follow the general guidelines for the business-letter format on pages 193–195. If the recipient purchased your product on behalf of his organization, include the recipient's title, organization name and organization address in the heading. Otherwise, write to the recipient at his home address and do not include his title or the name of his organization.

Content and Organization

Because debtors may be embarrassed by their situation, they may project blame onto you and your company. They also may be so deeply in debt that ignoring another creditor is easy. Successful collection of past due accounts is a process and may take a series of letters.

Notification Letter

Begin with a positive appeal that accentuates the benefits of prompt payment. A notification letter states the amount owed, the date and the penalties for late payment. It should be sent 15 days after the account is due.

March 15, 2005

Name
Title
Company
Address
City, State ZIP

Dear Mr. XYZ:

Thank you for your recent order. Our records indicate that payment of invoice number 23954 in the amount of $1,543.23 is past due.

We would appreciate payment by March 25, the point at which you would incur a five-percent charge as a late fee.

If you have already sent this amount, please disregard this notice.

Thank you again for doing business with Cogswell Sprockets.

Sincerely,

I.M. Boss
Customer Service Director

Reminder Letter

A few days after the date specified in the notification letter, send a reminder letter that restates the amount owed. The tone of this letter should be reassuring and acknowledge a minor problem in payment of the account. It is personal and assumes that something unusual must be preventing payment. It avoids any suggestion of customer dissatisfaction and offers to work out a payment plan.

March 31, 2005

Name
Title
Company
Address
City, State ZIP

Dear Mr. XYZ:

This is the second notice that your payment of $1,543.23 for invoice number 23954 was overdue on March 1, 2005. Please remit this amount immediately.

We invite you to contact our credit department to work out a payment plan if necessary. Cogswell Sprockets considers you a valuable customer, and we would like to continue our business relationship.

Thank you again for your prompt payment.

Sincerely,

I.M. Boss
Customer Service Director

Urgent Notice

This letter may be signed by the owner or chief executive officer. It indicates the negative consequences of failure to pay. It should leave an opening for payment without further penalty. It states the amount due and facts concerning collection efforts.

April 30, 2005

Name
Title
Company
Address
City, State ZIP

Dear Mr. XYZ:

I was surprised when your file reached my desk and indicted that your account of $1,543.23 for invoice number 23954 was 60 days past due.

Failure to pay this amount promptly will suspend further business between our two companies. If there are extenuating circumstances or we can set up a payment plan, please contact our credit department. Immediate payment will reinstate your credit account with Cogswell Sprockets.

Thank you for your prompt attention to this matter.

Sincerely,

I.M. Bigcheese
Chief Executive Officer

Ultimatum

This is the last letter sent before the account is turned over to a lawyer or collection agency. It states the exact consequences of failure to pay but avoids any hint of defamation or harassment. It encourages the debtor to re-evaluate his priorities and states facts sternly and directly.

May 15, 2005

Name
Title
Company
Address
City, State ZIP

Dear Mr. XYZ:

This is your final notice that your account of $1,543.23 for invoice number 23954 is past due. Payment was due on March 1, 2005.

If your payment is not received by June 1, 2005, or you do not contact our credit department to set up a payment plan, we will have no alternative but to turn your account over to a lawyer (or collection agency) for collection.

Thank you for your prompt attention to this matter.

Sincerely,

I.M. Bigcheese
Chief Executive Officer

TIPS

1. Consider an integrated campaign. Telephone calls sometimes complement collection letters. They correspond to the urgency of the similar letter and generally don't begin until the reminder letter stage.

2. If your series of collection letters has been unsuccessful, after the urgent notice consider sending a letter to the recipient's supervisor—but *only* if the recipient purchased the product on behalf of his organization. Do not contact a recipient's employer regarding a personal debt.

Section V
Strategic Writing in Business Communication

Objectives

*In Section V: Strategic Writing in Business Communication,
you will learn to write these documents:*

- Good-news letters
- Bad-news letters
- Request letters
- Job-request letters
- Résumés

- Memoranda
- Company announcements
- Policy and procedure documents
- Business reports

Business communication is the exchange of messages that help an organization complete its day-to-day functions. Business communication is sometimes called administrative communication because it helps an organization manage basic routines.

In a moment, we'll define business communication—and, more precisely, business writing—by the documents it includes. First, however, we might better understand business communication if we compare it to family communication. Let's imagine a mythical American family consisting of Mom, Dad, 2.5 kids, a dog and a goldfish. Think of all the communication required just to help that family function smoothly every day. Family members discuss what time dinner will be and when soccer practice is. Mom tells the kids to clean their rooms; the kids explain why they can't right now. Dad asks if anyone has fed the dog. The kids make suggestions for summer vacation. Both parents ask how the homework is going, and the kids ask for more allowance money. To keep the family functioning, its members also discuss family business with outside groups: neighbors, teachers, babysitters and others.

All that communication holds the family together. It helps family members sort out their priorities and schedules; it helps them plan, debate and establish policies that members will follow. And that's a lot like business communication. Employees of an organization are like family members, and business communication is the exchange of messages that allows the group to function effectively.

Often, the most effective method of business communication is face-to-face conversation. Studies conducted by the International Association of Business

Communicators show that face-to-face communication with the boss is usually an employee's favorite way to learn important news about the organization.

However, much of business communication needs to be written. Writing allows more than one person to see the same message. Writing creates a permanence that face-to-face communication can't match. As effective as face-to-face communication can be, organizations rely on good, clear, strategic writing to function from day to day.

Written communication also can help counter the effects of an unreliable channel of business communication: the grapevine. Many of us love to gossip, and offices supply ample opportunities for rumors and false stories.

The documents in this section help define business communication: business correspondence, memoranda, company announcements, policy and procedure documents and reports. This section also treats you as a business and includes two documents that are very important to your future: job-request letters and résumés.

Whatever your career interest is—public relations, advertising, sales or something else altogether—chances are strong that it will include many aspects of business communication.

Business Letters

Purpose, Audience and Media

The business letter is usually a one-page document that delivers a strategic message to a targeted individual. The business letter is one of the most common forms of business communication. There are several different kinds of business letters. Among the most common are

- The good-news letter (pages 197–199)
- The bad-news letter (pages 200–204)
- The sales letter (pages 171–175)
- The request letter (pages 205–207)
- The pitch letter (pages 50–53)
- The job-request letter (pages 208–212)

The audience of a business letter usually is one person. Very often, your organization wants something from that individual. Understanding the values and self-interests of the recipient of a business letter increases your chances of writing a successful letter.

Although business letters can be sent as e-mail messages, their usual medium is one sheet of your organization's stationery that you'll put in an envelope and place in the mail.

This first segment on business letters presents the standard format for such documents. This section also includes content and organization suggestions that apply to most business letters.

- **Key to Success:** Different business letters have different strategic organizations. For example, a bad-news letter is organized differently from a sales letter. The different ways to organize business letters support the strategic purposes of the different letters.

Format/Design

With rare exceptions, keep a business letter to one page.

Whenever possible, use your organization's stationery. Use your organization's stationery for the envelope as well.

Single-space between the lines of a letter. Double-space between

- The date and the other heading (recipient) information
- The recipient information and the "Dear Mr." or "Dear Ms."
- The paragraphs of the letter. (Don't indent the paragraphs.)
- The text of the letter and the "Sincerely"
- Your typed title at the bottom and any extra notes, such as "P.S." (for postscript) or "encl." (for enclosure)

Interactive Games
2010 Ridglea Drive
San Francisco, CA 55111

Today's date

Mr. or Ms. Recipient's First and Last Names
Recipient's Business Title
Recipient's Organization
Organization's Street Address
Organization's City, State (no comma) ZIP

Dear Mr. or Mrs. Last Name:

Thank you very much for . . .

(When you're writing a letter that isn't on your organization's stationery, such as a job-request letter, add your own street address and city, state and ZIP code to the date section, which is above *the recipient information. Note that you don't type your name in this section. Your typed name goes at the bottom.)*

Your Street Address
Your City, State (no comma) ZIP
Today's date

. . . .

Again, thank you very much for your time and effort. I look forward to meeting you next Friday.

Sincerely,

Your Legible Signature

Your Typed Name
Your Title

cc: Mary Jones (this is optional)
(If this is a personal letter, such as a job-request letter written by a college student, don't include a title below your typed name—you don't have a title yet!)

FIGURE 1

Align the proper headings (date and recipient information) along the left margin. Figure 1 shows sample headings.

Type "Sincerely" at the bottom left. Because "Sincerely" is traditional, that word is almost always the best sign-off. "Sincerely" is courteous and conservative. A less traditional sign-off might draw attention from your name and title.

After "Sincerely," skip down four to six spaces (enough room for a *legible* signature), and then type your first and last names. Under your name, type your title. Like the rest of the letter, these two lines should be aligned along the left margin. Don't type your organization's name under your title. Your organization's name is already on the stationery.

Remember to sign your name above your typed first and last names.

Notes at the bottom, below your typed title, are also aligned along the left margin:

- Adding *cc* means you've sent a copy to the person you name (for example, "cc: Mary Jones"). Because *cc* stands for "carbon copy" and is obsolete, you'll often see just *c* for copy.
- The abbreviation *encl.* stands for "enclosure" and means that you've enclosed another document, such as a brochure, in the envelope with your business letter. (Be sure that you remember to enclose the additional document.)
- *P.S.* means postscript and is a brief extra note that you add to a letter after you've signed it. A P.S. can be an important element of a sales letter.

Figure 1 shows a sample closing for a business letter.

Content and Organization

Avoid an unintentionally sexist greeting. For example, if you're writing to Lynn Jones, is that individual male? Or is Lynn Jones female? Should your salutation be "Dear Mr. Jones" or "Dear Ms. Jones"?

Don't use "Miss" or "Mrs." in salutations to female recipients unless you are certain that that is the person's preference. Ordinarily, use "Ms." for all women.

When you address the recipient by a courtesy title ("Mr." or "Ms.") and a last name, place a colon (not a less formal comma) after the last name. With such a formal beginning, be sure to sign both your first and your last names at the bottom of the letter above your typed name and title.

If you know the recipient well and your salutation is simply "Dear Lynn," then place a comma (not the more formal colon) after the recipient's first name. With such an informal beginning, be sure to sign *just your first name* at the bottom of the letter above your typed name and title.

TIPS

1. Within the first few sentences of most business letters, the recipient should know why she is reading the letter. In other words, tell her why you're writing to her. Sales letters, bad-news letters and pitch letters can be exceptions to this guideline.

2. The closing of a business letter (the last or next-to-last paragraph) often specifies or

suggests what the next action in the particular situation should be. When appropriate, this closing should say what you'll do next or what you hope the recipient will do next, or both.

3. Be courteous whenever possible. Opening and closing with a "thank you," whenever appropriate, is both good manners and good business.

4. Write like the warm, intelligent human being you are—not like a cold, unfeeling business machine. Avoid clichés such as "It has come to my attention" and "I regret to inform you." Such sentences are so overused that they sound insincere.

5. Sign legibly. An illegible signature can suggest carelessness or an oversized ego, which are not good qualities in a healthy business relationship.

6. Don't hand-letter the envelope. Use a good laser printer or a good, old-fashioned typewriter. The envelope should look as professional as your letter itself. In the upper left, devote two lines to your street address and your city, state and ZIP code. In the center of the envelope, devote four lines to the recipient's name, the name of the organization, the street address and the city, state and ZIP code.

Going Online

Formal business letters, particularly to individuals outside your organization, are rarely sent online as e-mail messages. Although e-mail messages are fine for informal correspondence, e-mail still lacks the formality and gravity of an old-fashioned paper letter.

Good-News Letters

Purpose, Audience and Media

The good-news business letter is a one-page business letter that conveys information that will please the recipient.

The audience of a good-news letter usually is one person. Occasionally, the good news may apply to an organization, such as an organization that has won an award. In that case, the recipient is a representative of that organization.

Although good-news letters can be sent as e-mail messages, their usual medium is one sheet of your organization's stationery that you'll put in an envelope and place in the mail.

> ■ **Key to Success:** A good-news letter should announce the good news in its first paragraph.

Format/Design

Follow the general guidelines for the business-letter format on pages 193–195.

Content and Organization

The good-news letter has three or four parts that usually translate into three to five paragraphs.

Part 1 of 4: Deliver the Good News

Open positively. Deliver the good news immediately. Or, if the recipient first wrote you with a request, you can thank her for contacting you. Then announce the good news: for example, a refund. If the good news involves an award, a promotion or something similar, offer congratulations. If you open with congratulations, be sure to immediately inform the recipient about the honor or award. Otherwise, your letter may sound as if you're congratulating her for something that you assume she already knows.

If your good-news letter is in response to a complaint, begin, as noted above, by thanking the individual for contacting you. Then, in one sentence, be understanding but don't apologize in a way that accepts blame. For example, you can write, "I regret that you're dissatisfied with the quality of our service." After the apology, concisely announce the good news.

Everything discussed in this "deliver the good news" section could be included in a three- or four-sentence opening paragraph. Do not include specific details about the good news, and do not make requests (such as asking the recipient if she will accept an award). The only function of this first paragraph is to announce the good news and, if appropriate, offer congratulations.

Part 2 of 4: Explain the Details

In a new paragraph, explain the details of the good news. For example, will you issue a refund check? If so, when will it be mailed? Are you inviting the recipient to an awards banquet? If so, when and where will it be? In this section, inform the recipient of any details she should know to take advantage of the good news. If this information includes a request to contact you, you may wish to save that until the last paragraph of the letter. This section can include more than one paragraph if needed.

Part 3 of 4: Say What the Good News Means to You (Optional)

If appropriate, in a new paragraph you may discuss your feelings (and/or the feelings of your organization) about the good news. For example, if your letter offers the recipient a job, this paragraph could mention how delighted you are to offer this job and how you look forward to working together.

Part 4 of 4: End Positively, Perhaps with Instructions

In your final paragraph, be courteous and positive. Consider specifying what the next action should be. Include details about how the recipient can contact you if necessary. If you are addressing a situation brought to your attention by the recipient, you may thank her again for contacting you. If congratulations are appropriate, you may again express them. Include a standard "Sincerely" sign-off.

TIPS

1. Keep the focus on the recipient. Don't write at length about you and your organization unless the recipient needs or desires that information.
2. If you're responding to a negative situation with good news, empathize. How would you feel if the roles were reversed?
3. When responding to a negative situation, don't disparage your organization. (It's tempting to deflect the recipient's anger by agreeing with her—that is, to share the recipient's anger so that it's not directed at you personally.)
4. When responding to a complaint, know what you can offer and what you can't. If you don't know, ask the appropriate person in your organization.
5. Remember that you represent your organization. Be courteous—even if you haven't been treated courteously by the recipient.
6. Make no commitment on behalf of your organization that it can't or won't keep.

Going Online

Good-news messages can be delivered via e-mail. Business acquaintances often use e-mail, or even a phone call, for minor good news. However, e-mail lacks the formality and keepsake value of a traditional letter on high-quality stationery. If the good news is important, or if you're sending it to someone you don't know well, be traditional and use paper (unless you know that the recipient prefers e-mail or a phone call).

GOOD-NEWS LETTER

Interactive Games
2010 Ridglea Drive
San Francisco, CA 55111
555·999·5555

January 18, 2005

Ms. Patricia Morris
Chief Executive Officer
Texas Mix Productions Inc.
1989 Binkley Ave.
Dallas, TX 87538

Dear Patty,

Congratulations! It is my great pleasure to tell you that MGS Interactive Games has named you and Texas Mix Productions its 2004 Supplier of the Year. The competition for this honor was impressive, but at its Jan. 10 meeting, our Management Council reviewed the list of finalists and selected Texas Mix Productions as our top supplier.

MGS Interactive Games invites you to be a guest of honor at our annual awards banquet March 15 at 7 p.m. at the Grand Royale Hotel in San Francisco. We'll gather for cocktails at 6 p.m. in the Casino Room. You are more than welcome to bring up to four guests. (If you'd like to bring a few more, we can certainly arrange that.) Please contact me to clarify what arrangements would be best for you.

At the banquet, David Mertz, our vice president of acquisitions, will present our Supplier of the Year 2004 trophy to you. At that time, we'll invite you to speak for two or three minutes. Your speech needn't be long or elaborate; we just want another chance to cheer for you.

I hope you know what an honor it is for me to write this letter. When we were roommates 10 years ago at Palmquist University, who knew our paths would cross again at such a wonderful moment? I'm proud to claim you as a business associate and a friend.

Again, congratulations on this significant achievement in your career. Please phone me at your earliest convenience to confirm a plan.

Sincerely,

Janet

Janet Walker
Special Events Coordinator

Bad-News Letters

Purpose, Audience and Media

The bad-news business letter is a one-page business letter that tells the recipient something that he doesn't want to hear: for example, no refund, no job opportunities at this time or no donation to a worthy charity.

The audience of a bad news letter usually is one person. Very often, your organization wants to maintain a good relationship with that person—or, at least, your organization wants to keep that person's goodwill. The need to preserve a good relationship while delivering bad news can make the writing of a bad-news letter difficult.

Although bad-news letters can be sent as e-mail messages, their usual medium is one sheet of your organization's stationery that you'll put in an envelope and place in the mail.

■ **Key to Success:** A well-organized bad-news letter explains the reason(s) for the bad news before it announces the bad news.

Format/Design

Follow the general guidelines for the business-letter format on pages 193–195.

Content and Organization

The bad-news letter has five parts that usually translate into three paragraphs.

Part 1 of 5: Begin Courteously, Focusing on a Positive Relationship

Part 1 usually is one paragraph. Thank the recipient for contacting you, if that's appropriate. Because you want to maintain a relationship with the recipient (or at least keep his goodwill), discuss the positive aspects of the relationship between your organization and the recipient. For example, to a customer you might describe how much you appreciate the opportunity to serve him. *In this opening paragraph, do not mention the bad news.* Do your best to focus on the value of the relationship. Don't talk about yourself or your organization too much. By discussing the recipient's role in the relationship, you show that you value him. In most bad-news situations, three or four sentences are sufficient to create this positive beginning.

Part 2 of 5: Explain the Reason for the Bad News

Part 2 usually is the beginning of the second paragraph. It can be more than one sentence. This concise description of the reason for the bad news is one of the most strategic parts of the letter: You offer an explanation for the bad news *before* you deliver the bad news. Therefore, if the bad news angers the recipient, at least he understands your reasoning. The recipient may even understand your reasoning so well that he graciously accepts the justice of the bad news.

For example, before telling a job applicant that you can't hire him, first explain that you have no available positions for someone with his qualifications. Deliver the explanation before you deliver the bad news.

The explanation of the bad news comes at the beginning of the second paragraph and is an important transition in the letter. The explanation is a bridge between the relationship-focused first paragraph and the upcoming delivery of the bad news. The explanation should avoid a sudden shift to a harsh tone from the courtesy of the first paragraph. An abrupt, stern tone at this point would make the first paragraph seem insincere.

Part 3 of 5: Deliver the Bad News

In the same paragraph as the explanation (usually the second paragraph), state the bad news clearly and concisely—in one sentence, whenever possible.

Don't set off the bad-news sentence as its own paragraph. One-sentence paragraphs get extra emphasis, and you don't want to emphasize the bad news. Ideally, the bad news sentence will appear in the middle of the second paragraph, which is a point of low emphasis. The bad news won't get the extra emphasis that paragraph openings and closings get.

Part 4 of 5: Cap the Bad News with Something Neutral or Positive

As noted above, don't let the bad-news sentence close the paragraph. Don't let it gain extra emphasis by echoing into the momentary silence that follows the end of a paragraph. Instead, "cap" the bad news. That is, close the paragraph with something neutral or positive.

For example, if you're turning down a job applicant, follow the bad-news sentence with the promise that you'll keep his résumé on file for one year and will contact him if any suitable jobs open.

Again, note that parts 2, 3 and 4 often go in the same paragraph: first the explanation; then the bad news; then the neutral or positive cap.

Part 5 of 5: Close Courteously, Focusing on a Positive Relationship

Sounds a lot like Part 1, doesn't it? It should: Just as you began the letter by focusing on a good relationship between your organization and the recipient, close the letter in the same way. Show the recipient that he has value to your organization.

This closing is usually one short paragraph, the last paragraph of the bad-news letter. *Do not refer to the bad news in this paragraph, not even indirectly.* You delivered the bad news clearly in the previous paragraph. Don't emphasize the bad news by repeating it, or even referring to it, in this closing paragraph. Instead, discuss the positive aspects of the relationship, or focus on preserving the goodwill of the recipient. Let the recipient finish reading the letter with a vision of a good relationship in his mind. Include a standard "Sincerely" sign-off.

Exceptions to the Standard Bad-News Letter Organization

The five-part bad-news letter, described above, works in almost every bad-news situation. However, when the bad news is devastating and recipient(s) already know some of the details, you might want to consider a different organizational strategy. This different strategy directly and boldly confronts the bad news in order to show that your organization takes the bad news seriously. For example, a CEO who must explain plummeting stock prices might want to use this more direct strategy in a letter to stockholders:

In the first paragraph, immediately announce the bad news. A brief explanation can come before the bad news, but you must announce the bad news in the first paragraph.

In a new paragraph or paragraphs, discuss in detail how the situation happened and what your organization is doing to improve the situation.

In the closing paragraph, express confidence about the future and announce any communication actions that should follow. Should the recipient(s) contact you? Will you phone the recipient? What other communications actions do you recommend to help address and resolve the bad news?

TIPS

1. Whenever possible, avoid personal pronouns (any form of *I* and *you*) in the explanation for the bad news and in the bad-news sentence—for example, "I must suspend your credit privileges." Those pronouns encourage the recipient to take the bad news personally, and you don't want him to do that. You want to preserve the relationship or at least the recipient's goodwill.

2. Don't be wordy. Don't attempt to hide the bad news in an avalanche of words. Avoid being blunt to the point of rudeness, but be concise.

3. Don't let personal feelings, such as anger or sympathy, excessively influence your letter. Your job is to protect and promote your organization by effectively managing the relationship with the bad-news letter's recipient. You might hurt that relationship by being overly emotional in your letter. For example, if you sympathize too much, you might sound as if you disagree with your organization's actions.

4. Never disparage your own organization. You may be tempted to defuse a recipient's anger by agreeing with him, but avoid writing something like "I agree that we didn't perform very well."

5. You can apologize to a recipient, but avoid doing so in a way that accepts legal responsibility or blame (unless your organization's legal team gives you permission to do so). Avoid writing, "I apologize for our poor performance in this area." Instead, you might write, "I regret that you're unhappy with the quality of our service."

6. Avoid clichés such as "It has come to my attention," "I regret to inform you" and "Pursuant to your request." These worn-out sentences are so overused that they sound insincere.

7. Consider using the five part bad-news organizational strategy in memos and speeches.

Going Online

Bad-news messages can be delivered via e-mail. However, e-mail lacks the formality and gravity of a traditional paper letter. If e-mail will not hurt the relationship with the recipient, you could consider using it to deliver a bad-news message.

Bad-news messages sometimes appear online in annual reports. Annual reports (pages 84–87) often begin with a letter to stockholders from the organization's CEO. If the CEO has bad news to deliver, that letter may use a strategic bad-news organization.

Interactive Games
2010 Ridglea Drive
San Francisco, CA 55111
555·999·5555

November 2, 2005

Ms. Molly Jones
President
Brand Z Software Systems
1876 Lancaster St.
Dallas, TX 76450

Dear Ms. Jones:

Thank you for your recent proposal explaining how Brand Z Software Systems could contribute to the new production processes at MGS Interactive Games. We thought your proposal was innovative, and it showed us why Brand Z is such a respected company in the software industry.

When MGS Interactive Games launched the new production processes, we signed a long-term contract with QN2 Software Supply Systems to maintain and monitor those processes. Therefore, MGS cannot offer Brand Z a maintenance contract at this time. However, MGS is continually expanding our lineup of interactive games, and we would be pleased to consider any proposals from Brand Z regarding future production processes.

Again, thank you for your interest in MGS Interactive Games. I would welcome an opportunity to meet with you and discuss future business opportunities.

Sincerely,

Mark Smith

Mark Smith
Executive Vice President

Request Letters

Purpose, Audience and Media

The request letter is a one-page business letter in which you ask someone outside your organization for something that you need—for example, information or special consideration.

Request letters can use different organizational strategies, depending on their purpose. If the letter is a request for funds, the organization for fund-raising letters (pages 182–185) works well. If the letter requests anything else, the organizational strategy presented below may be best.

The audience of a request letter usually is one person. That recipient generally has the power to grant your request—or at least to present your request to the members of his organization.

Requests can be sent as e-mail messages, particularly if you know the recipient well and can make the request in an informal manner. However, if the request is important and you do not know the recipient well (or at all), the usual medium of a request letter remains the traditional paper letter that you put in an envelope and place in the mail. The organization specified below also works for telephone calls in which you make a request.

■ **Key to Success:** Make your request courteously but promptly in the first paragraph. In later paragraphs, explain the request and close by noting future action.

Format/Design

Follow the general guidelines for the business-letter format on pages 193–195.

Content and Organization

To show respect for the time of the busy recipient, request letters usually follow a standard organization:

Part 1 of 4: Make the Request
In your first paragraph, make your request and briefly identify yourself. Getting right to the point is courteous. It shows respect for the recipient's time.

Part 2 of 4: Explain and Justify the Request
In a new paragraph, offer additional information if necessary. Briefly explain why you need the information, special consideration or whatever you are requesting. For

example, why do you need information on a particular production process? Or why do you deserve a refund? Without being defensive, justify your request.

Part 3 of 4: Describe Any Special Needs

In a new paragraph or still in the second paragraph, detail precisely what you hope the recipient will supply. What kind of details about the production process do you need to know? What action do you hope the recipient's organization will take in regard to a particular situation? Basically, what does the recipient need to know to meet your needs or wishes? If you have an important deadline for receiving the information, specify that deadline in a separate, following paragraph.

Part 4 of 4: Close with a Suggestion for Future Action

In your final paragraph, describe what action you will take next—or what action you hope the recipient will now take. Thank the recipient. Include a standard "Sincerely" sign-off.

TIPS

1. Be courteous. Don't issue orders on the assumption that the recipient will automatically grant your request. In Parts 2 and 3, as you describe your needs, consider phrases such as "We would appreciate" rather than "We need." Show gratitude for the extra effort you're requesting from the recipient.

2. Large businesses will use their own envelopes to reply to you if a formal letter is the proper response. But small organizations, nonprofit organizations or private individuals might appreciate a self-addressed, stamped return envelope enclosed with your letter.

Going Online

As noted above, requests can be sent as e-mail messages, particularly if you know the recipient well and can make the request in an informal manner. For requests made to members of your own organization, e-mail messages, phone calls or face-to-face meetings would be more traditional than the unusual formality of a paper letter.

Interactive Games
2010 Ridglea Drive
San Francisco, CA 55111
555·999·5555

May 13, 2005

Mr. Aubrey Tintrell
Event Director
Great Northern Exposition
Marlowe Place
Crossbridge, Surrey RL 17 TPN
ENGLAND

Dear Mr. Tintrell:

I am writing to request information on the Great Northern Exposition scheduled for Doncaster in July 2006. I am assistant marketing director for MGS Interactive Games, and we are considering registering for the exposition.

Specifically, could you tell me if you offer larger display areas than those specified in Plan B on your Web site? MGS would be interested in a space twice the size of Model 7. Also, could you tell me if MGS could purchase the back cover of the exposition's program for an advertisement? We're interested in participating in the Great Northern Exposition, and answers to these questions would assist our decision making.

We hope to make a decision by June 15. I'd greatly appreciate receiving answers to my questions before then.

Please feel free to phone me at the above number or e-mail me at rgreen@mgsintgames.com. Thank you very much.

Sincerely,

Robert Green

Robert Green
Assistant Director of Marketing

Job-Request Letters

Purpose, Audience and Media

The job-request letter is a one-page business letter in which the writer asks the recipient for a job.

The audience of a job-request letter usually is one person—a busy person who may be receiving several similar letters. This recipient may be nervous about the upcoming hiring decision. Although the job search can be nerve-wracking for you (the letter writer), the search also can be stressful for the employer. If she makes a good decision in hiring you, she has improved her stature within her organization. Her supervisors will see that she can recruit talented individuals. However, if she hires someone who doesn't perform well, her own supervisors may question her judgment and her abilities as a manager. Therefore, the recipient of a job-request letter wants something almost magical: She wants a letter that seems to promise that the writer would be the perfect employee.

Although job-request letters can be sent as e-mail messages or as attached files, their usual medium is one sheet of high-quality paper that you'll put in an envelope and place in the mail.

■ **Key to Success:** In a successful job-request letter, you should include specific research to explain why you want to work for that organization. Show the recipient that this isn't a form letter. With your research, show her that you seek more than just a job; show her that you truly want to work for *her* organization.

Format/Design

Follow the general guidelines for the business-letter format on pages 193–195. However, because your job-request letter will be on a blank sheet of paper rather than on organizational letterhead, you need to include your return address. Include that address at the top. Instead of beginning with the date, begin with your street address and then city, state and ZIP code. The first three lines of your letter, single-spaced and placed in the upper left corner, would look like this:

> 712 Custer St.
> Paderno, TX 80476
> January 18, 2005

Note that in this new heading, you do not include your name. You still will type your name at the bottom. After this heading, skip one line and then follow the traditional headings for a business letter, beginning with the recipient's name and, on the next line, her title.

At the bottom of the letter, do not include a title under your typed name.

Content and Organization

The job-request letter has four parts that usually translate into four paragraphs. In each paragraph, avoid sounding like a business-writing machine. Strive for a tone that shows you're an intelligent, articulate, friendly, ambitious job seeker.

Part 1 of 4: Tell the Recipient Why You're Writing

Begin by saying why you're writing and who you are. For example, you might begin this way:

> Please consider this letter to be my application for a position as account assistant at Jones & Jones. This May I will receive a bachelor of science degree, with honors in journalism, from Palmquist University. I share the commitment expressed in the Jones & Jones mission statement: "providing services that exceed expectations." That's why I would like to join the team at Jones & Jones.

Part 2 of 4: Explain Why You Want to Work for This Particular Organization

In this paragraph, demonstrate that this isn't just a form letter. Use specific knowledge of the organization to explain your eagerness to work there. To gain this knowledge, you'll need to do more than just examine the organization's Web site. Search online news databases for information about the company, such as awards and new projects. Learn where the company has been, where it is now and where it hopes to go. Your second paragraph may sound something like this:

> My interest in working for Jones & Jones began with your handling of the Fat Burger account. You not only won a Bronze Quill Award for excellence but also helped set record profits for that restaurant. Your pro bono work for City Children's Center has inspired our entire community, including me. And your recent remarks about business ethics at the Chamber of Commerce luncheon show why clients and competitors alike respect Jones & Jones for integrity as well as excellence. I'd like an opportunity to contribute to the continuing success of Jones & Jones.

Chances are, this paragraph will grab the recipient's attention because she's used to receiving form letters that could have gone to any organization. This second paragraph will help your letter stand out for a variety of reasons:

- You didn't write a form letter.
- In gathering organization research, you worked harder than other job applicants.
- You used a smarter, more sincere approach than other job applicants.
- You showed that you want more than just a job; you really want to work for the recipient's organization.
- You flattered the recipient by showing specific, well-informed interest in her organization.
- You eased the recipient's concerns about the hiring process. You've shown yourself to be smart, hard-working and diplomatic. The recipient may well believe that you'll help her gain a reputation for recruiting good employees.

Part 3 of 4: Describe Your Specific Accomplishments

In the third paragraph, sell yourself. Be specific about your accomplishments and what you can bring to the organization. Name former employers and particular successes. When possible, focus on results. Creating a public relations media kit is impressive—but creating a media kit that generated regional news coverage is better. It's fine to repeat parts of your résumé here:

> I believe that I have the skills to be part of the Jones & Jones success story. As I hope you'll see on my résumé, I . . .

Part 4 of 4: Show Initiative: Ask for an Interview

In the fourth and final paragraph, close by showing initiative:

> I will call next week to see if we can schedule an interview. Thank you very much for your time and consideration.
>
> Sincerely,
>
> *(Be sure to sign the letter legibly.)*
>
> Your typed name

By asking for the interview, you show polite aggressiveness, a good quality in a prospective employee. You don't simply say, *I hope to hear from you at your earliest convenience.* Instead, you show that you're the kind of person who tries to make good things happen. Rather than just hoping for an interview, you're willing to step up and ask for one. That polite aggressiveness may appeal to the recipient, who will think you'll carry that same initiative into the workplace. Include a standard "Sincerely" sign-off.

You may wish to send your letter to more than one person at the organization. If so, type

> cc: full name
>   full name

at the bottom left of the letter. Address each letter to each new recipient. Don't just send copies of the letter addressed to the original recipient.

TIPS

1. Proofread again and again, and have others proofread the letter. Just as with the résumé, a single error can be fatal.
2. Have a set speech ready when you make your follow-up call to try to schedule an interview. Remind the recipient of your letter, and ask if an interview is possible. If you get voice-mail, be ready with your concise, professional speech. One more call-back is all right, but don't leave more than two messages. If you get a secretary, explain why you're phoning and ask for the letter recipient to return your call. Be polite. A secretary's opinion of you can be very influential in whether you'll be hired.

3. Prepare for your interview. A good approach is to have a two-topic agenda for the interview: to show that you know the company and to show that you have the skills to do the job. When possible, steer your answers to those two areas. Do even more research on the organization, and prepare answers for potential questions. For example, what are your strengths? Your weaknesses? What's the most rewarding thing you've ever done? What are your pet peeves? Where do you want to be in 10 years? Be ready with questions of your own—questions that display your knowledge of the organization. Don't ask about salary and benefits; let the interviewer introduce those topics. An excellent resource for job interviews is the book *Knock 'Em Dead* by Martin John Yate.

4. Have a well-organized, diverse, professional-looking portfolio of your work. Such portfolios often are three-ring binders with zippers that help seal the notebook to prevent media kit folders or bound proposals from tumbling out. Use transparent sheet protectors to enclose your documents. Organize your portfolio by document categories, with a divider tab for each section—for example, news releases, newsletter stories, TV commercial scripts, and so on. To help show the diversity of the enclosed documents, include a table of contents (without page numbers) that names each section. Often, the first page of the portfolio is your résumé.

5. Dress appropriately for the interview. Select clothing in which you look and feel professional and comfortable. For job interviews, it's better to be overdressed than underdressed.

6. During the interview, have a firm handshake and maintain eye contact. Don't fidget. Fold your hands in your lap if necessary.

7. After the interview (on the same day), send a brief, typed thank-you letter in which you thank the recipient for the interview, mention something specific that you appreciated learning during the interview and gracefully ask for the job. Follow the general guidelines for business letters on pages 193–195. Write such a letter to everyone who interviewed you. Vary your wording so that the letters are not duplicates. Also write thank-you letters to anyone who helped you set up the interview, including secretaries and friends who recommended you. Handwritten thank-you letters used to be standard. Many employers still believe handwritten thank-you letters show old-fashioned courtesy. However, handwritten letters strike other employers as being unprofessional. Many employers consider e-mail thank-you letters to be too easy and too informal. Play it safe by typing and mailing thank-you letters.

Going Online

Employers increasingly seek job-request letters via e-mail. If you know that an employer prefers an e-mail request, you can skip the headings of a business letter and begin with the salutation *(Dear Ms. Jones:)*. After that salutation, follow the four-paragraph method described above.

If you send a formal letter as an attachment to an e-mail message (or, more common, if you attach your résumé), be certain to scan that document for viruses. E-mailing an infected document to a potential employer is a sure way to get fired before you're hired.

JOB-REQUEST LETTER

712 Custer St.
Paderno, TX 80476
January 18, 2005

Ms. Ivy Jones
President
Jones & Jones
1876 Lancaster St.
Dallas, TX 76450

Dear Ms. Jones:

Please consider this letter to be my application for a position as account assistant at Jones & Jones. This May I will receive a bachelor of sciences degree, with honors in journalism, from Palmquist University. I share the commitment expressed in the Jones & Jones mission statement: "providing services that exceed expectations." That's why I would like to join the team at Jones & Jones.

My interest in working for Jones & Jones began with your handling of the Fat Burger account. You not only won a Bronze Quill Award for excellence but also helped set record profits for that restaurant. Your pro bono work for City Children's Center has inspired our entire community, including me. And your recent remarks about business ethics at the Chamber of Commerce luncheon show why clients and competitors alike respect Jones & Jones for integrity as well as excellence. I'd like an opportunity to contribute to the continuing success of Jones & Jones.

I believe that I have the skills to be part of the Jones & Jones success story. As I hope you'll see on my résumé, I wrote a news release for the Flora County United Way that generated coverage from seven media outlets in the county. I've written more than eight newsletter stories for Central City Senior Center and have designed and written more than two dozen print ads for the *Palmquist University Daily News*. During my internship at United Marketing Corp., I helped prepare seven direct-marketing packages, and I helped plan special events. I'm a writer who gets results, and I'd like a chance to prove that at Jones & Jones.

I will call next week to see if we can schedule an interview. Thank you very much for your time and consideration.

Sincerely,

Taylor Jackson

Taylor Jackson

Résumés

Purpose, Audience and Media

A résumé is a short document that summarizes an individual's education, professional experience, professional abilities and other work experience. A résumé can include information on individual honors and on activities. Generally, a résumé is just one page.

A job seeker sends a résumé to a potential employer. Often, the job seeker also sends a job-request letter (also called a résumé cover letter; see pages 208–212), a list of references and some work samples.

Résumés generally exist on paper. However, they also can exist as computer files to be attached to e-mail messages or stored on job-search Web sites.

■ **Key to Success: A successful résumé is well-organized, specific and concise.**

Format/Design

Experts don't agree on one perfect format for a résumé. As many students know, if you ask three professors and three professionals how to organize a résumé, you may get six different answers. This chapter recommends a format that definitely works. The authors of this book have watched hundreds of students use this format in successful quests to land internships and jobs.

The easiest way to understand this format is simply to examine the sample résumé on page 216. Try to keep one-inch margins at top, bottom and both sides. To squeeze in more information, you can cut those to three-quarters of an inch. Certainly don't go lower than a half inch. A common typeface and size is 11-point Times or Times New Roman. Set the line spacing to 11 points or even 10 points. If you still lack space, consider an even smaller size of a sans-serif typeface such as Geneva. Let your eye be the judge. A résumé can be tight with information, but it shouldn't look overloaded. Again, keep your résumé to one page.

Single-space your résumé, and insert an extra space before each new section. Use boldface type to highlight key words, such as categories of information (for example, **Education**) and names of organizations that employed you. However, don't overuse boldfacing. If everything seems to be highlighted, then nothing gains emphasis.

Your résumé can include the following categories of information, often in this order: Education, Professional Experience, Other Employment, Skills, Honors and Activities. In the sample on page 216, note how those titles can appear boldface on the left side. This technique clarifies the organization of your résumé.

Unless you know that an employer seeks flamboyance and wild creativity, use a conservative paper color for your résumé: white, gray or cream. Use good cotton-fiber paper, not just photocopy paper.

Content and Organization

Type your name and contact information (address, phone number and e-mail) at the top. Students occasionally include both a school address and a permanent (family) address.

Beneath the contact information, summarize your "Education." Don't include information about high school. Do include all universities at which you've gained college credit, including any universities you attended during study abroad experiences. Include dates for each university. Include your graduation date or anticipated graduation date. Potential employers generally expect to see your grade point average, but it's not required. Chances are, employers will be more interested in your experience and your portfolio of professional work than in your GPA. If you list your GPA, show it as a ratio: 3.4/4.0.

Next comes "Professional Experience." In this category, include jobs since high school graduation that are relevant to your career goal. Be sure to include professional internships here. List them in reverse chronological order, beginning with the most recent. For each job, list your title and describe your duties. For each duty, begin with a strong, specific verb—or verbs. For example, don't say, "Worked for monthly newsletter" or "Responsible for monthly newsletter." Instead, say, "Wrote stories for monthly newsletter." If you still are employed in the job, use present-tense verbs; otherwise, use past-tense verbs. For each job, list your dates of employment. Listing those dates in the left margin allows an employer to easily scan the dates of your employment history to see if there are any long gaps.

In "Other Employment," include other jobs since high school graduation. These jobs may not relate directly to your career goal, but they help show work ethic, versatility and the ability to get along with others. Employers know that you're a college student. They'll expect to see jobs such as waiter, store clerk and lifeguard. List these jobs in reverse chronological order, beginning with the most recent. For each job, list your title and describe your duties. Again, use strong, specific verbs to describe your duties. Be sure to include any duties that show that an employer trusted you with money or with the business itself. For example, if you opened or closed the business, or if you totaled cash registers or trained other employees, be sure to include that information. For each job, list your dates of employment, just as you did in the previous section.

If you include a "Skills" section, list only skills that separate you from the normal employee. For example, don't include "Proficiency in Microsoft Word." That's a professional expectation, not a skill. Instead, include such skills as "Proficient in QuarkXPress, Dreamweaver and Microsoft Excel." Include fluency in foreign languages in this section.

If you include an "Honors" section, be concise. List only the name of the award and the date. If an explanation is necessary, consider including just the name of the organization that bestowed the honor.

Like an "Honors" section, an "Activities" section is not required. Include it only if space allows and if you believe the rest of the résumé fails to show that you're a well-rounded person. In "Activities," you can include organizations to which you belong and sports or other activities to which you devote time. As always in a résumé, be concise. Include just the names of organizations and activities.

TIPS

1. Keep your résumé to one page. More than one middle-aged employer has said, "If I can get my résumé onto one page, don't tell me that a college student can't do the same."

2. Proofread. Proofread. Proofread. Have others proofread your résumé. Then proofread it again. Proofread your résumé backward, one passage at a time. A single typo can be fatal to your job search.

3. If a job-request letter accompanies your résumé, you probably don't need a "Career Objective" just below the contact information at the top. That letter will specify your career objective. However, if a job request letter *doesn't* accompany your résumé, then a "Career Objective" can be a good idea. Put that section just below the contact information at the top. Treat the words "Career Objective" in the same way you treat other labels, such as "Education." In your objective, be concise. Don't be pretentious, and don't be self-centered, focusing only on what you hope to gain. A good career objective comes right to the point: "An entry-level position in events management."

4. Consider saving space by listing job duties, awards, honors and activities in paragraph form rather than giving one line to each entry. If you have space for one line for each of those items, consider introducing each item with a small bullet (•). However, as you gain more experience, chances are good that you'll lack the space for one line per item.

5. If you have room, consider listing references on your résumé. However, you may lack room. It's generally all right to send your references on a separate sheet of paper labeled "References" at the top. Under that label, put your name and contact information, just as you did on the résumé. For each reference, include name; title; organization; street address; city, state and ZIP code; phone number, including area code; and e-mail address. Don't staple this sheet to your résumé; don't create the appearance of a two-page résumé.

6. As noted above, don't include any information from your high school years. Some employers have the perception, fair or not, that high school students are not adults. Employers are interested in your achievements as an adult.

Going Online

Résumés can go online in three different ways. You can send an e-mail message requesting a job and include your résumé as an attached document. Use this method only if you know that the employer accepts online job requests. If you include your résumé as an attached file, include it as a Microsoft Word file whenever possible. Despite whatever word-processing program has your loyalty, the business world tends to use Microsoft Word—and you want your résumé file to open easily. Also, be sure to scan the file for viruses. An infected file either will be destroyed by the employer's safeguards—meaning no résumé to read—or it will infect your potential boss's computer. Either way, you lose.

Résumés also can go online through job-search Web sites, such as Monster.com. Each site has its own instructions for how to create and place your online résumé.

Finally, if you have your own Web site, consider posting your résumé—plus impressive items from your portfolio—there.

John Doe

Current Address	Permanent Address
3309 Frontier Rd.	4974 47th St. Terrace
Tonsing, FL 98638	Ink City, OK
(555) 253-9876	(555) 873-6524
jdoe@ucfla.edu	

Education

University of Coastal Florida, Tonsing, Fla.
B.S. in Journalism, with emphasis in Strategic Communication
B.A. in French
Degrees expected: May 2006
Current Grade Point Average: 3.85/4.0
City University, Paris, France
August–December 2004

Professional Experience

Jan. 2005–present **Advertising Intern,** Carter and Associates, Midway, Fla.
Develop strategic message planners for print, radio, television and Web ads. Write copy for print and radio ads. Assist with research and writing of proposals for clients. Assist with proposal presentations.

Jan. 2004–present **Freelance Projects**
Write newsletter stories for Compton County Senior Services newsletter. Write and distribute public relations media kits for Tonsing City Volunteer Fire Department. Write and produce videos for Midway Adult Learning Center.

Jan. 2004–Aug. 2004 **Corporate Communications Intern,** Coastal Power, Tonsing, Fla.
Wrote and distributed news releases. Wrote and edited weekly newsletter. Helped coordinate news conferences. Monitored local news coverage. Wrote print ads for weekly newspapers in Coastal Florida.

Other Employment

May 2003–Aug. 2004 **Store Clerk and Cashier,** Fashion Fun Stop, Tonsing, Fla.
Opened store. Closed store. Ordered inventory. Totaled cash drawers. Assisted approximately 30 customers per day. Named Employee of the Month nine times.

May 2002–Nov. 2003 **Waiter,** Old Doug's Fishing Shack, Ink City, Okla.
Assisted approximately 40 customers per day. Trained new employees. Edited new menu.

Skills

Proficient in QuarkXPress, Dreamweaver, Microsoft Excel and digital video-editing systems. Fluent in French.

Honors

William Allen Bowen Academic Scholarship (four years). School of Journalism Dean's List, 2004, 2003, 2002.

Activities

Public Relations Student Society of America. University of Coastal Florida Ad Club. St. John's Catholic Campus Center volunteer. University of Coastal Florida Water Skiing Team.

Memoranda

Purpose, Audience and Media

A memorandum is a written message to an internal audience—that is, to a person or people within your organization. Think of a memo as an in-house letter. Often, memos are informal and conversational, though not needlessly wordy. The memorandum can incorporate other forms of business writing. A memo can be a company announcement (pages 222–225), a modified good-news or bad-news letter (pages 197–204) or even a policy and procedure document (pages 226–228).

The audience for a memo, again, is a person or people within your organization. You can send memos to people outside your organization if you have a longstanding business relationship with them and you know them well. Memos are less formal than business letters and even business phone calls. Send memos outside your organization only when your relationship with the recipient allows such informality.

Memos generally are sent via e-mail. However, some memos still are written on paper and distributed through office mail. Paper memos also can be faxed to other locations within your organization.

> ■ **Key to Success:** A good memo shows respect for the reader. It specifies its message with the subject line and comes to the point quickly and gracefully.

Format/Design

The headings of a memo should specify the recipient, the sender, the date and the subject. E-mail systems, therefore, are effective media for memos. E-mail systems automatically specify the sender's name and address as well as the date. In addition, they prompt the sender to specify the recipient and the subject.

Some organizations still use paper memos when a message is important, will be frequently consulted or must be filed for legal records. Such organizations may still have a memo form that reminds you to include necessary information about

- The date
- The recipient (a *To* section)
- The sender (a *From* section)
- The subject

At the top of a paper memo, after you record the date, record the recipient's name and title in the *To* section.

In the *From* section, record your name, your title, your office location, your department name, your phone number and your e-mail address. Including all this *From* information is important. It provides the recipient several ways to contact you. All the *From* information even allows the recipient to write a brief answer on your memo, cross out the original *To* and indicate that the memo should be returned to you at the address listed in the *From* section.

If you send a paper memorandum to more than one person, include all the appropriate names and titles in the *To* section. You can, however, "cc" a memo if you want someone to see a memo that you've sent to someone else (see the business-letter guidelines, page 195). You also can simply write "All Employees" in the *To* section.

Always include a brief description of the subject in the memo's heading; this is true for e-mail as well as paper memos. (If you're writing a bad-news memo, strive for a neutral but accurate subject description.) The subject description usually is not a complete sentence.

Standard headings for a paper memo are single-spaced with an extra space between each section. Headings for a paper memo can look like this:

Date:	Nov. 20, 2005
To:	Melva Young, Director of Personnel
From:	Mike Smith
	Director of Communications
	Communications Dept.
	Building H, Office 427
	Ext. 3875
	msmith@mgsintgames.com
Subject:	Employee Handbook revisions

Single-space the paragraphs of a paper memorandum. Double-space between paragraphs. Don't indent paragraphs.

After you have carefully proofread a paper memo, write your initials next to your name at the top of the page. This is how you sign a paper memo. Unlike an e-mail memo, you generally don't sign your name at the bottom of a paper memo.

Content and Organization

In e-mail memos, the most common salutation is simply the recipient's name plus a colon. For example, "Sarah:" would be the salutation to a co-worker you know well. (If you write "Dear Sarah," you would use a comma.) Salutations such as "Ms. Hernandez:" or "Mr. Fulton:" are suitable for more formal situations.

The first sentence of a memo is traditionally a courteous greeting. After that, move quickly to the subject of the memo.

Because e-mail memos are less formal than business letters, they usually lack the "Sincerely" sign-off. A simple "Thanks!" or "Thank you" often suffices for a closing paragraph.

Below the "Thank you" in an e-mail, simply type your name. If your salutation was simply "Sarah," then type only your first name. However, if your salutation was more formal, such as "Ms. Hernandez:" then type your first and last names.

Ideally, you have used the options of your e-mail program to automatically add your name, title, address and phone number to the bottom of your e-mail messages.

This information would appear below where you have typed your name. (Because of the automatic information, your name may appear twice at the bottom of an e-mail message. No problem—that's traditional.)

Paper memos are different from e-mail memos. They have no salutation; the *To* information at the top of the memo serves as the salutation. Therefore, after completing the headings, begin the memo with the first sentence of your message.

Paper memos also have no sign off—no "Sincerely" line—nor do they have a signature and/or typed name at the bottom. Instead, the *From* information at the top of the memo, which includes your handwritten initials, serves as your sign-off and signature. Because of this lack of a traditional sign-off, the last words of your final paragraph should provide a sense of closure. Thanking the recipient or suggesting what the next communications action should be, or both, can provide closure.

Position Memos

Position memos are prepared for an organization's leaders. Position memos address issues that may require action. This type of memo often has a concise, three-part organization:

- Paragraph one: What is the issue? What is the problem? This section often is labeled "The Issue."
- Paragraph two: What are the possible solutions, courses of action or policies? This section often is labeled "Possible Actions."
- Paragraph three: What solution, course of action or policy do we recommend— and why? This section often is labeled "Recommendations" or "Recommended Position."

Position memos are concise. Consolidating so much information into three paragraphs demands skill in precision and editing.

Career Advancement Memos

In the following workplace situations, you can use memos to advance and protect your career:

- If your organization doesn't have a standard project-status meeting or form, get in the habit of writing a memo to your boss every Friday before you leave for the weekend. In that memo, briefly describe the status of all your projects. If you foresee problems with any of your projects, use your weekly memo to say so. If you announce a problem, also try to propose one or two solutions. Such memos often are called progress reports. Keep copies of these memos. If a problem does arise, you will at least have a record of your warnings.

- Similar periodic memos can be sent to in-house clients, updating them on the progress of projects. (An in-house client is a member of your company or organization.) Such memos can be particularly useful if you have an in-house client who misses deadlines or whose lack of performance is affecting the quality of a project. Never threaten an in-house client in such a memo. Diplomatically point out the consequences—financial and otherwise—of his actions. Such memos leave a record, showing that you've done your best to act in your organization's interest. You may wish to consult your boss before writing such memos.

If the client is someone outside your organization, a business letter may be more appropriate than a memo. However, if constant updates on an important project are advisable (as they often are), e-mail memos are increasingly acceptable as external documents—that is, documents sent to someone outside your organization.

■ If an in-house client or a boss asks you to act unwisely or, worse, unethically, and you're concerned that failing to comply will hurt your career, write that client or boss a memo detailing the requested action and ask if you understand correctly. If circumstances allow, consult your boss before writing such a memo to a troublesome in-house client. Seeing the request in print also may help the client or boss perceive the unwise or unethical nature of the request. Or, better, perhaps you have misunderstood the situation, and the memo will help resolve the confusion.

Such a memo increases the chances that the matter will be dropped—because, again, the memo begins to create a record of the situation. A business letter can fulfill the same purpose with an external client. If the client or boss responds to your memo with a phone call or personal visit, be sure to write yourself a memo about that conversation (see the next paragraph).

■ If you're in an unpleasant situation at work, such as giving an employee a poor evaluation—or, worse, having to fire an employee—write a memo to yourself, simply for your own files, describing what happened. Be brief but accurate and detailed. Be certain to date the memo. That memo can help refresh your memory later if you need to describe the situation to internal or even external authorities.

■ Keep paper printouts of all such e-mails.

TIPS

1. Although memoranda usually are internal documents, don't write anything in a memo that you wouldn't want to see on the front page of the *New York Times* or as the lead story on CNN. Internal information has a way of becoming external. Be careful how you phrase bad news and sensitive topics. An effective test is to ask yourself, "What damage could my worst enemy or my organization's worst enemy do with this memo?" (This is good advice for writing any sensitive document, not just a memo.)

2. *Memorandum* doesn't stand for "random memory." It's Latin ancestor is *memorare*, a verb meaning "to remember." Memoranda are relatively informal, but they still should be clear, brief and well-organized—not at all random.

Going Online

The great majority of memos are online e-mail messages. However, remember to print out paper copies of diplomatically sensitive or economically important memos. Keep those paper copies in your files.

MEMORANDUM

Interactive Games
2010 Ridglea Drive
San Francisco, CA 55111
555·999·5555

MEMO

Date: Nov. 20, 2005

To: All Employees

From: Andy Johnson aJ
                Director of Personnel
                Personnel Dept.
                Aberdeen Building, Office 427
                Ext. 3875
                aj@mgsintgames.com

Subject: Employee Handbook revision

This memo changes the last sentence of "Section Four: Applying for Promotions or Vacant Jobs" in your Employee Handbook. Please change the last sentence to read "The Personnel Dept. will respond to all applications within two weeks."

Please add this memo to the "Addenda" section of the three-ring binder that contains your Employee Handbook. We'll also make this change in the online version of the Employee Handbook.

At its last meeting, Management Council voted to change the responding procedure so that MGS employees wouldn't have to wait as long to learn about the status of promotion and other job-related requests.

Thank you very much.

Company Announcements

Purpose, Audience and Media

A company announcement delivers important information to all appropriate employees as quickly as possible. The reason is simple: The employees of your organization shouldn't hear the news elsewhere first.

The company announcement is difficult to define because it can address so many subjects—stock news, cafeteria menus, obituaries—and can be conveyed by so many different media (for example, old-fashioned bulletin-board posters, e-mail messages, memos read at meetings, Web-site entries and so on). Of these media, bulletin-board posters, Web-site entries and e-mail are perhaps used most.

> ■ **Key to Success:** Distribution of company announcements should be fast, and announcements must be accurate. Company announcements should be the best place for employees to learn accurate, breaking news about their organization.

Format/Design

Company announcements generally have a headline that describes the content. E-mail company announcements generally do not have a salutation. They begin with a headline.

Keep company announcements short. E-mail messages and Web-site entries should fill one screen or less. Bulletin-board posters or paper memos should be no more than one page.

Company announcements should always record the date of distribution. An e-mail message will do that automatically. A paper memo should include the date as part of its standard headings (page 218). A Web-site entry can include the date below the headline or, at the end of the message, can include a sentence such as "Posted Jan. 18, 2005." Old-fashioned bulletin-board posters can include a date at the bottom: "1/18/05."

Whatever medium they use, company announcements usually are single-spaced to save space. To save additional space, you may wish to indent paragraphs rather than double-spacing between them.

Company announcements often have a "###" or "end" after the last paragraph to show that the announcement has concluded. On bulletin-board posters, a date at the bottom can show that the announcement has concluded.

Content and Organization

Most company announcements begin with a headline that summarizes the main point of the story. As noted below, obituary headlines usually are simply the employee's name.

Company announcements usually follow the inverted pyramid organization (page 34), with the most important information coming first. As the story progresses, the information becomes progressively less important.

In company announcements, different messages require differences in content and organization.

Announcements That Affect Stock Prices

If the announcement could affect your organization's stock prices, timing is crucial. The announcement often is made when New York–based stock markets are closed—and the announcement is made simultaneously to the news media, major stockholders and employees. If your announcement were made to employees first and they were able to buy or sell their organization's stock with that insider knowledge, both you and they would have broken the law. Keep all such announcements strictly confidential until the moment of release. Never use your insider knowledge to purchase or sell stock. When possible, work with your organization's legal counsel on such announcements.

Company announcements that can affect stock prices usually are concise, factual and include a quotation from the leader of the organization.

Obituaries

The headline of an obituary announcement usually is just the employee's name. Most announcement obituaries do not list the cause of death. That omission can lead to speculation, but it also avoids occasionally awkward or private situations. Don't avoid the word *died;* it's generally better than *passed away* or other euphemisms.

An objective, factual tone is best. Leave the sentiment to a manager's quotation. (You won't sound heartless; the organization's grief will appear in the manager's quotation.)

In the first paragraph, note that the employee died, and include his title and age.

Traditionally, the second paragraph is a quotation from the employee's supervisor.

In later paragraphs, briefly outline the employee's career with your organization, listing the different jobs he may have had within your organization. List survivors. With the family's permission, include information on memorials and/or funeral arrangements. Memorial information sometimes can be a veiled reference to the cause of death: "The family requests that any memorial donations be made to the Cancer Program at City Hospital." Do not include information about who will succeed the deceased employee. That's a subject for a different, later company announcement.

New Employee/Retiring Employee

When a new employee joins your organization, use a company announcement to tell employees something about him. For example, what is the new hire's educational background and work experience?

Similarly, when an employee retires, announce her retirement and trace her career with the company. Consider including a quotation from a co-worker that praises the departing employee.

TIPS

1. Avoid speculation. In all company announcements, state nothing but the facts (and sometimes, as in obituaries, don't state all the facts). The only place for anything speculative is in an approved quotation.

2. In the first reference to an employee (except for a headline), include that person's title. A good policy is to always capitalize employee titles. The *Associated Press Stylebook* recommends capitalizing titles only when they come immediately before a name. However, if you follow AP style, employees may not understand why some titles are capitalized and others aren't. To avoid hurt feelings, consider capitalizing all employees titles in all instances.

3. Remember that many employees have families that can be affected by an important announcement. When appropriate and possible, include your awareness of that fact in the announcement. Discuss what the announcement might mean to families. (This can be a good policy for many internal documents besides company announcements.)

4. If the distribution of an announcement is complex, have a written timetable that specifies how each step of the distribution will be handled—that is, when each step should happen, how it will happen, and who is in charge of making it happen. A written timetable helps motivate members of your team to perform flawlessly their portions of the task.

   Take particular care to ensure successful distribution to high-ranking managers in your organization. They no doubt know about the announcement, but they'll want to see that the announcement plan works.

Going Online

E-mail messages and Web-site entries are effective ways to distribute company announcements, particularly in large organizations and organizations that have more than one location.

Interactive Games
2010 Ridglea Drive
San Francisco, CA 55111
555·999·5555

Kenneth Mikkalsen

Associate Director of Finance Kenneth Mikkalsen died Wednesday night. He was 62 and had served the company for 23 years.

"We've lost a true friend," said Director of Finance Sid Halley. "Ken was the kind of associate everyone wanted to work with. He was brilliant, funny, hard-working and a joy to be with. We'll miss him every day for a very long time."

Mikkalsen began his career at MGS Interactive Games as a Financial District Manager in 1982 and progressed steadily through positions of increasing responsibility to Associate Director of Finance. Before joining MGS, he served in financial positions at Worldwide Sprockets and McDaniel Inc.

Mikkalsen is survived by his wife, Marie; a son, Henry; and a daughter, Jill.

Funeral arrangements are pending. In lieu of flowers, the family requests donations be made to the Heartland Kidney Foundation.

6/26/05

Policy and Procedure Documents

Purpose, Audience and Media

Policy and procedure documents take many forms: binders, magazines, memos, brochures, Web-site entries, and so on. However, all share a common goal: to tell employees how something works or how something should be done. Policy and procedure documents are explanations for members of your organization. For example, a document telling employees how to arrange business travel would be a policy and procedure document.

■ **Key to Success:** Effective policy and procedure documents have consistent style, logical organization and clarity.

Format/Design

Because the media of policy and procedure documents can differ, formats also differ. However, because all policy and procedure documents explain something, some format guidelines do apply to all such documents:

- Avoid long paragraphs. Divide the explanation into small, clear parts.
- Use headlines and subheadlines to explain and announce upcoming passages.
- Use bullets (•) to signal the beginning of each part of a series of related short passages (just as this series of six bulleted parts does). You also can number each short, related passage, especially if the order of completion is important.
- Consider using descriptors. A descriptor is a very brief summary placed in the margin next to the passage it summarizes.
- Use illustrations or photographs to describe complex processes.
- Both on paper and online, use white space generously. Don't let the document get cluttered and compressed. That tight appearance can overwhelm readers.

Content and Organization

Policy and procedure documents need consistent sentence structure, logical organization and clarity.

Consistent Sentence Structure
Within the document, always address the same audience. Don't switch back and forth from "You should" to "The employee should."

Select either the indicative or imperative (command) mood, and, as much as possible, stick with that choice.

Indicative mood:	The employee should sign the voucher.
Imperative mood:	Sign the voucher.

Use active voice as much as possible. Some situations may require passive voice. In active voice, the subject does the action of the verb. In passive voice, the subject does not do the action of the verb.

Active voice: Sign the voucher. (The understood subject is "you.")
                 The employee should sign the voucher.

Passive voice: The voucher should be signed.

Logical Organization

Establish a logical order for the policy or procedure you're explaining—for example, order items chronologically, list them from most important item to least important or cluster related points.

Keep policy and procedure documents short and logical. In unavoidably long documents, look for logical ways to cluster the information into brief, well-labeled sections.

Clarity

Avoid "bizspeak"—that is, avoid inflated and pretentious words and phrases. Use clear English. In a policy and procedure document, you're not trying to impress; you're trying to explain.

Tighten flabby sentences. Come to the point, but avoid being so abrupt that you sound rude.

Again, avoid long sentences and paragraphs.

TIPS

1. Every document you write should be edited by someone other than you (of course, you always should be your own first editor). Such editing is particularly important for policy and procedure documents. An editor may discover passages that seem clear to you but that fail to communicate your message to others.

2. Though they are important, policy and procedure documents are rarely anyone's favorite documents. If appropriate, consider using humor—even humorous illustrations—to make the document more inviting.

3. Consider listing a contact person or a department that could answer questions related to the policy or procedure. Be sure to gain the person's or department's consent before including such information.

4. Policy and procedure documents are often revised and updated. Be sure to record the date on each document to prevent confusion about which version is current.

Going Online

Policy and procedure documents can exist as e-mail messages. Such documents can be particularly useful on internal Web sites—pages on so-called intranets that only employees can access.

Interactive Games
2010 Ridglea Drive
San Francisco, CA 55111
555·999·5555

Corporate Headquarters
Fire Evacuation Plan

When the fire alarm sounds and the emergency lights flash, please do the following:

1. **Don't panic.** The alarms sound at the first hint of fire. You will have ample time for a safe evacuation.

2. **Stop what you're doing, and walk calmly to the nearest stairwell.** Don't finish what you're working on. Please don't take work with you. Also, don't attempt to take the elevators because the power will be shut off.

3. **Walk down the stairs to the first floor.** Don't run down the stairs. Please assist any associates who may require help. Again, you should have plenty of time, and the stairwells are fire resistant.

4. **Use the south exits at the bottom of the stairwells.** For your own protection, do not attempt to enter the first-floor lobby.

5. **Gather in the southernmost part of the south courtyard.** Please await further instructions there.

Special Instructions for Floor Monitors
1. When a fire alarm sounds, calmly ensure that all employees exit to the stairwells.
2. Remind employees, as needed, of the five points listed above.
3. Ensure that no one remains in any office or restroom on your floor.
4. Use the stairwells to exit to the south courtyard.
5. Please ensure that all stairwell doors are closed.

Revised: Dec. 24, 2004

Business Reports

Purpose, Audience and Media

Business reports communicate facts and sometimes opinions or recommendations based on those facts. Business reports communicate information that shows the relative effectiveness of an organization. They also can communicate information designed to improve the effectiveness of an organization.

The audience for a business report is usually a manager or managers within an organization. Most business reports are internal documents, although some organizations—such as think tanks—prepare reports for general distribution.

Business reports appear in a variety of media. The most traditional medium is paper, which often is bound together with a staple or a binder. Business reports also can be delivered as CDs or DVDs and as Web-site entries.

■ **Key to Success:** Whether formal or informal, good business reports are clear, concise, detailed and well-organized.

Format/Design

The format of a business report should clarify its organization and aid readability. The text of a business report is single-spaced. Double-space between paragraphs, and do not indent paragraphs. Number the pages of the report, beginning with the first page of the actual text; do not number the title page or the table of contents. The formats of business reports often include the following features:

■ Boldfaced, larger-than-ordinary type for the title on the title page (18-point Times is a standard size and typeface for report titles)
■ Boldfaced type for section titles and subheadlines
■ Margins of at least one inch
■ White space (extra spacing) between sections. In long reports, new sections often begin on a new page.
■ Colorful charts and graphs, when appropriate, to reinforce and clarify meaning. Most word-processing programs offer user-friendly ways to create and insert charts and graphs.

Content and Organization

Before beginning to write a report, ask yourself these questions:

■ What is the purpose of this report? Does everyone involved agree?
■ Who is the audience? What does it expect, want and need to learn from this report?

Let the answers to these questions guide the information that the report should contain.

A formal business report contains, in order, the following sections, each of which often begins on a new page. (Less formal versions can discard some of the following sections.)

Memo or Letter of Transmittal

The memo or letter of transmittal typically goes with paper reports and is paper-clipped to the title page or cover of the report. Such a memo or letter essentially says, "Attached is the report you requested. If you have questions, please contact me." (This page is a matter of courtesy—almost always an important part of strategic communications.)

Title Page

The title page is often the cover of the report. It includes a title; a descriptive subtitle, if necessary; the name(s) of the author(s); and the date. The title page should clearly communicate that the document is a report on a specific topic. If the title is vague—such as "A Time for Action"—then include a specific subtitle: "Recommendations for Improving Safety in the Central City Factory."

Table of Contents

A table of contents lists each section, in order, and its starting page. (Do not list the span of pages for each section; just list the starting page.) Don't include the memo or letter of transmittal or the title page in the table of contents. With a headline, clearly label this page as the table of contents.

Table of Charts and Graphs

This optional section lists the names and page numbers of the charts and graphs in the report. This section generally is not listed in the table of contents. It generally does not have a page number.

Executive Summary

An executive summary is a concise, one-page (if possible) overview of the report's highlights. In general, include an executive summary if the report is formal and will take more than 15 minutes to read. Executive summaries highlight the key findings of the report. For example, the executive summary of a problem–solution report would include the most important details of the problem as well as the most highly recommended solutions.

Do not use your executive summary as the introduction to your report. A reader may skip the executive summary. Your report needs a separate introduction (see next segment). You can avoid this hazard by writing the executive summary last, after you have completed the rest of your report, including its official introduction.

Text of the Report

The text generally consists of an introduction, a body (which delivers most of the details) and a conclusion. These three sections follow the organizational cliché of "Tell 'em what you're going to say, say it and tell 'em what you've said."

Introduction. The introduction states the report's purpose and main point(s). The introduction also establishes the tone of the report (that is, how formal it will be) and the level of language used.

If your introduction seems too brief, consider two things:

- Brevity in a report is an asset as long as it's not confusing or rude.
- If the introduction seems so brief that it's ungraceful, beef it up by announcing the organization of the report. That is, use the introduction to forecast the order of the sections to come. This may repeat some of the table of contents, but such repetition can be useful, reinforcing the report's organization.

Body. The body delivers the specifics. It explains and develops the main point(s). In most reports, the introduction and conclusion are short; the body is comparatively long.

In most reports, the subject-restriction-information paragraph-organization technique can help keep the body focused on the report's subject. Here's how the subject-restriction-information model works: Each time a new section of the body begins, the opening sentence refers to the subject of the report and to the restriction of that subject covered in the new section. Specific information follows. For example, here is a subject-restriction opening sentence: "A second reason for the inefficiency of the Arcadia factory [subject] is obsolete equipment [restriction]." The information following this sentence would prove that the equipment is, indeed, obsolete.

The sections of the body should be organized logically—for example, from the first event in time to the last; from the most important information to the least; from the best solution to the worst; and so forth. Consider using headlines to label sections or chapters in the body.

If the report makes recommendations, present them in the body, not the conclusion. You may wish to announce them in the introduction; you certainly would announce them in an executive summary. In the body, you either can put the evidence first so that when the recommendations appear, they seem logical—or, if there are several recommendations, you might wish to make them one at a time and, after each, provide evidence to support it. A good model is a financial audit report, which first presents evidence, usually a description of an organization's financial practices and financial health. The financial audit report then makes recommendations and, after each recommendation, includes a brief explanation of the problem to be solved or prevented.

Conclusion. The conclusion reasserts the report's purpose and main point(s) in light of all the information in the body. The conclusion also can note the next action that will or should be taken. If the conclusion seems too short, it can briefly note the most useful sources of information. Remember: Unless brevity seems rude or ungraceful, it is an asset, not a problem.

Endnotes (Often Called Footnotes)

Endnotes cite specific sources of information. They're needed only in very formal reports. Each endnote requires a previous marker in the text, usually a small, elevated number like this.[17]

List of Works Consulted

Like endnotes, a list of works consulted is reserved for very formal reports.

Appendix

An appendix would contain articles, tables, charts and other related information. An appendix is optional.

TIPS

1. Avoid the temptation to pad a report with wordiness, useless information and unneeded sections. Reports should be long enough to thoroughly fulfill their purpose— and no longer.
2. If possible, show drafts of your report to your manager as you progress. Reports are important documents, and you should avoid distributing an unedited, unapproved report.
3. Long reports often are written by teams. If you are the team leader, assign specific tasks to specific individuals. Assign a deadline for each task. Make these assignments in writing—in a memo—to avoid any misunderstandings. If the report will take several days or weeks to complete, hold quick progress meetings or ask that members of your team send you periodic progress memos.

Going Online

Business reports still exist primarily as paper documents. Many reports are confidential; distributing them through online media can undermine security. However, business reports can be distributed as attached files or placed on an organization's internal Web site—its intranet.

A Concise Guide to Punctuation

Important! Read this: To understand several rules of punctuation, you must understand what a **clause** is.

A clause is any group of words that has a subject and a verb that has tense. By "a verb that has tense," **we mean a verb that sends a time signal, such as past, present or future.**

For example, *She wrote a speech* is a clause. It has a subject (*She*) and a verb that has tense (*wrote*)—in this case, past tense. However, *writing the speech* is not a clause. *Writing* can be a verb form, but it doesn't show tense; it's not past, present or future. And *writing the speech* doesn't have a subject, a doer of the action. No one here is doing the writing. Therefore, *writing the speech* is not a clause.

Basically, there are two kinds of clauses: **independent clauses** and **dependent clauses.** An independent clause can stand all by itself as a complete sentence. *She wrote a speech* is an independent clause.

A dependent clause, like all clauses, has a subject and a verb that has tense—but it cannot stand all by itself as a complete sentence. *When I was young* is a clause. However, because it cannot stand all by itself as a complete sentence, it is a dependent clause. A dependent clause must attach itself to an independent clause; otherwise, it becomes an incomplete sentence, also known as a sentence fragment. For example, *When I was young, I studied advertising* is a complete sentence. It consists of a dependent clause and an independent clause.

Here's the last part of the grammar lesson: There are two kinds of dependent clauses: **subordinate clauses** and **relative clauses.** A subordinate clause begins with a subordinate conjunction. The list of subordinate conjunctions includes such words as *because, if* and *when. When I was young* is a subordinate clause.

A relative clause begins with a relative pronoun. There are five basic relative pronouns: *that, which, who, whom* and *whose.* In the sentence *The account executive who wrote the proposal won an award*, the words *who wrote the proposal* are a relative clause.

Understand these terms—**clause, independent clause, dependent clause, subordinate clause** and **relative clause**—and you're ready to understand and explain several punctuation rules.

In the rules below, the "PM" simply stands for punctuation mark.

Commas

PM1 When a coordinating conjunction (*and, but, or, for, so, nor, yet*) connects two independent clauses, put a comma before the coordinating conjunction.

EXAMPLE   *She wrote the news release, but he distributed it.*

PM2 In most cases, if *and* is not connecting two independent clauses, do not put a comma before it.

EXAMPLE   *She wrote the news release and put it on the Web site.*

EXAMPLE   *He writes news releases, radio ads and speeches.*

PM3 Do not connect two independent clauses with only a comma. That error is called a comma splice.

EXAMPLE   *She wrote the news release, he distributed it.* (INCORRECT: The comma connects two independent clauses. This is a comma splice.)

EXCEPTION   A comma can connect two independent clauses when there is a series of at least three independent clauses: *She wrote the news release, he distributed it and they both left to celebrate.*

PM4 Set off an opening subordinate clause with a comma.

EXAMPLE   *If you understand clauses, you'll understand more about punctuation.*

EXAMPLE   *Because you understand clauses, you understand punctuation better.*

TIP   The list of subordinate conjunctions includes *if, when, although, though, because, while, unless, as soon as, before* and *after*.

PM5 Do not (usually) put a comma before a subordinate clause that ends a sentence. The comma isn't wrong; it's optional and usually not used.

EXAMPLE   *You'll understand more about punctuation if you understand clauses.*

EXAMPLE   *You understand punctuation better because you understand clauses.*

PM6 If a relative clause narrows down the meaning of the noun that comes before it, do not set it off by commas.

EXAMPLE   *The account executive <u>who wrote the proposal</u> won an award.*

EXPLANATION   The relative clause *who wrote the proposal* narrows down what we mean by the noun *executive*. In other words, the clause is essential to what we mean by *executive*. We don't mean just any executive; we mean the one who wrote the proposal.

TIP Sometimes the relative pronoun and its verb are deleted from the sentence: *My favorite song sung by Lenny Kravitz is "Fields of Joy."* (In this sentence, *that is sung by Lenny Kravitz* has been reduced to *sung by Lenny Kravitz.*)

PM7 If a relative clause does not narrow down the meaning of the noun that comes before it, set it off with commas.

EXAMPLE *My father, <u>who lives in London,</u> works in corporate communications.*

EXPLANATION The relative clause *who lives in London* does not narrow down what we mean by the noun *father.* The speaker has only one father.

TIP Sometimes the relative pronoun and its verb are deleted from the sentence: *My favorite song, sung by Lenny Kravitz, is "Fields of Joy."* (In this sentence, *which is sung by Lenny Kravitz* has been reduced to *sung by Lenny Kravitz.* This differs from the tip in Rule PM6. In that guideline, the song is the speaker's favorite just among Kravitz's songs. In this tip, for Rule PM7, the song is the speaker's favorite song among all songs.)

PM8 Use commas to set off nouns and noun phrases when they immediately follow a noun or noun phrase that means the same thing.

EXAMPLE *Julie Smith, our new president, will address the stockholders.*

EXAMPLE *Our new president, Julie Smith, will address the stockholders.*

TIP If you can drop the second noun (or noun phrase) from the sentence and the sentence still works grammatically, set the second noun (or noun phrase) off by commas.

PM9 Do not put a comma between a title and a name when you can substitute *Mr.* or *Ms.* for the title.

EXAMPLE *President Julie Smith will address the stockholders.* (Ms. Julie Smith will address the stockholders.)

EXAMPLE *Director of the Western Region Arnold Jones will address the stockholders.* (Mr. Arnold Jones will address the stockholders.)

PM10 Do not set off a noun (or noun phrase) with commas when it narrows down the meaning of a preceding noun.

EXAMPLE *My associate Arnold Jones will address the stockholders.* (The noun *Arnold Jones* narrows down the noun *associate;* it tells which associate.)

EXAMPLE   *Our newsletter* Employees Today *just won a national award.* (This is accurate only if the company has more than one newsletter. In that case, *Employees Today* narrows down the noun *newsletter*; it tells which of your organization's newsletters won the award.)

PM11 Set the number designating a year off with commas when the number follows a month and a date. When a date follows a day of the week, set the date off with commas.

EXAMPLE   *Jan. 1, 2000, was a memorable day.*
Wednesday, Jan. 1, was a memorable day.

EXAMPLE   *I remember Jan. 1, 2000.*
I remember Wednesday, Jan. 1.

TIP   Most stylebooks agree that when only the month and year are specified, commas are unnecessary:
January 2004 was a profitable month for our company.

PM12 Set off state names with commas when they follow city names.

EXAMPLE   *Weslaco, Texas, is near Mexico.*

EXAMPLE   *She works in Weslaco, Texas.*

PM13 Use a comma to separate adjectives that modify a following noun. (If you can substitute *and* for the comma, the comma usage is correct.)

EXAMPLE   *The direct-mail campaign was an effective, timely tactic.*

EXCEPTION   *He wrote an excellent annual report.* (Do not put a comma between the adjectives *excellent* and *annual* because *annual* is considered to be part of the noun phrase *annual report*. *Excellent* modifies the entire noun phrase *annual report*.)

PM14 Do not use a comma before the final item in a series. (Stylebooks differ on this point. The *Associated Press Stylebook* prefers no comma in this situation.)

EXAMPLE   *The campaign includes a TV ad, a radio ad and a magazine ad.*

EXCEPTION   Even the *Associated Press Stylebook* recommends inserting a comma when an item in a series includes an *and: The campaign includes a news release, a speech, and print and TV ads.*

EXCEPTION   When the items in a series are highly detailed, the *Associated Press Stylebook* recommends including a comma before the final *and.*

PM15 Use a comma before opening quotation marks when (a) the quotation immediately follows *said* (or a similar word) and (b) when the quotation answers the question *said what?*

EXAMPLE   *She said, "Our annual report is a stunning example of computer graphics."*

EXAMPLE   *She said that the annual report was "a stunning example of computer graphics."* (In this second example, do not put a comma before the opening quotation marks. The quotation does not immediately follow *said*. Also, the quotation by itself does not answer the question *said what?* The quoted passage needs the help of the words *the annual report was* to answer that question.)

TIP   Do not automatically put a comma before quotation marks. Follow Rule PM15.

PM16 When the attribution (the *she said*) follows a quotation or a paraphrase, set the attribution off with a comma.

EXAMPLE   *"Our annual report is a stunning example of computer graphics," she said.* (Remember that the comma goes inside the closing quotation marks. See Rule PM20.)

EXAMPLE   The company's annual report is superb, she said.

PM17 When an attribution (the *she said*) follows a quotation that ends with a question mark or an exclamation point, do not include a comma.

EXAMPLE   *"Our annual report is superb!," she said.* (INCORRECT)

EXAMPLE   *"Did she praise the annual report?" he asked.*

PM18 When you place the attribution (the *she said*) within a quotation, put a comma before it. If the attribution comes at the end of a sentence, put a period after it. If it does not come at the end of a sentence, put a comma after it.

EXAMPLE   *"Our annual report is superb," she said. "I love the computer graphics."*

EXAMPLE   *"Our annual report is superb," she said, "but we'll do even better next year."*

EXAMPLE   *"Our annual report is superb," she said, "I love the computer graphics."* (INCORRECT: This is a comma splice. See Rule PM3.)

PM19 Do not put a comma after an attribution (the *she said*) that introduces a paraphrased quotation.

EXAMPLE   *She said that the annual report was superb.*

PM20 When a comma is next to a closing quotation mark, put the comma inside the quotation—even if that seems to make the comma part of a title.

EXAMPLE   *"I'll address the stockholders," she said.*

EXAMPLE   *His favorite song, "Fields of Joy," sung by Lenny Kravitz, is on that CD.* (Why is there a comma before the song title? See Rule PM8. Why is *sung by Lenny Kravitz* set off by commas? See Rule PM7.)

PM21 When someone is directly addressed by name (or a substitute for the name), set that name off by commas. (This is called "direct address" because, of course, you're directly addressing someone.)

EXAMPLE   *Stockholders, I welcome you.*

EXAMPLE   *Good morning, class.*

EXAMPLE   *I think, Mr. Jones, that you'd better sit down.*

PM22 When the word *yes* or the word *no* is used to answer someone, set it off with commas.

EXAMPLE   *"Yes, our annual report is superb," she said.*

EXAMPLE   *"But, no, I must disagree," he said.*

PM23 When someone's age follows his or her name, set the age off by commas.

EXAMPLE   *Julie Smith, 47, is our new president.*

PM24 When an *-ing* phrase (a participial phrase) modifies the subject of a sentence but is not essential to the meaning of the subject (meaning the *-ing* phrase could be dropped), set the *-ing* phrase off by commas.

EXAMPLE   *Finishing the annual report, he laughed with delight.*

EXAMPLE   *He laughed with delight, waving the annual report excitedly.*

EXAMPLE   *He ran into the office and, waving the annual report excitedly, began to shout.*

PM25 Rule PM24 also applies to phrases beginning with a past participle, most of which end in *-ed*. When such a phrase modifies the subject of a sentence but is not essential to the meaning of the subject, set it off by commas.

EXAMPLE   *Finished with the annual report, he laughed with delight.*

EXAMPLE   *He slumped in exhaustion, finished at last with the annual report.*

EXAMPLE   *He rose and, finished at last with the annual report, shouted with joy.*

PM26 When a phrase of four or more words opens a sentence, set it off by a comma. Also, set off a shorter opening phrase with a comma if doing so reduces ambiguity.

EXAMPLE   *In a little more than three hours, he finished writing the sales letter.*

TIP   This guideline is a matter of style, not a grammatical rule. Ask your professor or boss what her policy is. Some professionals set off every opening phrase: *In this office, we set off even short opening phrases with a comma.*

EXAMPLE   *Ever since, I was afraid of cats.* (This comma reduces ambiguity.)

PM27 When an adverb (most end in -*ly*) begins a sentence, set it off with a comma.

EXAMPLE *Generally, direct-mail campaigns are inexpensive.*

PM28 When the word *not* introduces a contrary idea in a sentence, put a comma before *not*.

EXAMPLE *The annual report was successful, not at all a failure.*

PM29 Set interjections off by commas. Interjections include words such as *um* and *well* and phrases such as *by the way* and *you know*.

EXAMPLE *Our annual report was, well, a little too expensive.*

EXAMPLE *Our annual report, by the way, was a little too expensive.*

PM30 Set off by commas the so-called conjunctive adverbs: *however, therefore, furthermore, consequently, moreover* and similar words. Be careful, however, to avoid comma splices (Rule PM3).

EXAMPLE *Therefore, he proposed an advertising campaign.*

EXAMPLE *Our sales brochures, consequently, have been effective.*

EXAMPLE *Our sales brochures are effective; however, our telemarketing needs revision.* (Note how a semicolon is used here to avoid a comma splice. See Rules PM3 and PM32.)

PM31 Do not set off an opening coordinating conjunction with a comma.

EXAMPLE And, we never saw her again. (INCORRECT)

EXAMPLE But, that's for you to decide. (INCORRECT)

EXCEPTION The comma is correct when it works with a following comma to set off a phrase: *And, after that, we never saw her again.*

Semicolons

PM32 Use a semicolon to connect two closely related independent clauses when a period seems to be too harsh a separation.

EXAMPLE *He likes our current strategy; she distrusts it.*

PM33 Use a semicolon to separate different items in a series in which all or some of the items include commas.

EXAMPLE *We'll revise our media kits, which have been too expensive; our direct-mail packages, which haven't been well targeted; and our print ads, which haven't included enough selling points.*

Colons

PM34 Use a colon only after an independent clause. (In other words, an independent clause must come before a colon.)

EXAMPLE *She has one great strength: punctuation.*

TIP   When a complete sentence follows a colon, most stylebooks recommend beginning that sentence with a capital letter.

EXCEPTION   In the title of a document, a colon need not follow an independent clause—*Changing Our Image: A Blueprint for a New Marketing Campaign.*

PM35 Do not put a colon before a list unless the colon follows an independent clause.

EXAMPLE   *Her strengths include: grammar, punctuation and spelling.* (INCORRECT: The colon does not follow an independent clause.)

EXAMPLE   *Her strengths include grammar, spelling and punctuation.* (No punctuation follows *include.*)

EXCEPTION   Sometimes an incomplete sentence introduces a bulleted list. A colon at the end of the incomplete sentence has become traditional. Ask your professor or boss what her policy is.
In our office, we produce:
- *newsletters;*
- *policy and procedure documents; and*
- *annual reports.*

Quotation Marks

PM36 When a quotation appears within a quotation, use single quotation marks within the original double quotation marks.

EXAMPLE   *"I love the song 'Fields of Joy,'"* she said.

TIP   Rules PM20 and PM47 apply to single quotation marks as well as double quotation marks. (When a comma or a period is next to a single closing quotation mark, it will go inside the mark.)

PM37 When a quotation continues beyond one paragraph, begin each new paragraph with opening quotation marks. Do not insert closing quotation marks until the quotation has concluded.

EXAMPLE   *"Our annual report is superb," she said. "I love the computer graphics.*
"Our direct-mail packages also have been effective. Our new databases have helped significantly.
"Finally, our advertising campaigns have been good, but we must try to target them more effectively."

PM38 When quotation marks appear in a headline, use single quotation marks to save space.

EXAMPLE   *Chairman predicts 'brilliant future'* (headline)

PM39 Quotation marks sometimes are used to signify titles of creative works such as books, songs and movies. Some stylebooks recommend italics for those situations. Ask your professor or boss what her policy is.

> EXAMPLE *My favorite old Beatles song is "In My Life" from the "Rubber Soul" CD.*

> TIP The *Associated Press Stylebook* recommends using quotation marks for the titles of books (except the Bible and reference books such as catalogs and dictionaries); computer games (but not software); movies; operas; plays; poems; songs; TV shows; lectures; speeches; and works of art.

PM40 Put quotation marks around unfamiliar words

> EXAMPLE *In his speech, he used a stylistic device called an "antimetabole."*

Question Marks

PM41 Put a question mark inside closing quotation marks when the quotation is a question. When the quotation is not a question, put the question mark outside the quotation.

> EXAMPLE *"Do you like our annual report?" she asked.*

> EXAMPLE *"Did he say, 'I love your annual report'?"*

> TIP See also Rule PM17.

PM42 When a sentence culminates in two questions, use only one question mark.

> EXAMPLE *"Did he ask, 'Where is your annual report?'"*

PM43 Realize that although a question mark can end a sentence (like a period), it also can function like a comma and allow the sentence to keep going.

> EXAMPLE *"Do you like our annual report?" she asked.*

> EXAMPLE *If he were to ask, "Was your annual report effective?" I know what I would answer.*

PM44 Do not put a question mark at the end of a paraphrased question that actually is a statement.

> EXAMPLE *She asked how they planned to finish the annual report.*

Exclamation Points

PM45 Put an exclamation point inside closing quotation marks when the quotation is an exclamation. When the quotation is not an exclamation, put the exclamation point outside the quotation.

> EXAMPLE *"I love this annual report!" she shouted.*

> EXAMPLE *I'm devastated that he called the annual report "mediocre"!*

TIP See also Rule PM17.

TIP Journalists dislike exclamation points in news stories. Avoid them in news releases and media kits.

PM46 Realize that although an exclamation point can end a sentence (like a period), it also can function like a comma and allow the sentence to keep going.

EXAMPLE *"I love this annual report!" she shouted.*

EXAMPLE *If he were to shout, "I love this annual report!" would you be surprised?*

Periods

PM47 When a period is next to a closing quotation mark, put the period inside the quotation—even if that seems to make the period part of a title.

EXAMPLE *She said, "This annual report is superb."*

EXAMPLE *He said, "My favorite song is 'Fields of Joy.'"*

EXCEPTION When a parenthetical phrase follows a quotation at the end of a sentence, put the period after the parenthetical phrase: *Our annual report includes a page titled "Projections for the Next Decade" (p. 22).*

PM48 When an abbreviation with a period ends a sentence, do not add a second period.

EXAMPLE *Bert lives at 123 Sesame St.*

TIP A period that follows an abbreviation does not necessarily end a sentence. *Janet Smith, Ph.D., is our new CEO.*

PM49 When words in parentheses close a sentence, the period goes inside the parentheses only if the entire sentence is in parentheses. If the beginning of the sentence is not in parentheses, the period goes outside.

EXAMPLE *(We distributed that media kit in August.)*

EXAMPLE *We distributed that media kit this past summer (in August).*

Dashes

PM50 Use dashes to set off a sudden thought that interrupts the progress of a sentence.

EXAMPLE *Our annual report—did you know it won a national award?—is superb.*

PM51 Use a dash to create a dramatic pause in a sentence.

EXAMPLE *Our annual report will win a national award—if we finish it on time.*

PM52 Use dashes to set off the expansion of a word or concept when that expansion interrupts the progress of the sentence.

> EXAMPLE   *The qualities that made our annual report a winner—conciseness, accuracy and infographics—characterize all of our investor relations publications.*

PM53 Use a dash as an informal substitute for a colon. (See Rule PM34.)

> EXAMPLE   *She has one great strength—punctuation.*

Hyphens

PM54 Use a hyphen to connect two or more modifiers when (a) they act as one word to modify a following noun and (b) when the absence of the hyphen could lead to confusion.

> EXAMPLE   *The XYZ Corp. announced first-quarter profits of $4.7 million Thursday.*
>
> EXAMPLE   *Our easy-to-assemble products need no instructions.*
>
> EXCEPTION   The *Associated Press Stylebook* recommends not using a hyphen with *very* compounds and compounds that involve adverbs that end in *-ly: Our very successful annual report was a heavily edited document.*

PM55 Use a hyphen when a prefix might cause confusion by creating a word identical to—but with a meaning different from—the word you want.

> EXAMPLE   *His re-creation of the situation was impressive.*

Apostrophes

PM56 Use apostrophes in contractions to indicate where a letter or letters have been deleted.

> EXAMPLE   *We're proud of our annual report.*
>
> EXAMPLE   *It's never too late.*
>
> TIP   Remember that the word *it's* (with an apostrophe) is the contraction of *it is*. Without the apostrophe, *its* is a possessive personal pronoun: *The company introduced its new chairman.*

PM57 Use an apostrophe to indicate possession.

> EXAMPLE   *The company's outlook is excellent.* (singular common noun)
>
> EXAMPLE   *The officers' spouses will join them after the meeting.* (plural common noun)
>
> EXAMPLE   *The boss's word is law.* (singular noun ending in *s*)
>
> EXAMPLE   *Davis' report was impressive.* (singular name ending in *s*)

TIP   Rules and style guidelines for using apostrophes are extensive and complex. For a detailed list, see the *Associated Press Stylebook*. Also, ask your professor or boss what her policies are.

PM58 Do not use an apostrophe with possessive personal pronouns.

EXAMPLE   *You believe that the credit is yours; however, your associates believe it is theirs.*

TIP   The possessive personal pronouns include *yours, his, hers, its, ours* and *theirs.*

PM59 Do not use an apostrophe when a plural noun acts as an adjective for a following noun.

EXAMPLE   *The conference will be in the teachers lounge.*

TIP   A word like *teachers* will not be possessive (and therefore will not have an apostrophe) if you can reverse the phrase and add the word *for,* as in a lounge for teachers. This shows that the lounge does not belong to teachers; rather, the lounge is for them.

PM60 Use an apostrophe with decade abbreviations.

EXAMPLE   *That strategy was successful during the '90s.*

Parentheses

PM61 Use parentheses to set off comments or citations that are grammatically nonessential.

EXAMPLE   *A successful document (such as our annual report) is the result of extensive planning.*

TIP   Don't overuse parentheses. Often, dashes can substitute for them.

TIP   See Rule PM49 for period placement and parentheses.

A Concise Guide to Grammar

Grammar may not be your favorite subject. In fact, grammar may not be in your Top 100 favorite subjects. However, strategic writers must have a solid command of grammar. Great ideas sometimes don't survive bad grammar. Also, a shaky knowledge of grammar can cause strategic writers to avoid problems by avoiding certain sentence structures that might otherwise be effective.

A second reason to improve your knowledge of grammar is to improve your career prospects. When you know what is correct grammatically and you also can explain it to others, you have a rare, marketable talent.

In this brief section, the authors describe the seven most common grammatical errors we find in student (and, sometimes, professional) writing. We've numbered the items so that you and your professor can easily refer to them. For additional information on good grammar, please see Appendix A: A Concise Guide to Punctuation. That appendix includes punctuation-related grammatical errors such as the comma splice.

G1 Pronoun Disagreement

Don't replace a singular noun with a plural pronoun. For example, don't write *That company loves their employees.* The noun *company* is singular, but the pronoun that later replaces it (*their*) is plural. Avoid a singular-to-plural shift like that.

The problem of pronoun disagreement has two basic solutions: Either make both terms plural, or make both terms singular. If both terms are plural, your sentence could be something like *The leaders of that company love their employees.* Now we move from a plural noun (*leaders*) to a plural pronoun (*their*). If both terms are singular, your sentence could be something like *That company loves its employees.*

Making both terms singular can sometimes lead to awkward *his/her* decisions. Avoid writing *Each employee should speak with their supervisor.* In that sentence, the noun *employee* is singular, but the pronoun that later replaces it—*their*—is plural. Replace *their* with *his, her* or even *his or her*—or avoid the whole mess and change *Each employee* to *All employees.*

G2 False Series/Lack of Parallelism

This problem occurs in sentences that include a series, such as *Strategic writing requires research, creativity and diligence.* In that sentence, the series consists of three nouns: *research, creativity* and *diligence.* A false series—also known as a lack of parallelism—occurs when we try to mix different parts of speech (such as nouns and verbs). The breakdown often comes in the last item in the series. For example, this sentence has a false series or a lack of parallelism: *Strategic writing requires research, creativity and to work hard.* In that sentence, our series is noun, noun, verb—an ungrammatical lack of parallelism.

Probably the most common form of false series happens like this: *Our employees value hard work, dedication and we especially value honesty.* In this sentence, our series is noun, noun, complete sentence. To fix the problem, we need to downsize our series from two items to three items and add a new clause: *Our employees value hard work and dedication, and we especially value honesty.* Or *Our employees value hard work, dedication and especially honesty.*

G3 Subject–Verb Disagreement

Verbs have to reflect the number of the subject. In other words, a verb has to reflect whether its subject is singular or plural. It often are easy to tell when you makes a mistake in subject–verb agreement (as this sentence illustrates). However, when the verb is a long way away from its subject—or when we're not sure if the subject is singular or plural—subject–verb disagreement can occur.

Consider this sentence: *A herd of wombats are stampeding in the streets.* Disagreement? Yes, because *herd* is our subject, and in American English (though not in British English), *herd* is singular. In American English, collective nouns such as *herd, group, jury* and *team* are singular (in British English, they're plural). So unless you're having lunch with Prince William of England, you'd say *A herd of wombats is stampeding in the streets.* (In this sentence, *wombats* is not our subject. *Wombats* is the object of a preposition; therefore, it can't be our subject.)

Now try this sentence: *His ability to analyze problems and develop solutions make him an outstanding leader.* That verb should be *makes,* not *make.* The verb's subject is *ability*—but the subject is so far away from the verb that we can lose sight of the connection. Don't let distance lead you into subject–verb disagreement.

Here's another tough one: *My talent plus your ambition are a good combination.* Disagreement? Yes, because *plus* doesn't equal *and.* *Plus* doesn't give us a plural subject. The correct version would be *My talent plus your ambition is a good combination*—an ugly sentence that you probably should revise. The same principle applies to *as well as:* That phrase doesn't equal *and.* It doesn't give us a plural subject. We would have subject–verb disagreement if we were to write *The CEO as well as the CFO are in the room.* Unfortunately, it should be *The CEO as well as the CFO is in the room*—again, an ugly sentence that you probably should revise: *The CEO and the CFO are in the room.*

One last disagreement: *Either the vice presidents or the CEO have leaked this information to the news media.* When you have a two-part subject united by the word *or,* whichever part of the subject sits closest to the verb controls the verb. In this case, *CEO* sits closest to the verb—and so the verb should show a singular subject: *Either the vice presidents or the CEO has leaked this information to the news media.* Once again, this is an ugly sentence that you probably should revise.

G4 *Who* and *Whom*

Believe it or not, there's an easy shortcut for this one—but first, let's do the basic grammar. (Sorry: The authors are professors, after all.) *Who* and *whom* are pronouns. *Who* is a subject pronoun (a so-called nominative pronoun). Because of that, *who* almost always will be the subject of a verb that has tense (such as past, present or future). *Whom* is an objective pronoun. Because of that, *whom* can never be the subject of a verb. Instead, *whom* will always be an object, such as a direct object or the object of a preposition.

That knowledge gives us one solution to the *who/whom* problem: If the word is the subject of a verb, we know it must be *who*. If it's not the subject of a verb, we know it must be *whom*.

Now for that shortcut, also known as the chop method. Because *who* is a subject pronoun, it is grammatically equal to *he*. Because *whom* is an objective pronoun, it is grammatically equal to *him*. To use the chop method,

1. Read the sentence in question and stop right before the who/whom word.
2. Now throw that first part of the sentence away.
3. Mentally substitute *he* and *him*, instead of *who* or *whom*, in the next several words that follow (in the next clause, if you remember the definition of clause from page 233).
4. If *he* works, you need *who*. If *him* works, you need *whom*.

For example, try the chop method on this sentence: *Give it to whoever/whomever wants it.*

1. [*Give it to*] *whoever/whomever* wants it.
2. *whoever/whomever wants it.*
3. *He wants it* or *Him wants it.* (Clearly, it's *He wants it.*)
4. The answer is *Give it to whoever wants it.*

Try it again on this sentence: *We'll award the contract to whoever/whomever we trust.*

1. [*We'll award the contract to*] *whoever/whomever we trust.*
2. *whoever/whomever we trust.*
3. *He we trust* or *Him we trust*—or, better, *We trust him.* (Clearly, it's *We trust him.*)
4. The answer is *We'll award the contract to whomever we trust.*

With practice, you can learn to do the chop method quickly and accurately.

G5 **Dangling Participles, Dangling Modifiers**

This one sounds awful, but it's not too hard to understand. Basically, two kinds of participles exist (don't ask us why): present participles and past participles. Present participles are verb forms that end in *-ing*: *Running, praising, screaming* and *writing* all can be present participles. Past participles are verb forms that complete this phrase: I have _____. The words *run, praised, screamed* and *written* all can be past participles.

Here comes the rule: When these participles introduce or help introduce a phrase that opens a sentence, that phrase modifies the subject. In other words, the phrase modifies the first noun or pronoun to follow the phrase. A dangling participle or dangling modifier occurs when the wrong word or words become the subject. For example, here's a classic dangling modifier from English 101: *Flying over the North Pole, an iceberg was seen.* We all know what the writer meant—but tough luck. *Flying over the North Pole* is an opening participial phrase; therefore, it modifies *iceberg.* Hence, the amazing flying iceberg.

Here's another one: *Screamed into the wind, he knew his words were lost.* Again, we know what the writer meant. But *Screamed into the wind* is an opening participial phrase; therefore, it modifies *he.* Hence, he—not his words—was screamed into the wind.

There's no easy way to fix a dangling modifier. You have to tear down the sentence and try again. Solutions to the above dangling modifiers could be *Flying over the North Pole, we saw an iceberg* and *He knew that his words, screamed into the wind, were lost.*

G6   *That* **and** *Which*
That and *which* are versatile words with many duties. But when they introduce clauses (see page 233), *which* sometimes gets confused with *that,* which leads to a minor grammatical error. (PM6 and PM7 on pages 234–235 cover this same concept.)

Use *that* to introduce a group of words (a clause) that is essential to the meaning of an immediately previous noun. In other words, use *that* when the clause narrows down, or restricts, the meaning of the previous noun: *The horse that won the race has been stolen.* In the previous sentence, not just any horse has been stolen—it's the horse *that won the race.* That information is essential; it restricts and narrows down which horse we mean.

In the same situation, we would not write *The horse which won the race has been stolen.* With clauses, *which* introduces nonessential, nonrestrictive information. Also, you should always set a *which* clause off with a comma or commas: *This grammar section, which we hope you enjoy, is getting pretty long.* In the previous sentence, the *which* clause doesn't narrow down what we mean by *This grammar section.* The clause is nonessential, so it uses *which* and is set off with commas. Sometimes, a *which* clause closes a sentence and requires only one comma: *She loves the movie "Casablanca," which I've seen many times.*

G7   *I* **and** *Me*
I and *me* can seem like the city kid and his country cousin. *I* seems distinguished and refined; *me* can seem like a hick. *I* is proper grammar, as in *King Henry and I will dine now, Jeeves. Me* can be an embarrassment, as in *Me and him are fixin' to chew some tobacco.* (In case we sound prejudiced against country folks, much of this book was written in Kansas and North Carolina.)

If you're lucky, you don't suffer from this weird distrust of *me.* If you're unlucky, get over it. *Me* is a perfectly good word; just don't use it in the wrong place (as in the tobacco sentence).

The difference between *I* and *me* is the difference between *who* and *whom,* discussed in G4. *I* almost always will be the subject of a verb that has tense (such as past, present or future). *Me* is an objective pronoun. Because of that, *me* can never be the subject of a verb. Instead, *me* will always be an object, such as a direct object or the object of a preposition.

Probably the most common *I/me* error is the avoidance of *me* as an indirect object: *The CEO told Dave and I that we would be promoted.* You can avoid this problem by testing the sentence without Dave. You wouldn't say *The CEO told I that I would be promoted.*

A second common error is the avoidance of *me* in preposition phrases: *Our new chief financial officer sat at the table between Marion and I.* You probably can spot the problem: *I* needs to be the subject of a verb, and there's no verb nearby. We need to use *me* because the word is the object of the preposition *between.* Objects need to be objective pronouns.

Appendix C

A Concise Guide to Style

Sorry, no fashion tips here. This brief chapter focuses on writing style. Like grammar, style provides guidelines for good writing. Unlike grammar, however, style doesn't consist of rules that everyone accepts. For example, we all can agree that *Her and me don't write so good* is bad grammar. But what about something like a state abbreviation? Should the abbreviation of *California* be *Calif.*? Or *Cal.*? Or *CA*? Grammar doesn't cover such matters. That's why we need style.

Organizations need consistent writing style to avoid the sloppy appearance of stylistic disagreements among their strategic writers. Imagine, for example, four different strategic writers working for the same newsletter. Unless they use the same style for things such as state abbreviations, numbers and company names, their editor will spend needless hours enforcing consistency. Any inconsistencies that escape the editor and appear in print can make the organization look careless and inattentive.

Newspaper journalists were among the first groups to adopt so-called stylebooks—that is, books that specify the style an organization will use. Many newspapers in the United States use the *Associated Press Stylebook and Libel Manual* (more commonly called the *AP Stylebook*). Because that manual is well-known, well-organized and easy to use, many organizations have adopted the *AP Stylebook* for their own written communications. The style tips that follow are just a few of the hundreds of guidelines in that book. If you don't already have a copy of the *AP Stylebook*, we recommend that you get one. We've numbered the tips below so that you and your professor can easily refer to them. In each entry, we supply only the basics. The *AP Stylebook* goes into greater detail.

S1 Business Titles

Your organization may wish to overrule AP style for business titles. AP recommends capitalizing a person's business title only when it comes before the person's name (when you can substitute the word *Mr.* or *Ms.* for the title): *Chief Executive Officer Alvin Fernald.* In all other cases, AP recommends lowercase letters for business titles: *Alvin Fernald, chief executive officer, will address the board of directors. The chief financial officer also will speak.*

In news releases and other documents sent to journalists, you should follow this style (again, many journalists use AP style). But for communications within your own organization, you might be wise to capitalize all titles all the time. Otherwise, you'll constantly explain to Employee A why his title *wasn't* capitalized when Employee B's title *was*. And even after you explain AP style to Employee A, he'll say, "OK, I understand. But you still capitalized *her* title and not *mine!*"

AP style isn't like grammar. You can overrule it. Just be sure everyone on your communications team knows and agrees.

S2 Abbreviations in Company Names

In formal company names, abbreviate the following words:

Brothers: Bros.

Company: Co.

Companies: Cos.

Corporation: Corp.

Incorporated: Inc. (Do not put a comma before or after *Inc.*)

Examples of AP style include *Smith Bros. Co.* and *Bingo Corp. Inc.*

S3 Second Reference

When you use a generic term for a second reference to an organization, lowercase that term: *The Flora Family Foundation donated $2 million. Last year, the foundation donated $1 million.*

When a second reference uses the initials of an organization, do not put those initials in parentheses after the first reference: *The Flora Family Foundation donated $2 million. Last year, FFF donated $1 million.*

S4 Numbers

Spell out the numbers zero through nine. Use figures for 10 and above. When you get to millions and above, use figures and words—for example, *1 million; 4 billion; 12 trillion.*

AP lists several exceptions to this policy. Use figures instead of words for ages, money, percentages, room numbers, temperatures (except zero) and weights. AP lists more exceptions in its *numerals* entry.

For fractions smaller than one, spell out the amount and use a hyphen: *three-fourths.* For numbers larger than one, use a decimal point and figures (not words) when possible: *1.75.* Don't extend numbers past hundredths. In other words, don't include more than two numbers to the right of the decimal point.

S5 Abbreviation of Month Names

When the name of a month appears with a date, as in *Sept. 1,* use these abbreviations: *Jan., Feb., Aug., Sept., Oct., Nov.* and *Dec.* Spell out the names of the other months. When the name of a month stands alone without an accompanying date, always spell out the full name.

S6 Abbreviation of State Names

AP doesn't use two-letter postal codes. People can be confused about whether MI is Michigan or Minnesota. And MA—is that Massachusetts or Maryland?

AP recommends different abbreviations for 42 states. It recommends spelling out *Hawaii* and *Alaska* and spelling out state names of five or fewer letters: *Idaho, Iowa, Maine, Ohio, Texas* and *Utah*. AP recommends these abbreviations:

Alabama: Ala.	Nebraska: Neb.
Arizona: Ariz.	Nevada: Nev.
Arkansas: Ark.	New Hampshire: N.H.
California: Calif.	New Jersey: N.J.
Colorado: Colo.	New Mexico: N.M.
Connecticut: Conn.	New York: N.Y.
Delaware: Del.	North Carolina: N.C.
Florida: Fla.	North Dakota: N.D.
Georgia: Ga.	Oklahoma: Okla.
Illinois: Ill.	Oregon: Ore.
Indiana: Ind.	Pennsylvania: Pa.
Kansas: Kan.	Rhode Island: R.I.
Kentucky: Ky.	South Carolina: S.C.
Louisiana: La.	South Dakota: S.D.
Maryland: Md.	Tennessee: Tenn.
Massachusetts: Mass.	Vermont: Vt.
Michigan: Mich.	Virginia: Va.
Minnesota: Minn.	Washington: Wash.
Mississippi: Miss.	West Virginia: W. Va.
Missouri: Mo.	Wisconsin: Wis.
Montana: Mont.	Wyoming: Wyo.

S7 Percent

Spell out the word *percent*—as one word. Don't use the % symbol. As noted above in S4, use figures, not words, for percents: *8 percent*.

S8 Commas in a Series

Use a comma to separate items in a series, but do not use a comma before the final *and* or *or: We need more computers, printers and scanners.*

Do use a comma before the final *and* or *or* when elements in the series use *and* or *or: We invited three couples: Ann and Marcus, Claudia and Wayne, and Kay and Duncan.*

Whether your organization uses the *AP Stylebook* or a different book—or even composes its own guidelines—your organization should have a stylebook. Inconsistent or illogical style can distract a reader and lessen the impact of your document's strategic message.

The ACT Agenda: An Editing and Proofreading System

The ACT Agenda helps you edit and proofread strategic documents. Using it, you can deliver a document that is

- Accurate
- Correct (grammatically)
- Thorough

- Audience-Focused
- Coherent
- Thematic

- Assisted
- Confirmed
- Timely

The ACT Agenda has three stages: ACT One, ACT Two and ACT Three. Each stage has three steps (shown above), and the initial letters of each stage's three steps spell ACT.

This memory trick can help you remember the nine steps of the ACT Agenda. Please read on: This *will* become clear.

Ideally, you should memorize the basic nine steps of the ACT Agenda. When you periodically review the steps as your document progresses, you'll be rewarded with something that's too rare: an excellent strategic document. The next sections describe each ACT in greater detail.

The ACT Agenda: ACT One

Accurate information, correct grammar and thorough coverage are fundamental to every strategic document. ACT One ensures the fundamentals.

Accurate
- Double-check every supposed fact in the final draft: names and spellings of people, companies, products, programs and so on. Also check job titles, arithmetic, quotations—anything that could be wrong.

- In your copy of the final draft, place a check mark over each fact as you verify it. (These check marks needn't be in the copy you deliver to your client or your boss.) The check marks allow you to keep track of what you've verified and what you haven't.
- Proceed one sentence at a time. Don't be overwhelmed by the entire document. Begin with the first sentence, verify the supposed facts, if any, and then move to the second sentence.
- Remember that accuracy alone sometimes isn't enough. Facts should appear in the proper context. For example, a newsletter story praising a filled quota shouldn't overlook the fact that the quota had been lowered because it couldn't be filled earlier. Remember: Good ethics mean good business.

Correct

- Use flawless grammar, including spelling and punctuation—unless there's a good reason for bad grammar (such as sentence fragments in print ads). Mastering grammar is a never-ending challenge, so resign yourself to the pleasures (?) of being a perpetual student. A knowledge of grammar also allows you to explain the logic of your word choice and sentence structure to others. If you need help, Strunk and White's book *Elements of Style* is a good place to start.
- Keep a written list of your grammatical errors (a personal Hall of Shame), including a separate list of words you have misspelled or frequently look up. Review those lists often. Proofread for those particular errors.
- Proofread backward one sentence (not one word) at a time. That is, carefully review the document's last sentence for good grammar, then the second-to-last sentence and so on. Proofreading backward breaks up the narrative flow and lets you focus on each sentence. (Don't combine this process with the separate fact-checking step. That's asking too much of yourself, and the document could suffer.)
- Ensure that everyone on your strategic communications team has a copy of and is using the same stylebook (the *Associated Press Stylebook* works well) and the same dictionary.
- Be diplomatic in correcting others' grammar. A first-rate knowledge of grammar and a keen sense of diplomacy will help make you an indispensable, promotable member of any strategic communications team.

Thorough

- Before, during and after writing, review the document's audience, purpose and strategic message. Don't simply pay lip service to this step. Do it painstakingly, because knowledge of audience, purpose and message will tell you how thorough the document should be. Stay focused on the audience's self-interest: What does it want to learn from the document? Do you supply that information?
- Challenge each draft in terms of *who, what, when, where, why* and *how.* Perhaps not each of these concepts will apply to your document—but consider each, and thoroughly develop those that are relevant.

■ Beware of being too thorough. Too many details can be as annoying as too few. Deliver only those that are necessary and/or interesting.

The ACT Agenda: ACT Two

Audience-focused information, coherent organization and thematic unity create a document that keeps the audience interested.

Audience-Focused
■ Respect your readers. Strive for brevity, courtesy, effective word choice and effective word order.

■ Avoid stereotypical, discriminatory or insulting language in these (and all) areas: age, gender, disability, race, religion and national origin.

■ Avoid inflated, pompous and jargony words that, superficially, sound important.

■ Avoid inappropriate timing. For example, during times of military conflict, some companies pull back lighthearted or frivolous advertisements.

■ Avoid "you and us" situations with your audience. For example, "When you joined our company, you . . . " can make readers feel that they're not part of the team.

■ Avoid the pronouns *I* and *you* when delivering bad news. For example, "I found 12 errors in your document." Instead, consider saying, "This document contains 12 errors. Please review and correct."

Coherent
■ Don't confuse this word with clear or comprehensible. Coherent basically means that all the parts cohere—that is, they fit together logically and gracefully. Coherent organization means that the document flows well.

■ Ask yourself if the document is well-organized. Is the arrangement of the parts logical? Is there a reason for the chosen order?

■ Now ask yourself if the document flows well. Are the transitions from point to point logical and smooth? Does sentence lead effectively to sentence? Paragraph to paragraph? Section to section?

■ When appropriate, consider using transitional words such as *however, therefore, also* and so on.

■ When appropriate, seek transitions that clarify the relation of one paragraph to the previous paragraph. At this level, transitional devices usually occur in the first sentence of the new paragraph. A common technique for effective transitions is the subject-restriction device, discussed on page 231.

■ When appropriate, use other devices and techniques that support coherence: a table of contents; main headlines and subheadlines; descriptors (descriptive notes placed in the margins); and bullets, such as the dots used on this page.

Thematic
■ Be able to state the strategic (goal-oriented) message of your document. Ideally, you should be able to do so in one sentence. Your entire document should

support this strategic message—every word, sentence and paragraph. Staying on message is the focus of this entire book.

■ Examine all passages that don't support your strategic message. Either they don't belong—or you should redefine your purpose to include them.

■ Challenge all first-person singular pronouns (the *I's* and *me's*). Are they absolutely necessary? When you write, "I know this plan will work," you ask your audience to focus on two things: you (you've referred to yourself); and the plan (which will work). The focus on you, usually, is unnecessary. You don't want readers to have double vision. You want their attention to be solely on the fact that the plan will work.

■ In short, strive for what Edgar Allan Poe, a master of the short story, called "totality." Poe believed that a good composition should have a clear purpose and that everything in that composition should support that purpose. Stay on message.

The ACT Agenda: ACT Three

Assisted work, confirmed work and timely work ensure that the review and distribution of your document will be successful.

Assisted

■ Keep informed of the progress, or lack thereof, of all associates assisting you with the document. Don't let your hard work be ruined by someone else's lack of effort.

■ If you're in charge of the team creating the document, clearly establish each associate's task; set reasonable deadlines; and schedule frequent meetings. Your sustained interest will create incentive for others to perform well. They won't want to face you every day with admissions of failure.

■ If you're not in charge of the document team, don't run to the team leader to report an associate's poor performance or missed deadlines. See if you can assist your colleague. If necessary, suggest to the team leader that a progress-review meeting be held.

■ Be diplomatic as you monitor others' progress. A friendly, competent team player is usually more valuable to an organization than a sullen, unpopular genius.

Confirmed

■ Realize that your document usually will be reviewed at several levels including, sometimes, a legal department—before it is released to its audience. Do your best work, because many high-ranking managers will examine your document.

■ Be sure that the document's production schedule includes time for the review process. If you're in charge of the review process, know who and where the reviewers are and know the order of review. Will all reviewers see the document simultaneously? Or will they see it one at a time with requested revisions made between each transfer? (If there's time, this second method can be effective—especially if you let the current reviewer know who has already approved the document.)

■ Attach to each document a polite memo asking the reviewer to examine the document. Include a diplomatically expressed deadline for the reviewer's response, and indicate that silence on his part will be taken to mean that the document is fine. (If you mail the document draft to a client outside your organization, a letter would be more appropriate than a memo.)

■ Keep a record of the review process: who should see the document, who has seen it, when they received it, what their deadlines were and when they returned the document.

■ During this involved process, do your best to prevent reviewers from weakening the document. Some reviewers may try to inject pompous jargon, which will harm readability. Some readers may try to remove potentially controversial information that the audience ought to know—and this, of course, could harm credibility.

■ Be prepared, however, to graciously accept reasonable changes. Be a team player.

Timely

■ Don't miss deadlines. Don't miss deadlines. Don't miss deadlines. If deadlines are vague, clarify them. If you're going to miss a deadline, communicate that fact as soon as possible. Don't wait until the due date to say, "Sorry . . ."

■ Devise a calendar with periodic deadline reminders. For example, an entry for one day might be "Document X due in one week." Large wall-chart calendars can display several months at a glance. Computers, cell phones and personal digital assistants can beep reminders at you.

■ Don't forget to allow time for the nonwriting part of the creative process: brainstorming, reviewing, printing, binding, distributing and so on.

■ Finally, be aware of the time lapse between publication or broadcast. If you are describing an event that hasn't yet taken place but *will* have occurred by publication or broadcast date, be sure to describe it in past tense (and cross your fingers that you were right).

Appendix E

Tips for Oral Presentations

Strategic writers sometimes must stand up and present their work to a group. For example, you might help explain a new ad campaign to a client's management team. Or you might lead the presentation of a proposal for a new marketing strategy.

Confidence in oral presentations comes from experience. But until you gain that experience, you might be uncomfortable speaking in front of groups—many of us are. This short chapter offers tips for making successful oral presentations. We recommend a four-step process that works for all forms of strategic communication: research, planning, communication and evaluation.

Research

In the earlier sections of this book, each segment that describes a document begins with an analysis of purpose, audience and media. You need to study those three areas before you make your presentation.

In researching your purpose,

- Identify the main reason for the presentation. What do you hope to accomplish?
- Pinpoint your strategic message. What is the one main point of your presentation that all your information will support?
- Find the information that best supports your strategic message.

In researching your audience members,

- Learn who they are. What unites them? Why are they a group?
- Learn what they hope to gain from your presentation.
- Identify the leaders and decision makers. You'll want to devote extra attention to them.
- Determine how long you're supposed to speak. What is your time limit? Do audience members hope to ask questions when you're done?

In researching your media,

- Determine what technology will be available. Will you be able to use computer projection? Or will it just be you and a flip chart?

■ Learn about the layout of the presentation room. Will you stand at the head of a table? Or will you present from a lectern in an auditorium? Will you need a microphone? Will a pitcher of water and a glass be available?

Planning

Begin by planning to be yourself. If you try to act like someone else during the presentation, you carry the double burden of acting and presenting. Just be yourself at your best. In addition,

■ Consider how to combine your strategic message with your audience's self-interest. Audience members want to hear about themselves and what your message means to them.

■ Write an outline for your presentation. (Write a script, if necessary, but remember: You'll need to maintain eye contact with audience members.)

■ Consider writing a brief introduction—a biography of yourself—for the person who will introduce you.

■ Think twice about beginning with a joke. Professionals often discourage such a beginning. If the joke falls flat, your presentation has a shaky start.

■ Consider this traditional beginning: After you have been introduced, thank the audience. Pause. Smile. Look at the people in the room. Show them that you're confident, ready and excited about the information you're about to deliver. Don't rush. When audience members see that you're relaxed, they'll relax.

■ Consider using visual aids to emphasize your main points. Studies show that well-designed visual aids increase an audience's comprehension of your information. If you use such aids, keep them simple. You don't want audience members reading while you're talking.

■ Plan a presentation that consumes about three-fourths of the allotted time. Allow for surprises and questions. Know where you can cut your presentation if necessary.

■ Practice your presentation—first alone and then in front of colleagues who will evaluate your performance. No, that's not fun—but it's necessary. Better to learn about errors during trial runs than during the real performance.

■ If possible, practice in the room where you will deliver the presentation. If that's not possible, practice in a similar room.

■ During your final practices, wear the clothing that you'll wear during the presentation—usually clothing at or just above the level of formality of your audience's attire.

■ Finally, plan for problems. What will you do if the computer projection system fails? (Have transparencies and an overhead projector ready.) What will you do if you lose your outline or script? (Have a second copy with you or with a colleague in the room.)

Communication

OK, it's show time. As you deliver your presentation,

- Again, avoid reading from a script. (Formal speeches are an exception; they generally have word-for-word scripts.) If necessary, have an outline. If possible, memorize your opening and closing so that you can maintain unbroken eye contact with audience members at those key moments.
- Maintain eye contact. Look at one person at a time, letting your gaze linger so that he knows you were speaking directly to him. Single out leaders and decision makers for extra eye contact.
- Unless you're making a formal speech from a lectern, move about the front of your presentation area. Your graceful movements will help keep audience members engaged and attentive.
- If your technology fails, don't try to hide the fact. Move smoothly to your backup solution. Your preparation and grace under pressure will impress audience members. They'll appreciate how seriously you've taken this opportunity to speak with them.
- When appropriate, close by asking for questions. After answering the last question, deliver a brief closing statement—just a few sentences, but make them as dramatic as the situation allows.
- Consider this closing strategy. When you've finished your presentation, deliver your closing statement. Then pause, maintain eye contact and simply say, "Thank you." This strategy often triggers applause.

Evaluation

You're done! When you're finally alone, relax and congratulate yourself. But don't get too comfortable. Before your sharpest memories of the presentation fade,

- Ask yourself what worked well. What didn't work well? How did the technology perform?
- Ask yourself if anything in the presentation surprised you. Was the audience responsive? If so, when? Why?
- Analyze your clock management. Did you finish on time? Did you allow time for questions? Did you feel rushed? Or did the presentation go too quickly? If so, why?
- Give yourself a grade. Was the presentation an *A*? *B*? *C*? Try to score a higher grade next time.
- Learn from your successes and your failures. Build on what went well. Revise what didn't work.

As you gain experience, your presentations will become better and better. Who knows? You might even learn to enjoy them.

The Gunning Fog Index

The Gunning Fog Index evaluates the readability of a written passage. Similar systems exist, but the Gunning Fog Index is easy to use and easy to explain to clients. It has become an industry standard. (However, check your word-processing program to see what readability-score functions may be included in its Tools menu.)

Consistent use of concise, graceful sentences and clear, direct language will help ensure an acceptable score on the Gunning Fog Index.

Using the Index

1. In a representative two- or three-paragraph stretch of text, determine the average number of words per sentence.
2. In the same passage, mark off the first 100 words. In that group, how many words of three or more syllables are there? Don't count
   - Names of people, organizations and so on
   - Verbs with *-ed* or *-es* endings when that suffix creates a third syllable
   - Easily recognizable compound words such as *marketplace*.
3. Add the average sentence length to the number of long words. Multiply the sum by 0.4.
4. The score reveals the school grade level of the prose. For example, an 8 suggests the prose is understandable to eighth graders. Generally, strategic documents should score in the 8 to 12 range—but much depends on the nature of the target audience.
5. Consider doing this for several representative passages to be sure that your original Gunning Fog score fairly represents the document.

Source: The Technique of Clear Writing, by Robert Gunning (McGraw-Hill).

Index

265